The Fort Pillow Massacre

On April 12, 1864, a small Union force occupying Fort Pillow, Tennessee, a fortress located on the Mississippi River just north of Memphis, was overwhelmed by a larger Confederate force under the command of Major General Nathan Bedford Forrest. While the battle was insignificant from a strategic standpoint, the indiscriminate massacre of Union soldiers, particularly African-American soldiers, made the Fort Pillow Massacre one of the most gruesome slaughters of the American Civil War, rivaling other instances of Civil War brutality.

The Fort Pillow Massacre outlines the events of the massacre while placing them within the racial and social context of the Civil War. Bruce Tap combines a succinct history with a selection of primary documents, including government reports, eyewitness testimony, and newspaper articles, to introduce the topic to undergraduates.

Bruce Tap is an independent scholar and the author of *Over Lincoln's Shoulder: The Committee on the Conduct of War.*

Critical Moments in American History

Edited by William Thomas Allison, Georgia Southern University

The Assassination of John F. Kennedy
Political Trauma and American Memory
Alice L. George

The Battle of the Greasy Grass/Little Bighorn
Custer's Last Stand in Memory, History, and Popular Culture
Debra Buchholtz

Freedom to Serve
Truman, Civil Rights, and Executive Order 9981
Jon E. Taylor

The Battles of Kings Mountain and Cowpens
The American Revolution in the Southern Backcountry
Melissa Walker

The Cuban Missile Crisis
The Threshold of Nuclear War
Alice L. George

The Nativist Movement in America
Religious Conflict in the 19th Century
Katie Oxx

The 1980 Presidential Election
Ronald Reagan and the Shaping of the American Conservative
Movement
Jeffrey D. Howison

The Fort Pillow Massacre
North, South, and the Status of African-Americans in the Civil War Era
Bruce Tap

The Fort Pillow Massacre

North, South, and the Status
of African-Americans in the
Civil War Era

Bruce Tap

Routledge
Taylor & Francis Group

NEW YORK AND LONDON

First published 2014
by Routledge
711 Third Avenue, New York, NY 10017

and by Routledge
2 Park Square, Milton Park, Abingdon, Oxon OX14 4RN

Routledge is an imprint of the Taylor & Francis Group, an informa business

Library of Congress Cataloging in Publication Data
Tap, Bruce.
   The Fort Pillow massacre: north, south, and the status of
African-Americans in the Civil War era/Bruce Tap.
   pages cm. – (Critical moments in American history)
   Includes bibliographical references and index.
   1. Fort Pillow, Battle of, Tenn., 1864.   2. United States—History
—Civil War, 1861–1865—African Americans.   I. Title.
   E476.17.T37 2013
   973.7′415—dc23
   2013013170

ISBN: 978-0-415-80863-7 (hbk)
ISBN: 978-0-415-80864-4 (pbk)
ISBN: 978-0-203-08146-4 (ebk)

Typeset in Bembo and Helvetica Neue
by Florence Production Ltd, Stoodleigh, Devon, UK

Printed and bound in the United States of America by Publishers Graphics,
LLC on sustainably sourced paper.

Contents

Series Introduction   vii
List of Figures   viii
Timeline   ix

Introduction   1

1   Means to an End   12

2   No Quarter   41

3   Controversy   66

4   Historians and the Fort Pillow Massacre   100

    Conclusion   120

Documents   127
Notes   174
Selected Bibliography   187
Index   192

Series Introduction

Welcome to the Routledge *Critical Moments in American History* series. The purpose of this new series is to give students a window into the historian's craft through concise, readable books by leading scholars, who bring together the best scholarship and engaging primary sources to explore a critical moment in the American past. In discovering the principal points of the story in these books, gaining a sense of historiography, following a fresh trail of primary documents, and exploring suggested readings, students can then set out on their own journey, to debate the ideas presented, interpret primary sources, and reach their own conclusions—just like the historian.

A critical moment in history can be a range of things—a pivotal year, the pinnacle of a movement or trend, or an important event such as the passage of a piece of legislation, an election, a court decision, a battle. It can be social, cultural, political, or economic. It can be heroic or tragic. Whatever they are, such moments are by definition "game changers," momentous changes in the pattern of the American fabric, paradigm shifts in the American experience. Many of the critical moments explored in this series are familiar; some less so.

There is no ultimate list of critical moments in American history—any group of students, historians, or other scholars may come up with a different catalog of topics. These differences of view, however, are what make history itself and the study of history so important and so fascinating. Therein can be found the utility of historical inquiry—to explore, to challenge, to understand, and to realize the legacy of the past through its influence of the present. It is the hope of this series to help students realize this intrinsic value of our past and of studying our past.

William Thomas Allison
Georgia Southern University

Figures

2.1   Map of Fort Pillow   44
2.2   Engraving of Fort Pillow Massacre   50
3.1   Drawing by Thomas Nast, August 5, 1865   92
3.2   Editorial cartoon by Thomas Nast, March 14, 1874   95
4.1   Editorial cartoon by Thomas Nast, September 5, 1868   102
4.2   Editorial cartoon by Thomas Nast, September 7, 1872   104

Timeline

April 12, 1861	Confederate bombardment of Fort Sumter.
May 23, 1861	General Benjamin F. Butler, Union commander at Fortress Monroe, Virginia, refuses to return three escaped slaves to rebel masters, thus inaugurating the "contraband" policy.
July 21, 1861	The 1st battle of Bull Run.
July 22 and July 25, 1861	Congress passes the Crittenden-Johnson Resolution, stating the North fought with no intention of overturning the institution of slavery.
August 6, 1861	Passage of the 1st Confiscation Act, allowing the confiscation of any slave directly assisting the Confederate war effort.
August 30, 1861	John C. Fremont issues a decree of Emancipation and Martial Law, freeing the slaves of all enemy slaves in the Department of the West.
October 14, 1861	War Secretary Simon Cameron allows Department of the South commander, Brigadier General Thomas W. Sherman to recruit fugitive slaves as soldiers.
March 13, 1862	Congress adopts new articles of war forbidding Union officers from returning fugitive slaves.
April 10, 1862	Congress passed Lincoln's requested resolution offering compensation for any slave state in the Union that would abolish slavery.
April 16, 1862	Congress passes a plan to abolish slavery in the Washington, D.C., offering $300 compensation to slave owners.
May 9, 1862	Major General David Hunter, commander of the Department of the South, issues an Emancipation Proclamation abolishing slavery in South Carolina, Georgia, and Florida. Hunter's decree was countermanded by President Lincoln on May 22.
July 17, 1862	Congress passes the Militia Act, allowing blacks to be used in non-combat roles in the military.
July 17, 1862	Congress passes the 2nd Confiscation Act, providing for the seizure and emancipation of any slave owned by a disloyal master.
September 17, 1862	Union victory at the battle of Antietam, Maryland.
September 22, 1862	Lincoln issues the preliminary Emancipation Proclamation giving rebellious states 90 days to come back into the Union or risk the emancipation of slaves.

January 1, 1863	Emancipation Proclamation issued, which includes specific provision for the enlistment of African-American soldiers.
May 22, 1863	Bureau of United States Colored Troops created.
May 27, 1863	Battle of Port Hudson becomes one of the first major Civil War engagements to involve black soldiers.
June 7, 1863	The 9th and 11th Louisiana Corps of African Descent distinguish themselves at Battle of Milliken's Bend (Mississippi).
June 1–3	The battle of Gettysburg.
July 18, 1863	Battle of Fort Wagner (South Carolina) involves the black 54th Massachusetts and suffers 262 casualties.
February 8, 1864	Major William Bradford stations the 13th Tennessee Cavalry at Fort Pillow, Tennessee.
March 24, 1864	Major General Forrest subordinate Colonel W. L. Duckworth, uses the threat of "no quarter" to secure the surrender of the Union garrison at Union City, Tennessee.
March 26, 1864	Forrest launches unsuccessful attack on Union garrison at Paducah, Kentucky.
March 28, 1864	Major General Stephen Hurlbut orders the 6th USCHA under Major Lionel F. Booth to Fort Pillow.
April 12, 1864	Fort Pillow Massacre.
April 13, 1864	Truce negotiated by Confederate officer Colonel Charles Anderson and Acting Master William Ferguson allows Union dead and wounded to transfer to Union vessels *Platte Valley* and *Olive Branch*.
April 16, 1864	Congressional debate concerning the Fort Pillow Massacre.
April 17–20	Battle of Plymouth, North Carolina, where accusations of a slaughter of African-American troops were raised.
April 18, 1864	Battle of Poison Springs, Arkansas results in African-American soldiers being executed instead of taken prisoners.
April 18, 1864	President Lincoln gives public speech in Baltimore and hints at retaliation for the Fort Pillow Massacre.
April 19, 1864	Daniel W. Gooch and Benjamin F. Wade leave to investigate the Fort Pillow Massacre, visiting Cairo and Mound City, Illinois, Columbus, Kentucky, Fort Pillow and Memphis, Tennessee.
April 21, 1864	Joint Resolution of Congress officially authorizes an investigation by the Joint Committee on the Conduct of the War. War Department starts its own investigation.
May 4–6, 1864	Cabinet members submit opinions on a response to the Fort Pillow Massacre.
May 6, 1864	Official publication of the report of the Joint Committee on the Conduct of the War with witness testimony.
May 6, 1864	40,000 additional copies of the Joint Committee on the Conduct of the War's report on the Fort Pillow Massacre are approved for publication.
May 17, 1864	President Lincoln directs Edwin Stanton to issue formal response to the Confederate government for the Fort Pillow Massacre.
June 10, 1864	Battle of Brice's Cross Roads, Mississippi, where the actions of African-American troops prompts Forrest to initiate an explanation from Union General Cadwallader Washburn.

June 15, 1864	Congress passes equal pay provision for black troops, but applies it only to those black soldiers free at the beginning of the war.
July 30, 1864	Battle of the Crater (Petersburg, Virginia): African-American troops, 4th division, 9th corps are slated to lead attack but withdrawn prior to the attack.
October 2, 1864	Battle of Saltville, Virginia where accusations of Confederate slaughter of African-American troops were made.
November 1864	Re-election of Abraham Lincoln.
January 31, 1865	House of Representatives passes the thirteenth amendment to the Constitution abolishing slavery (ratified on December 18, 1865).
March 3, 1865	Congress enforces equal pay provision on all African-American soldiers.
April 15, 1865	Death of Abraham Lincoln.
December 18, 1865	Thirteenth amendment ratified.
June 16, 1866	Passage or the Fourteenth amendment (ratification 1868).
March 2, 1867	Passage of the 1st Military Reconstruction Act.
March 23, 1867	Passage of the 2nd Military Reconstruction Act.
July 19, 1867	Passage of the 3rd Military Reconstruction Act.
March 12, 1868	Passage of the 4th Military Reconstruction Act.
February 27, 1869	Passage of the 15th amendment (ratified, 1870).
May 31, 1870	Passage of the 1st Force or Ku Klux Klan Act.
February 24, 1871	Passage of the 2nd Force or Ku Klux Klan Act.
April 19, 1871	Passage of the 3rd Force or Ku Klux Klan Act.
March 2, 1877	Congress declared that Rutherford B. Hayes the winner of the contested presidential election of 1876, thus leading to the end of Reconstruction.
October 15, 1883	The United States Supreme Court rule in the *Civil Rights Cases*.

Introduction

On April 12, 1864 a small military engagement, involving approximately 1,500 Confederate soldiers and slightly less than 600 Union soldiers, took place at Fort Pillow, a small fort on the banks of the Mississippi river, north of the city of Memphis, Tennessee. In many respects, the battle that transpired at Fort Pillow was not unlike many similar small-scale engagements that took place throughout the southern states during the American Civil War. One side won; one side lost. Casualties might be high or casualties might be low. When many Americans think of important Civil War battles, Fort Pillow does not come to mind. They think of Antietam, Gettysburg, or any number of other important military engagements. The battle of Antietam, for instance, is often associated with the advancement of the cause of emancipation; whereas Gettysburg is typically associated with the high tide of the Confederacy. What transpired at Fort Pillow, however, was different from what transpired in many Civil War battles because it involved accusations of slaughter and massacre, in particular, the deliberate slaying of African-American soldiers recruited to serve in the Union armies. Fort Pillow was certainly not the first battle in which Confederate soldiers encountered African-American troops. By the time it took place, African-Americans had taken part in any number of engagements on the field of battle, many of which were well known to northerners: Fort Wagner, Port Hudson, and Milliken's Bend. Nor was Fort Pillow the only battle in which charges of indiscriminate slaughter were raised. There were allegations of mistreatment of black soldiers before and after the Fort Pillow engagement. The Fort Pillow Massacre, nonetheless, became one of the most prominent symbols of the refusal of Confederate authorities and Confederate soldiers to recognize blacks as legitimate soldiers engaged in lawful enrolment in their nation's armed forces; moreover, it also served as a cruel reminder to black soldiers about the risks that their military service entailed. Above all, Fort Pillow represented or symbolized the attempt by northern society to alter the status quo on racial relations. By enlisting African-Americans in Union armies, the Lincoln administration warned southerners in rebellion that it not only rejected the institution of slavery but also was inching toward a position of social and political equality between the two races. While most white northerners did not envision a bi-racial society that was based on equality, the emancipation and arming of African-Americans suggested that the status quo social order in the southern states was passing away.

More than any other issue, slavery was at the root of the American Civil War. While historians of past generations have put forth a number of other interpretations for the cause of the war that have minimized the impact of slavery—states' rights, high protective tariffs, or differing economic systems—slavery was the foundation for the South's dissatisfaction in the Federal Union. When southerners raised the issue of states' rights, it was usually to defend the institution of slavery from Federal encroachment. One the other hand, when it came to protecting the sanctity of slavery, most states' rights southern political leaders had no qualms in demanding that the Federal government intervene and protect slave property. The most flagrant example of this was the 1850 passage of a revised Fugitive Slave Act, whereby the Federal government would intervene on behalf of southern slaveholders and assist in the recovery of runaway slaves. When the issue of the tariff was put forward as the fundamental issue that caused sectional division and the outbreak of war, slavery still played a role in this divisive issue. Southerner's dissatisfaction with a high protective tariff was that it favored—in their opinion—the development of northern manufacturing and commercial interests as opposed to the agricultural, plantation economy of the South, whose foundation was the slave system. Whatever contemporaries or subsequent historians have said to deflect from slavery being the direct cause of the American Civil War, slavery was always at the forefront of sectional conflict.

Throughout the first 80 years of the young American republic, the slavery issue emerged as a divisive factor time and time again. It divided the Founding Fathers during the writing of the Constitution. At various critical junctures in the life of the young republic, the slavery issue would erupt and threaten to fatally divide the young country. The crisis over the admission of Missouri as a slave state in 1819 was one such moment. A few decades later, during the Mexican war, Pennsylvania Democratic congressman, David Wilmot, unsuccessfully introduced a proviso (the Wilmot Proviso) in August 1846 that would have banned slavery from any lands taken from Mexico during the course of the war. In 1848, when the United States took possession of the Utah and New Mexico territories at the conclusion of the war with Mexico, the debate over the expansion of slavery into the territories of the United States became so intense that it eventually could not be managed by the political system of the 1850s and the American Civil War erupted. With the exception of a few abolitionists, however, the central debate over slavery was not typically a debate over whether slavery should be abolished in the southern states where it already existed. Many northerners, even those who belonged to the Republican party, a new born political party that had emerged in 1854–1855 to combat the expansion of slavery, had little interest in abolishing slavery per se. While more radical abolitionists wanted to exterminate the institution of slavery from all of the United States, many anti-slavery Republicans were simply anti-extentionists, that is, they could accept slavery in the existing southern states, but they were adamant that no new slave states should come into the Federal Union.

For southerners, the movement to block the expansion of slavery seemed like a threat to both their political power as well as the southern way of life. While Republicans claimed that they had no intention of abolishing slavery in any southern state, southerners also knew that blocking the expansion of slavery into the American West would eventually give the free states a distinct numerical advantage in the United States Congress. With that numerical advantage would come increased political power, and, at some future date, opponents of slavery might be able to marshal the numbers to abolish slavery via a constitutional amendment. Sensing that political power was slipping away from them, radical southerners, known as "fire eaters," were determined to force the issue with the election of Abraham Lincoln in 1860 and used Lincoln's election as a pretext to secede from the Union.

Southerners were also concerned that efforts to chip away at the institution of slavery threatened the southern way of life, which was built on the premise of white supremacy. Indeed, many southerners, from the poorest subsistence farmers to the wealthiest plantation owners, believed that whites were intrinsically superior to blacks. During the antebellum period, a number of southern writers and intellectuals had carefully constructed a pro-slavery argument that provided an intellectual framework to support this idea. The southern writer Thomas Roderick Dew, for instance, argued in the aftermath of the Nat Turner slave revolt in Virginia, that blacks were incapable of living in freedom because of inferiority; therefore, it was better for them to live as slaves. A life of freedom would undoubtedly lead to crime, dissipation, and pauperism for most African-Americans. Josiah Nott, a southern writer and physician, argued that whites and blacks did not, in fact, share common ancestry. Arguing that physical differences supported this contention, Nott maintained that blacks had less brain capacity than whites and that, therefore, they were well suited for lives as slaves or laborers.

Some of the most extreme and provocative thinking on slavery and southern society was performed by men such as George Fitzhugh, a southern philosopher and writer, and James H. Hammond, a South Carolina politician. Fitzhugh, in a series of books such as *Cannibals All!* and *Sociology of the South* constructed an extremely complex and elaborate argument justifying the institution of slavery. According to Fitzhugh, slavery was simply a more traditional form of social organization where the rich and powerful recognized their obligations to the poor and less powerful. Modern readers, when first acquainted with Fitzhugh's ideas, are likely to be shocked as well as outraged; however, Fitzhugh believed his theories had a certain amount of validity when readers considered the plight of free blacks in the north as well as the condition of the average northern wage earners. According to Fitzhugh, when the economy suffered a decline, northern workers were simply cut from payrolls and left to fend for themselves. By contrast, the southern slaveholder continued to provide food and shelter to the dependent slave regardless of the condition of the economy. For Fitzhugh, the modern economy that was developing in the free states allowed the rich to "cannibalize" the poor, but the southern economy, organized on a more traditional social arrangement, made sure that the strong did not completely destroy the weak. Fitzhugh often used colorful language to reinforce his points:

> Our slaves till the land, do the coarse and hard labor on our roads and canals, sweep our streets, cook our food, brush our boots, wait on our tables, hold our horses, do all hard work, and fill all menial offices. Your freedman at the North do the same work and fill the same offices. The only difference is, we love our slaves, and we are ready to defend, assist and protect them; you hate and fear your white servants, and never fail, as a moral duty, to screw down their wages to the lowest, and to starve their families, if possible, as evidence of your thrift, economy and management—the only English and Yankee virtues.[1]

Reinforcing and building on the ideas of George Fitzhugh, South Carolina Senator James Hammond popularized similar ideas in the halls of the United States Congress. Hammond argued that all history proved that involuntary labor was the most appropriate organization for laborers. Hammond and others referred to this as the "mudsill" theory of labor, which Hammond popularized in an 1858 speech before the United States

Senate. In the American South, however, the "mudsill" theory had been improved because the lower class had been exclusively identified with African-American slaves. By relegating blacks to the mudsill class, every white, even the most illiterate and uneducated, still had a place in society that was higher than the most elevated black. Thus by equating slavery with most productive form of economic organization and, at the same time, defining slavery in terms of race alone, southern theorists had developed a social and political framework that seemed to justify the plantation system, but, at the same time, give every white, even the most ignorant and impoverished, an important role in preserving the status quo. J. D. B. DeBow, the southern journalist, wrote at length about how the slave system elevated non-slaveholding whites in the South. "The poor white laborer at the North is at the bottom of the social ladder," remarked DeBow, "whilst his brother here [in the South] has ascended several steps and can look down upon those who are beneath him, at an infinite remove." Or as the southern historian of the early twentieth century, Ulrich Bonnell Phillips, argued, every white had an interest in making sure that the South was and remained a white man's country. Why then would southern whites, who owned no slaves and seemingly shared no conceivable economic or political interest with the upper class, fight and die to preserve the South's plantation system? Because even the lowest white, in this theory, had a place that was always at least one wrung on the ladder higher than the best African-American. As Phillips stated:

> Yet it [the South] is a land with a unity despite its diversity, with a people having common joys and common sorrows, and, above, all, as to the white folks a people with a common resolve indomitably maintained—that it shall be and remain a white man's country. The consciousness of a function in these premises, whether expressed with the frenzy of a demagogue or maintained with a patrician's quietude, is the cardinal test of a Southerner and the central theme of Southern history.

Reinforced in the press and from the pulpit, it is little wonder that southern whites fighting for the Confederacy would be enraged when they confronted African-Americans, donning blue uniforms, who seemed to challenge and contradict the very notion of innate white superiority.[2]

Southern ideas on race and the inferiority of African-Americans were not obviously exclusive to the South. Indeed, given the northern treatment of its own small population of free African-Americans during the antebellum period, one could make the argument that northerners and southerners held almost identical views on black inferiority and the position of blacks in American society. At the same time, northern writers, theorists, and politicians were also developing a unique set of ideas about northern society and how it differed from the social and economic organization of the south. According to advocates of what would become known as the "free labor" argument, northern society was dynamic, progressive, and constantly evolving for the good. The reason, as proponents argued, was that the northern society had jettisoned slavery and developed a dynamic culture based on free labor, not only the freedom of labor but the ability that freedom provided for ordinary workers and laborers in the antebellum United States. Under the plantation economy of the South, reasoned northern advocates of free labor ideology, the slave would always remain a slave; the master would always remain a master. While there might be some small slaveholders who might develop into large planters or some non-slaveholders who might acquire a few slaves, southern society was a model of the status quo. It was a static and lacked innovation as well as social mobility. Class lines were relatively fixed and, so the argument went, it was lacking in productivity and dynamism. By contrast, a northern free laborer might begin as a mere wage earner, but through hard work, savings, and diligence might become a business owner in the future. One of the most prolific speakers on the free labor argument was the sixteenth president of the United States, Abraham Lincoln. Addressing an audience at the Wisconsin state fair in 1859, Lincoln took direct aim at the mudsill theory of southern pro-slavery theorists and contrasted it with his own ideas of free labor. The proponents of the mudsill theory, argued Lincoln, believed that the condition of each laborer was fixed for life:

> They [southern advocates of the mudsill theory] further assume
> that whoever is once a *hired* laborer, is fatally fixed in that
> condition for life; and thence again that his condition is as bad as
> or worse than that of a slave. This is the "mudsill" theory.

But, maintained Lincoln, the beauty of the free labor northern economy was that the laborer was not in a permanent, fixed position. As Lincoln stated in a particularly cogent passage:

> The prudent, penniless beginner in the world, labors for wages
> awhile, saves a surplus with which to buy tools or land, for
> himself; then labors on his own account another while, and at
> length hires another new beginner to help him. This, say its
> advocates, is *free* labor—the just and generous, and prosperous
> system, which opens the way for all—gives hope to all, and
> energy, and progress, and improvement of the condition to all. If

any continue through life in the condition of a hired laborer, it is
not the fault of the system, but because of either a dependent
nature which prefers it, or improvidence, folly, or singular
misfortune.[3]

In order for the theory of free labor to function correctly, however, its
advocates had to ensure that American expansion into the western
territories of the United States promoted the conditions of free labor. If
slavery and the plantation system, with its rigid class lines, were allowed
to take root in the territories on the United States, the free labor society
that had revolutionized the north would not be duplicated in the west.
Beginning with the 1848 formation of the Free Soil party, preventing the
spread of slavery into the territories of the United States became a major
political position for large numbers of northern politicians and citizens.
With the formation of the Republican Party in 1854–1855, the United
States political system now had one major political party whose principal
position, whose raison d'être, was to stop the expansion of slavery into
the western territories of the United States.

For many Republican leaders, the political conflicts that had taken
place between the northern free states and the southern slave states in the
last 30 years were the result of competition between a slave system and a
free labor system. Many anti-slavery leaders also believed that the two
systems were incompatible. They had existed side by side for many years,
but could not peacefully co-exist into the indefinite future. As William
Henry Seward, the Republican Senator from New York put it, the two
radically different systems were headed for collision, and, moreover, that
collision was inevitable, even necessary. As Seward stated:

It is an irrepressible conflict between opposing and enduring
forces, and it means that the United States must and will, sooner
or later, become either entirely a slave-holding nation, or entirely
a free-labor nation. Either the cotton and rice-fields of South
Carolina and the sugar plantations of Louisiana will ultimately be
tilled by free labor, and Charleston and New Orleans become
marts for legitimate merchandise along, or else the rye-fields and
wheat fields of Massachusetts and New York must again be
surrendered by their farmers to slave culture and to the
production of slaves, and Boston and New York become once
more markets for the trade in bodies and souls of men.[4]

The fundamental ambiguity of the Republican Party was its moral
equivalence about slavery and African-Americans. Students relatively new

to the study of history and only superficially aware of the major contours of the sectional conflict and the American Civil War, often assume that the opposition to slavery expressed by northern Republicans and many northerners in general also represented feelings of sympathy toward African-Americans. In fact, except for small numbers of abolitionist and radical anti-slavery advocates within the Republican party, many Republicans did not necessarily have positive feeling toward blacks; many were not supporters of political and social equality for African-Americans; and many were content to prevent the spread of slavery into the territories, but were relatively unconcerned about the existence of slavery in the states where it already existed. In theory, it was certainly true that Republicans looked forward to a day when slavery did not exist in the United States, but this was fundamentally different than a vision of a bi-racial society where whites and blacks interacted on terms of equality. Many northerners were as committed to preserving white supremacy as the most ardent advocates of southern nationalism.

Northern ambiguity on the status of blacks was one reason it took so long for the Lincoln administration to support and implement the recruitment of African-Americans as soldiers. When it finally decided to use African-Americans in the United States armies, they were first accepted only into non-combat roles. When they were finally accepted into combat roles, they were not allowed to be commissioned officers and were paid significantly less than their white counterparts. Even more significantly, the reasons cited for use of black troops were often more pragmatic than ideological. Blacks may as well take bullets that were intended for whites. If whites failed to enlist in sufficient numbers, only the recruitment of blacks could offset potential manpower shortages. If African-Americans expected military service to advance the cause of their civil rights, the Lincoln administration, northern governors, and the bulk of the white population was far less enthusiastic about such prospects. Even with the adoption of emancipation as a formal war goal and policy, northerners were ambivalent about blacks and their position in northern society in a post Civil War country.

When news about the Fort Pillow Massacre spread throughout the north, there was a tremendous outpouring of anger toward the Confederate President Jefferson Davis and the rebel officers—Major General Nathan Bedford Forrest and Brigadier General James R. Chalmers—considered most responsible for the perpetration of the Fort Pillow Massacre. Although there would be demands for retaliation as well as negative public comment on Forrest for many years to come, in the end nothing concrete was really accomplished on behalf of African-American soldiers. No retaliation took place; no rebel officers were ever captured and tried for alleged war crimes. President Lincoln would issue a strong demand for accountability and an explanation from the Richmond government, promising the implementation of harsh measures if the government of Jefferson Davis did not address the alleged atrocities committed at Fort Pillow. When the Richmond government simply ignored the demands of the Lincoln administration, the issue was never pursued again in any meaningful sense.

Why did the Lincoln administration fail to follow up on the Fort Pillow atrocities? Why did the issue of retaliation, which was so much in the forefront of public opinion in the days and weeks after the Fort Pillow Massacre, so quickly become dead letter in the minds of many northerners? In searching for an answer to this question, one might also consider a parallel question. Why did a society that had incorporated emancipation as a war goal fail, during the Reconstruction period, to adequately protect the rights of African-Americans in the Reconstruction period, making a second Reconstruction period—the modern Civil Rights movement of the mid-twentieth century—necessary to advance the cause of black freedom and equality? The answer, I believe, lies in the northern ambiguity toward blacks. Antebellum American society, whether northern or southern, had almost universally held that African-Americans were fundamentally inferior to white Americans. In the four short years of the American Civil War, was it really realistic to expect a fundamental change in attitudes and outlooks? The events of the war caused the Lincoln administration to advocate and endorse positions that would have been considered radical and unrealistic prior to the war—even revolutionary. Once the war had ended, northerners had the opportunity to re-evaluate their thoughts on African-Americans. While most were not unhappy about the end of slavery, the slave as citizen was still something that made many Americans uncomfortable.

The Fort Pillow Massacre tells the story of America's complicated and conflicted attitudes on race. The southern anger and hostility expressed that day symbolized the frustration southerners felt about how the American Civil War was altering traditional southern social values, the role of white males, and a common commitment to white supremacy. The northern outrage over the massacre symbolized northern "theoretical" rejection of slavery and the slave system. The failure of a concrete response to the outrages of the massacre along with the shortcomings of the Reconstruction period in general, however, show an American society that was still uncomfortable with the notion of racial equality or, at best, was still struggling to define what racial equality meant in terms of social, political, and economic relationships. Northerners may have hated slavery, but they were not necessarily enthralled with the idea of the slave as an equal citizen. Again and again, throughout the war, in the statements of white northerners and African-Americans, one sees a divergence in the purpose and reasons for the use of African-American soldiers. Whites are typically pragmatic and cautious when it comes to implication of black participation in winning the Civil War. African-Americans, on other hand, were confident, hopeful, and in some cases, even adamant, that their military contributions should entitle them to full citizenship in the American Republic.

The present volume is divided into five chapters. The first chapter defines the context in which the Civil War took place, particularly from the perspective of the North. It also delineates the political debates that took place surrounding the use of African-Americans in combat as well as discrimination that many African-Americans experienced during their tenure in the armies in the United States. The second chapter provides a detailed account of the massacre at Fort Pillow, discussing the attitudes of southern generals, such as Nathan Bedford Forrest, as well as the attitudes and emotions of Confederate soldiers towards the African-American soldiers they faced at Fort Pillow. The description of the battle is based largely on eyewitness accounts from testimony of military officials as well as the Joint Committee on the Conduct of the War, a congressional committee assigned to investigate the massacre. Chapter 3 analyzes northern reactions to the massacre as well as the response of the Lincoln administration. It also discusses how African-American soldiers interpreted the massacre and modified their behavior in subsequent military engagements. This chapter also discusses how the failure of the northern government to take action as a result of the Fort Pillow Massacre parallels, in a broad sense, the failure of government in the aftermath of the Civil War to permanently secure the rights of African-Americans in American society. Chapter 4 discusses how historians have interpreted the Fort Pillow Massacre over the last 150 years, particularly how changing interpretations of historians have been influenced by broader societal trends, not simply by the fruits of scholarly research. Chapter 5 presents the reader a series of primary documents, most of which represent eyewitness accounts of the massacre as well as contemporary comment.

Students reading this volume are asked to draw their own conclusions about the significance of the Fort Pillow Massacre and how it should be interpreted as a critical event in American history. In reading and interpreting, however, students should also be aware of the different voices and points of view that are expressed in the narrative. In particular, why would southern soldiers in the Confederate army act the way they did? How would African-Americans, reading about the Fort Pillow Massacre, interpret the event and why? How would the interpretation of white northerners differ from both African-Americans and white Confederates and why? Why has it taken historians so long to adopt the point of view that a brutal massacre did take place at Fort Pillow? Finally, as students of history as citizens of the United States, what do we, as men, women, citizens of the United States, or simply human beings, ultimately conclude about a brutal and tragic event such as the Fort Pillow Massacre? The purpose in studying a brutal massacre such as Fort Pillow is not simply to pass judgment on the perpetrators; rather it is to understand motives, beliefs, and the emotions of the various actors in this pivotal and critical event in American history. History is a messy business, and the history of atrocities can be an even messier business. People act from a variety of emotions, motives, beliefs, and a host of other influences. The role of the student of history is to examine these conflicting bits and pieces of information and make the best judgment about what happened and why.

CHAPTER 1

Means to an End

After the election of Abraham Lincoln to the presidency in November 1860 and the eventual secession of seven southern states of the Deep South in the winter of 1860–1861, the linkage between the eventual eruption of the American Civil War and the institution of slavery was obvious. The election of Abraham Lincoln, the first Republican presidential candidate to win the presidency, was something that obviously threatened the South, and the reason southerners were threatened was the position that the Republican party took on the slavery—particularly its determination to block the expansion of slavery in the American West. Indeed, almost every attempt to resolve the national crisis brought about by the act of secession, whether the so-called congressional plan known as the Crittenden Compromise or the February 4, 1861 Washington Peace Conference was intimately connected to issues that involved the "peculiar institution," as slavery came to be known. The Crittenden Compromise, named for Kentucky Senator John J. Crittenden, proposed a series of amendments to the Constitution that hoped to resolve the conflict over slavery. Two of the proposed amendments, however, could not be accepted by congressional Republicans.

One amendment would extend the Missouri Compromise line to the Pacific Ocean. By doing this, United States territories south of the Missouri Compromise line would be open to the spread of slavery, something that violated the fundamental purpose of the Republican Party to prevent the spread of slavery into the territories of the United States. Another amendment would have prevented the abolition of slavery by the Federal government in any current slave state. Similarly, the Washington Peace Conference attempted to use the principles of the Crittenden Compromise as a framework for national reconciliation. When several northern and southern states boycotted the proceedings, this effort at compromise collapsed.[1]

The 1850s was a volatile decade for the United States. Although cultural issues such as the battle over temperance, immigration, and control of public education occupied a great deal of public debate throughout local communities and states, some of the most volatile events of the decade concerned slavery, particularly its potential expansion into the western territories of the United States. The passage of the Kansas-Nebraska Act in 1854, the brainchild of Illinois Democratic Senator, Stephen A. Douglas, fueled a national debate over the expansion of slavery since the measure proposed to abolish the Missouri Compromise line when applied to the territories of Kansas and Nebraska. Each of these territories was north of the Missouri Compromise line. In addition, each territory was also part of the Louisiana Purchase territory. Douglas's bill introduced the principle of "popular sovereignty" as a mechanism to referee the question of the expansion of slavery. If the residents of a territory wanted slavery, they would choose by democratic means to establish the institution. If they did not want slavery, they would do the opposite. Unfortunately, as popular sovereignty played out on the plains of Kansas in the 1850s, it was transformed into popular savagery. As pro-slavery and anti-slavery forces competed to organize Kansas as a slave or Free State, violence escalated. In 1857, the controversy culminated when pro-slavery forces, then in charge of the Kansas territorial legislature, through various acts of political chicanery, attempted to bring Kansas into

The Missouri Compromise of 1820 temporarily resolved one the first major disputes in the early American Republic over the expansion of slavery. When northern members of Congress attempted to block the admission of Missouri into the Union as a slave state, a sectional crisis erupted in the nation's capitol. Eventually a compromise was negotiated that allowed the admission of Missouri with slavery but was balanced by the admission of Maine as a free state. Since Missouri was part of the Louisiana Purchase territory recently acquired from France, Congress also put forward a mechanism to govern the admission of future states carved out of the Louisiana territory, establishing a northern latitude line of 36, 30. Future states could not come into the Union as slave states if they were north of this line.

Source: EEATW: 2: 377–378.

Abbreviations:
EACW: *Encyclopedia of the American Civil War: A Political, Social, and Military History*. David S. Heidler and Jeanne T. Heidler, eds. 5 vols. Santa Barbara, California: ABC-CLIO, 2000.
EEATW: *Encyclopedia of Emancipation and Abolition in the Transatlantic World*. Junius Rodriguez, ed. 3 vols. Armonk, New York: Sharpe Reference, 2007.
WWWCW: *Who Was Who in the Civil War*. Stewart Sifakis, ed. New York: Facts on File, 1988.

the Union as a slave state under the fraudulent document known as the Lecompton Constitution. While the said Constitution was rejected by the United States Congress—meaning Kansas was temporarily denied statehood, the fight over the ratification of the Lecompton Constitution was another example of the divisiveness of the slavery issue in the 1850s.

Probably the most controversial event of the 1850s involved the United States Supreme Court when it rendered its *Dred Scott v. Sanford* decision on March 6, 1857. Not only did the case decide that African-Americans were not entitled to citizenship, the Court also rejected the central tenet of the Republican Party when it determined that not even Congress could pass laws to prevent slavery from spreading into the territories of the United States. According to the court and its chief Justice, Roger B. Taney, southern slaveholders had the right to migrate to United States territories with their slave property. To deny this right was to violate the Fifth Amendment to the constitution, which guaranteed that citizens could not be denied their property rights without due process of law. Since slaves were property, telling a potential southern settler that he was not allowed

---

Sidebar 1.1

The *Dred Scott v. Sanford* Supreme Court decision of March 1857 was one of the most controversial Supreme Court decisions in all of American history. Dred Scott, a Missouri slave, had belonged to an army surgeon named Emerson, who, in the course of his travels for the army, transported Scott to both Illinois and Wisconsin territory, the former a free state and the latter part of the Louisiana territory that was north of the Missouri Compromise line. Scott originally filed suit for his freedom in Missouri courts in 1846, but the case, after 11 years, ended up in the United States Supreme Court. In a majority opinion written by chief Justice Roger B. Taney, a Maryland resident sympathetic to the rights of slaveholders, the Court declared that Scott was not a citizen and, therefore, was not entitled to sue in Federal court. Although Taney's arguments were factually incorrect—some blacks had, in fact, been considered citizens at the time the Constitution was ratified—he could have let the case rest with the Court's refusal to grant Scott an audience with the Court. Instead, Taney also weighed in on the constitutionality of the Missouri Compromise of 1820. Because the fifth amendment to the Constitution stated that citizens could not be deprived a property without due process of law, Taney declared congressional prohibitions on slavery in federal territories were unconstitutional. Hence, the Missouri Compromise of 1820 was declared null and void. While southerners applauded this decision, many residents of the North, particularly members of the Republican Party, were appalled and determined to work toward a reversal of the Court's decision in the future.

Source: EEATW: 1:182–184.

to take slaves into a Federal territory deprived the citizen of property without due process.

Shortly after the Dred Scott decision was handed down, a number of southern Senators made the demand that the Federal government back up the court's position in the Dred Scott case by providing a Federal slave code that would protect the peculiar institution in all territories of the United States. The adoption of a territorial slave code would mean that southerners could settle into the territories of the United States and take slaves along with them.

With the election of Republican presidential candidate, Abraham Lincoln, in the election of 1860, politicians of the Deep South states reached a crisis point in their assessment of their relationship within the Federal Union. While Lincoln garnered nearly 40 percent of the popular vote in a four-candidate race, he had not even been on the ballot in any of the states of the Deep South. Additionally, his electoral majority was based on carrying the larger, more populous northern states, without carrying a single slave state. For many southern political figures, this was a moment of crisis. Accustomed to dominating the national government for years, the South now saw a sectional political party, whose avowed goal was to limit and eventually eliminate the institution of slavery, achieve political power. For many southern political leaders, the handwriting was on the wall. With the secession of the southern states, the firing on Fort Sumter, and Lincoln's call for 75,000 90-day volunteers to put down the insurrection, the American Civil War had begun.[2]

Since disagreements over slavery and its expansion had played an important role in bringing about the crisis, one might reasonably conclude that the Union's attempt to put down the southern rebellion would also include provisions to eliminate and eradicate the peculiar institution. As the first Republican president in American history, Abraham Lincoln had come to national prominence in the senatorial campaign of 1858. Opposing the much more popular and well-known Democratic incumbent, Stephen A. Douglas, Lincoln had captured the imagination of many anti-slavery supporters throughout the country with his soaring moral rhetoric about the evils of slavery. At the joint debate with Douglas at Quincy, Illinois on October 13, 1858, Lincoln tried to define the difference between himself and the Democrat Douglas. He stated:

> I suggest that the difference of opinion, reduced to its lowest terms, is no other than the difference between the men who think slavery a wrong and those who do not think it a wrong. The Republican party think it wrong—we think it is a moral, social, and a political wrong.

A few days later, while debating Douglas at Alton, Illinois Lincoln again crystallized the issue, stating:

> the real issue in this controversy—the one pressing upon every mind is the sentiment on the part of one class that looks upon the institution of slavery as a wrong, and of another class that does not look upon it as wrong.[3]

Yet Lincoln himself, in different debate venues throughout the state of Illinois, said different things to different audiences that seemed to mitigate the moral fervor of his public denunciations of slavery. Speaking at Charleston, Illinois on September 18, 1858, Lincoln sounded more traditional, stating:

> I will say then that I am not, nor ever have been, in favor of bringing about in any way the social and political equality of the white and black races—that I am not nor ever have been in favor of making voters or jurors of negroes, nor of qualifying them to hold office, nor to intermarry with white people.

Although twenty-first-century Americans may be shocked to read such sentiments from a president popularly known as the "Great Emancipator," in reality Lincoln's point of view was conventional, even mainstream, in the United States of the mid-nineteenth century. Despite a small population of abolitionists who were dedicated to eradicating the institution of slavery and even bringing about a measure of social and political equality for African-Americans, the vast majority of the northern population, at the

Sidebar 1.2

In the early republic, Northern states abolished slavery in the following order:

Vermont, 1777
Pennsylvania, 1780 (gradual abolition)
Massachusetts, 1783 (decree of the state Supreme Court)
Connecticut and Rhode Island, 1784 (gradual abolition)
New York, 1799 (gradual abolition)
Ohio, 1802
New Jersey, 1804 (gradual abolition)
Indiana, 1816
Illinois, 1818

onset of the Civil War, was much more tentative in their opinions on African-Americans. While believing slavery was wrong, many northerners were equally anti-black and negrophobic in outlook.[4]

If many northerners disliked the institution of slavery, they still, nevertheless, had an unfavorable opinion of African-Americans. Viewed as inferior to whites in intelligence, ambition, and morality, many whites viewed blacks as lazy, indolent, and incapable of self-direction. In the popular culture of the day, blacks were portrayed as closely resembling animals, named Zip Coon or Jim Crow in the popular minstrel shows of the antebellum period. Black speech was often ridiculed in newspapers and editorial cartoons. Above all, many whites believed that blacks really did not want freedom. Believing that African-Americans were incapable of self-direction, many northerners thought that African-Americans were better off under the slave system. In many respects, northern ideas on blacks and black nature resembled the thinking of the southern pro-slavery apologists, such as the southern theorist George Fitzhugh, who reasoned that slavery was a beneficent institution in which philanthropic white slaveholders cared for childlike blacks.[5]

The population of African-Americans in the United States on the eve of the Civil War was approximately four million. Nearly 10 percent of African-Americans were free, residing in some of the large cities in the south such as Charleston, Baltimore, and New Orleans. In the northern states, where slavery was largely extinct by 1830, the free black population was largely an urban phenomenon. And freedom, as the historian Leon Litwack observed, did not confer citizenship on African-Americans. Despite the relative insignificance of the free black population from a numerical perspective, many states, particularly in the Midwest, adopted anti-black laws that severely limited the rights of the African-American population. Save for a handful of New England states, blacks were not allowed to vote in the majority of northern states. In almost every state, blacks were forbidden to serve on juries, testify in trials, and perform military or militia service. Several states such as Illinois and Indiana adopted exclusion measures that forbade free blacks from migrating into the state on penalty of fines or even imprisonment. Midwestern states like Ohio had a special class of black laws that forbade African-Americans from any type of public assistance, forbade serving on juries, and discouraged blacks from coming into the state. At the Federal level, African-Americans prior to 1855 had difficulty acquiring passports for travel abroad. For the sake of balance, it must also be pointed out that for many Americans, the idea of contact with African-Americans in the mid-nineteenth century was almost an abstraction. In the Midwest, the population of free blacks was so miniscule that many residents probably passed their entire lives without coming into contact with blacks. Still, because of deep-seated prejudices, anti-black rhetoric and anti-black measures were popular in most of the northern states. As several historians point out, the anti-slavery platform of the Republican Party, particularly the determination to keep the territories of the United States free from slavery was a double-edged sword. Many Americans certainly wanted to keep slavery out of the territories, but they also wanted to keep African-Americans— slave or free—from these "virgin" lands.[6]

Even many anti-slavery advocates believed that the abolition of slavery would not lead to an integrated society. As a result, there was widespread support for the colonization of free blacks in the north and even in portions of the border slave states where a modicum of anti-slavery sentiment continued to persist in the antebellum time. The primary argument for colonization was the inability of blacks to compete in white society. Driven by the assumptions of black inferiority in almost every relevant aspect of human activity, colonization advocates believed that sending free African-Americans to reside in Africa or other tropical, humid environments would benefit both blacks and whites. Formed in 1816, the American Colonization Society promoted the gradual emancipation of slavery coupled with colonization of free blacks to Africa. Although the society would found the country of Liberia in West Africa, colonization was not successful for many reasons, the primary one being the determined resistance of free African-American leaders such as Frederick Douglass, a prominent Rochester, New York editor and abolitionist and James Forten, a prominent member of Philadelphia's free black community. Rejecting the notion of innate black inferiority, free black leaders argued that they were Americans and entitled to the same rights and opportunities as white Americans. While a few African-American leaders such as Martin R. Delany would endorse colonization on the grounds that white society would never fully accept African-Americans, the majority of blacks on the eve of the Civil War continued to hope for a better seat at the table of American democracy.[7]

Martin Robison Delany is considered one of the founders of Black Nationalism. Born on May 6, 1812 in Charles Town, Virginia (present day West Virginia), he was born a free man, although all of his grandparents began life as slaves. Because he suffered from racial oppression, particularly in his attempt to study medicine, Delany became a vigorous advocate of repatriation of American blacks, although he opposed the efforts to establish a free black country in Liberia, which was the project of the American Colonization Society. Serving in the American Civil War, Delany was the first African-American to become a commissioned major in the United States Army. He died in Ohio in 1885.

Source: EEATW: 1: 171–174.

Even though the debate over slavery was intimately connected with the eruption of the American Civil War and despite outcries from radicals within the Republican Party to link the suppression of the rebellion with the abolition of slavery, President Lincoln proceeded cautiously when outlining his goals for the war. A native of Kentucky and a long time resident of Illinois where negrophobia was widespread, the President knew that early and aggressive action against the peculiar institution would be unpopular with many northerners. In the first place, as Lincoln tried to make clear from the beginning of the conflict, the "war" was not really a war but the suppression of a civil insurrection. In wars between two foreign nations or belligerent powers, there was precedent for the confiscation of enemy property. Since slaves were considered property—at least by most slave owning southerners, there was support for the position that the president, using the war powers, could issue proclamations of emancipation as consistent with the established laws of war. In fact, this was the position of such radicals as Republican Senator Charles Sumner of Massachusetts, a famous anti-slavery legislator who urged Lincoln to consider such action as soon as the bombardment of Fort Sumter had taken place. Since the Lincoln administration denied that this was a war between two belligerent powers, the exercise of the president's war power was unwarranted. "Slave owners in particular," writes historian Burrus Carnahan, "could not deny that, in their view, slaves were another form of property, entitled to no greater protection from enemy action than any other property." Yet, if the civil war was an insurrection and not a war between two belligerents, the right to confiscate or emancipate slaves could not be legally asserted.[8]

For several practical reasons, Lincoln, in the early days of the war, contradicted his policy of viewing the war as an insurrection as opposed to a war between two belligerent powers. For instance, shortly after the firing on Fort Sumter, Lincoln announced, on April 19, 1861 a naval blockade of southern ports. Such an action directly contradicted statements that the war was merely a civil insurrection. Typically a nation would not blockade its ports during the suppression of an internal civil war. To declare a blockage was, in fact, granting a certain de facto recognition of the Confederacy as an independent nation. When it came to the confiscation of enemy property, however, Lincoln took a much different approach, especially as it concerned the institution of slavery. A number of prominent Republicans including the president and his Secretary of State, William Henry Seward, were convinced the secession lacked traction among many southerners. According to this point of view, the southern masses had been whipped into secessionist frenzy by demagogic southern extremists. Once the gravity of secession and civil war set in, many southern civilians would come to their senses and a latent Unionism would emerge in many southern states, particularly the Border States. It was imperative, therefore, that northern leaders did not overreact to the situation. To do this, Union leaders initially pursued a policy known as conciliation. Conciliation meant that as northern forces attempted to subdue the South militarily, they would do so with minimal impact on southern civilians. By so doing, the spirit of rebellion might collapse of its own volition. It was important, under this point of view, that no action be taken to disturb slavery. Not only did Lincoln initially practice conciliation, Congress also approved, passing the Crittenden-Johnson resolution in the aftermath of the Union defeat at the first battle of Manassas in July 1861. The resolution stated that the war had nothing to do with overturning or abolishing the institution of slavery.[9]

An even more pressing reason why the northern government hesitated to attack slavery was the lack of popular consensus. Most northerners, Democrat or Republican, were more interested in saving the Union than in abolishing slavery. "Except among abolitionists and some Radical Republicans," writes historian Gary Gallagher, "liberation of enslaved people took a back seat to saving the Union." To allow the seceded states to break up the Union as a result of Lincoln's election would mean that popular democracy had failed, that the experiment with popular government could not be maintained. If the Lincoln administration had decided to attack the institution of slavery from the onset of the conflict, it would have lost the support and the resources of many of the border slave states that had remained loyal to the Union. Additionally, the opposition party, the northern Democrats, would have turned against the war. Early on in the conflict, the president had worked tirelessly to construct a pro-war Union coalition. Premature action against slavery might have compromised his efforts.[10]

Despite Lincoln's determination to steer clear of the slavery issue in the early stages of the war, at critical moments during the early years of the American Civil War, individual military commanders attempted to take an aggressive policy towards slavery, a policy that was much in advance of the views of the Lincoln administration. In the opinion of the president, these actions threatened to erode the fragile war coalition that he had carefully constructed during the first months of the conflict. On August 30, 1861, for instance, Department of the West commander, Major General John C. Fremont, issued a proclamation of martial law and emancipation for the Department of the West. Fremont's proclamation made all rebel slaves in his area of jurisdiction free, something that directly contradicted the administration's policy. As previously stated, such a measure, it could be argued, had the precedent of international law, and, moreover, such proclamations were not unheard of in the annals of military history. Although the measure touched a chord of popular support, Lincoln officially countermanded the measure on September 8, 1861, reasoning that such a policy could not be instituted without his approval as commander-in-chief. More importantly, Fremont's proclamation might have driven the Border State of Kentucky, a slave state that had stayed within the Union, into the arms of the Confederacy. As Lincoln stated to Orville Hickman Browning, a Senator from Illinois and close political confident of the president, "I think to lose Kentucky," Lincoln told Browning,

> is nearly the same as to lose the whole game. Kentucky gone, we can not hold Missouri, nor, as I think, Maryland. These all against us, and the job on our hands is too large for us. We would as well consent to separation at once, including the surrender of this capitol . . . You must understand I took my course on the proclamation because of Kentucky.[11]

Just seven months later, Lincoln faced a similar action from another of his generals, when Department of the South commander, Major General David Hunter, issued a proclamation on May 9, 1862 that declared that all slaves in the Department of the South (which consisted of Union controlled areas of South Carolina, Georgia, and Florida) were emancipated. Again overruling one of his generals, Lincoln reminded his Secretary of the Treasury, Salmon P. Chase, who defended Hunter's course of action, that only he, the president, had the authority to take such a measure against the South. Yet, the passage of a few months between the actions of Fremont and those of Hunter was significant. Even though Lincoln reversed Hunter's proclamation, his thinking on the relationship between the war and slavery was changing. As Union battlefield fortunes sagged, Lincoln, the Republican Party, and public opinion was beginning to accept the idea that action against slavery, as a means to defeat the Confederacy, was not only necessary but desirable.[12]

Despite the many reasons for trying to sidestep the slavery issue early on in the war, there were a number of individuals, events, and situations that kept the peculiar institution in the spotlight. First, a number of radical Republicans, abolitionists, and prominent free African-American leaders continued to lobby for aggressive action against slavery. Second, as the war continued, the number of instances where Union forces had to deal with fugitive slaves coming into Union lines increased; moreover, as the conflict dragged on, it assumed the character of a conventional war between two belligerents. The precedents from the laws of war would certainly justify actions that would result in the confiscation and emancipation of slave "property." Finally, lackluster Union military performance created pressure for northern political leaders to take additional measures to defeat the Confederacy. If southern slaves worked plantations and performed labor to assist the Confederacy, and, moreover, if the Richmond government used slaves to help build fortifications and other military tasks, perhaps it was time for northern political leaders to take action to eliminate this valuable resource so it could weaken and eventually defeat its military opponent.

Even before hostilities erupted between the North and the South, some anti-slavery advocates viewed the outbreak of war as an opportunity to rid the nation of slavery. Although initially such demands were muted in the aftermath of the firing on Fort Sumter, by the end of the summer 1861, radicals such as Senator Charles Sumner of Massachusetts became more outspoken in linking the cause of the North with the abolition of slavery. "People who ask for peace should be told," Sumner wrote to abolitionist Wendell Phillips, "that peace is impossible while Slavery exits. Abolition is the Condition Precedent." The female African-American abolitionist, Harriet Tubman, was well aware of the connection between slavery and the cause of the war. As she told her friend, Lydia Maria Childs:

> Suppose there was an awfully big snake down there on the floor.
> He bites you. You send for the doctor to cut the bite; but the
> snake, he coils up there, and while the doctor is doing it, he bites
> you again. The doctor cuts down that bit, but while he is doing it
> the snake springs up and bites you again, and so he keeps doing
> it till you kill him. That's what Mister Lincoln ought to know.

The African-American abolitionist Frederick Douglass, likewise, believed that the only way to win the war and to restore the Union was to make war on the slaveholder and slavery. Unlike other anti-slavery radicals, however, Douglass and other African-American leaders also recommended the enlistment of black soldiers in the cause of the Union. Arguing that the Confederacy was using slaves and slave labor to assists its military endeavors, northern armies should do the same.[13]

Even though the Lincoln administration had pledged to wage a war for the restoration of the Union without interfering with slavery, the Union military was tasked with the delicate duty of what to do with fugitive slaves that came into Union lines. Despite the secession of 11 slave states, the 1850 Fugitive Slave Law was still the law of the land.

This meant that southern slaveholders still had an expectation that the Union military would return runaway slaves to masters, even if those masters were no longer loyal to the Union government. Although Lincoln would overrule both the emancipation proclamations of Fremont and Hunter, in May 1861, an event transpired that would begin to alter the Lincoln administration's position on slavery. With Brigadier General Benjamin F. Butler, a Massachusetts political general, commanding Union forces at Fortress Monroe, three fugitive slaves came across into the fort on May 19, 1861, when a Confederate officer attempted to retrieve the three fugitives on the basis of the Fugitive Slave Law. Butler refused, stating that the aforementioned law did not apply to a foreign nation. "Butler's action," writes historian Eric Foner, "did not imply a broad attack on slavery. He recognized the fugitives as property but used that very status to release them from service to their owners."[14]

Congress, in effect, codified Butler's actions a few months later

> The Fugitive Slave Act of 1850 was one of the most controversial pieces of legislation passed by the Congress in the 1850s. Part of a series of compromise measures known collectively as the "Compromise of 1850," the law addressed southern concerns that the 1793 Fugitive Slave Act was too lenient. The law allowed slave owners to reclaim runaway slaves and penalized those citizens who sought to interfere with recovery of fugitive slaves. Perhaps the most controversial portion of the law required federal marshals to assist in the apprehension of runaways and could deputize ordinary citizens to assists in these tasks, regardless of their personal beliefs about slavery. As a result, many northern states passed personal liberty laws that forbade citizens of the state to render assistance to Federal authorities.
> Source: EACW: 2: 794–796.

when it passed the 1st Confiscation Act in August 1861. Butler's actions were justified on the grounds that the fugitive slaves had, in fact, been working on Confederate fortifications. The law allowed slaves to be seized by Union military officials if they were being used to support the Confederate war effort. The law did not free slaves. In fact, the status of confiscated slaves was ambiguous. As legal historian Burrus Carnahan notes, "the First Confiscation Act was designed more to punish slave owners than to free slaves." Although slaves freed under this act could not be returned to a master through the provisions of the Fugitive Slave Act, slaves did not automatically inherit rights such as the right to give testimony or vote; moreover, the offspring of slaves freed under this act were not free. Finally, any slave owner who felt slaves were illegally seized could certainly sue the Federal government for the return of confiscated "property."[15]

Despite the limited provisions of the 1st Confiscation Act, as the war entered its second full year, members of the Republican Party became more impatient on taking action against slavery. A good deal of this impatience stemmed from uneven military progress. During the early days of the conflict, a wild enthusiasm had invigorated communities throughout the northeast, the Atlantic mid-section, and the Middle West, as it was widely assumed that northern armies would quickly suppress the southern rebellion. As 1861 yielded many Union defeats and few victories, the early enthusiasm for the conflict atrophied. Although victories in the western theatre, particularly the capture of Fort Henry and Fort Donelson in Tennessee in February 1862 by Union forces under Ulysses S. Grant, temporarily revived northern hopes for a short war, the military situation in the east continued to worry the public as well as the Lincoln administration. The massive Army of the Potomac had remained inactive for several months under the command of Major General George McClellan. Determined not to be pushed into a campaign until he was ready, McClellan resisted moving south until March 1862 when he embarked on an ambitious amphibious expedition to take the Confederate capital of Richmond, known as the Peninsula Campaign. After several battles in which McClellan and his Army of the Potomac surrendered the military initiative to the smaller Army of Northern Virginia under Joseph Johnston but eventually Robert E. Lee, by early July, the Army of the Potomac languished at Harrison's landing on the banks of the James River, east of the Confederate capital of Richmond. Demanding sizeable reinforcements before he could move again on Richmond, McClellan's lack of success had a negative impact on Union recruiting and the ability of the North to continue the war. It was under these circumstances that the president began to consider harsher measures, actions that in 1861 would have been considered out of bounds. In effect, Lincoln was determined to jettison the early policy of conciliation that had shaped his policy on slavery in the early days of the war.

Even before McClellan's campaign had been labeled a failure, both Congress and the president had taken aim at slavery. On March 13, 1862, the president signed a resolution passed by both houses of Congress that made it illegal for Union officers to return fugitive slaves to rebel masters. A week earlier, the president tried to jump start the emancipation movement in the loyal slave states by sending a resolution to Congress promising financial compensation to any loyal state that voluntarily decided to end slavery. Lincoln believed that the war would eventually doom the peculiar institution; however, to ensure that the Border States would remain loyal to the Union, Lincoln hoped to offer financial compensation to slaveholders for giving up their slaves. Although both houses of Congress passed the resolution, no Border State representative was interested in the measure. Similarly in early April, 1862, Lincoln signed a measure to abolish slavery in the District of Columbia, where the federal government was allowed to take such action without violating state prerogatives. The bill provided slave-owners with financial remuneration for emancipated slaves, and, additionally, provided $100,000 for the colonization of slaves freed under the provisions of the law.[16]

With the refusal of the Border State congressmen to respond to Lincoln's proposal, the president was now free to consider alternative measures. The evolution of Lincoln's thought on the war and its relationship with slavery had come a long way since the early days of the war and the philosophy of conciliation. From the perspective of George McClellan, the highest ranking general in the northern army and rising political star of the Democratic Party, little had changed. Writing Lincoln from Harrison's landing in early July, 1862 McClellan outlined his views on the conduct of the war:

> The rebellion has assumed the character of a War; as such it should be regarded; and it should be conducted upon the highest principles known to Christian Civilization. It should not be a War looking to the subjugation of the people of any state, in any event. It should not be, at all, a War upon population; but against armed forces and political organizations. Neither confiscation of property, political executions of persons, territorial organizations of states or forcible abolition of slavery should be contemplated for the moment.

Lincoln never responded to McClellan's appeal. McClellan's approach and philosophy had been found wanting. It was time to try a new approach, one that would allow the Union to avail itself of the laws of war and include a more rigorous confiscation of enemy property, the emancipation of slaves, and eventually, the use of slaves as soldiers to help put down the rebellion.[17]

Shortly after McClellan's Harrison's landing letter was received by Lincoln, both the president and Congress undertook a series of measures that took aim at the institution of slavery. In late July, 1862, Congress passed and Lincoln signed the Militia Act of 1862. This bill allowed the recruitment of African-Americans into the army for non-military roles. The thought behind the provision was that African-Americans could perform labor and other non-combat types of duties that would allow a higher percentage of white troops to be available for combat. Paid $10 per month minus a clothing allowance of $3, African-Americans were paid significantly lower than whites in the armed services, who earned $13 minus the clothing allowance. Although the president stated that he would not consider using black troops in combat roles, there were elements in the Republican Party and the free African-American community that urged the president to reconsider. Conversely within conservative circles and the Border States, there were howls of protest. The use of blacks in non-combat roles, argued critics of the legislation, simply presaged the use of black troops. Democratic critics of the administration, known as Copperheads or Peace Democrats, sensed that the character of the conflict and the goals of the war were subtly changing. Despite assurance to the contrary by Lincoln, who clearly articulated his policies on the war in a public letter to Horace Greeley, the radical editor of the *New-York Tribune*, critics of the administration were not satisfied. "My paramount object in the struggle," Lincoln wrote,

> *is* to save the Union, and is *not* to save or destroy slavery. If I could save the Union without freeing *any* slave I would do it, and if I could save it by freeing *all* the slaves I would do it; and if I could save it by freeing some and leaving others alone I would also so that. What I do about slavery and the colored race, I do because I believe it helps save the Union.[18]

In fact, as early as July 13, 1862 Lincoln had made the decision to emancipate; however, since the military situation was not favorable, particularly in the aftermath of the failed Peninsula campaign; Lincoln was persuaded by Secretary of State Seward to withhold such a proclamation until a military victory transpired. In Seward's opinion, using emancipation in the present situation might appear as an act of desperation. In the meantime, however, Congress passed the 2nd Confiscation Act, a more aggressive piece of legislation than the earlier Confiscation Act. The 2nd Confiscation Act allowed all property—including slaves—to be seized from anyone who supported the rebellion. Under section nine of this law, slaves that came across Union laws were free. Although Lincoln had some reservations about the law, he eventually signed the bill on the grounds of military necessity. It would only be a few short weeks until Lincoln accomplished the same thing by issuing his preliminary Emancipation Proclamation after the Union victory at Antietam. "Congress had adopted emancipation as a means of economic warfare," notes Burrus Carnahan, "and the president would carry this policy to its logical conclusion."[19]

Lincoln would get the opportunity to take executive action after the battle of Antietam in western Maryland on September 17, 1862. When George B. McClellan's Army of the Potomac was able to stop Robert E. Lee's invasion of the North in what proved to be the bloodiest single day of the war in the small western Maryland town, Lincoln believed he had the appropriate military momentum to take action. Hence, on September 22, 1862, Lincoln issued the preliminary Emancipation Proclamation. The document gave rebellious states 90 days to put down arms and rejoin the Union. If states did not heed Lincoln's warning, then slaves in areas of rebellion against the United States would be considered forever free. Lincoln made little mention of the moral issue of slavery in the document; instead military necessity was the principal motive. If slavery was directly attacked, the Confederacy's ability to wage war would be weakened. There was also no mention of arming black troops in the preliminary Emancipation Proclamation. Although Lincoln had done little more than Congress had already accomplished in the 2nd Confiscation Act, the preliminary Emancipation Proclamation created a howl of protest among Democrats throughout northern cities and the rural Middle West.[20]

Ethnic groups such as the Germans and Irish along with the so-called "butternuts" of the lower Middle West had initially supported the war; however, their support for the war was based on restoring the Union and had nothing to do with the abolition of slavery. Republicans, too, had been wary of attacking slavery initially; but as the military situation grew grim, those skeptical of emancipation were able to expand their definition of the Union to incorporate the abolition of slavery. "Lincoln's proclamation," writes John David Smith, "had indeed transformed the war from a constitutional struggle over the maintenance of the Union to one of black liberation." Many members of the opposition party could not make this transformation and some spoke out in vociferous terms against the preliminary Emancipation Proclamation. For opponents of emancipation, the measure was simply a prelude to a society where miscegenation would be commonplace; where inexpensive black workers would deluge the north and displace white workers; where indolent and ignorant African-Americans would become wards of the state and lower the quality of life for white residents. One small town Democratic paper ridiculed the preliminary Emancipation proclamation in colorful terms:

> The long agony is over—the days of the war are numbered! Abolitionists will join the ranks now—they will go "flaming" with the grand object of hugging niggers to their bosoms—they will be "giants" in accomplishing the ends for which they instigated the war. Hoop de-dooden-do! the niggers are free![21]

Like the decision to emancipate, the Lincoln administration cautiously moved toward a position of using blacks in combat roles. There was already much ridicule and opposition from the ranks of the Democratic Party. In Lincoln's home state of Illinois, the president's political ally, Governor

Richard Yates, on July 12, 1862, published a letter that endorsed more vigorous war measures and hinted at the necessity of arming black troops. For this, Yates was widely ridiculed in Democratic papers throughout the state. The *Chicago Times*, for instance, accused Yates of possessing "a combination of negro and whiskey on the brain fearfully." The paper also mocked Yates for even suggesting that somehow white troops would want the help of African-Americans. "Never will they [Union troops] cry out, 'Help us, negroes, or we sink.'" Worried that blacks on the battlefield might also alienate Border States such as Kentucky, Lincoln's initial attitude toward blacks in the military was cautious. When a delegation of western Republicans visited Lincoln at the White House in early August 1862 and offered the president two regiments of black soldiers, the president refused, stating "that he was not prepared to go the length of enlisting negroes as soldiers. He would employ all colored men offered as laborers, but would not promise to make soldiers of them." In fact, the administration's policy on arming black soldiers was not always consistent as the War Department had authorized a limited use of blacks for military purposes as early as October 1861, when the War Department authorized Brigadier-General Thomas Sherman, commander of the Department of the South, to recruit anyone to assist in the invasion of the sea islands of South Carolina. Yet the Lincoln administration was cautious and skeptical of any attempts to go beyond this limited policy. When then Secretary of War, Simon Cameron, in his annual report in December 1861, argued for a more general policy of freeing and arming slaves in the south, his endorsement was quickly criticized and countermanded by the president. Cameron's unorthodox position on arming black troops was a factor in his removal from his position in early 1862.[22]

When Major General David Hunter assumed command of the Department of the South on March 31, 1862, he asked permission of Secretary of War, Edwin Stanton, to organize African-Americans into military units. Although Lincoln would publicly reprimand Hunter when the latter issued his Proclamation of Emancipation, Hunter continued his efforts to organize runaway slaves from the coastal regions into military units, using former Secretary of War Cameron's order to Thomas W. Sherman as his authorization. That Hunter was organizing blacks into military units set off a wave of comment in the northern press, both positive and negative. In early July 1862, a spirited debate took place in the United States House of Representatives between Kentucky congressman, Robert Mallory, and Pennsylvania Republican, Thaddeus Stevens. Mallory, along with his Kentucky colleague, Charles A. Wickliffe objected to the work of General Hunter in organizing black troops. Although Mallory had no objection to using African-Americans as laborers who might perform menial work, he objected to blacks being used in combat roles. Armed blacks would slaughter their former masters along with the master's families. "When armed," stated Mallory, "they will be turned loose against those who have been heretofore their masters, and that when they get the ascendancy their practice will be the indiscriminate slaughter of men, women, and children, wherever they go." At the same time, Mallory paradoxically maintained that blacks lacked the necessary discipline to be organized as soldiers. "One shot of a cannon would disperse thirty thousand of them," maintained Mallory. Thaddeus Stevens, meanwhile, ridiculed Mallory for relegating blacks to exclusively menial roles. "I am glad that the gentleman from Kentucky is for employing them for some purpose . . . I suppose they would be kept employed till after peace is made, and," Stevens added with his usual savage irony, "then sent back to their masters unhurt, under the fugitive slave law." Stevens then stated his own position:

> In the mean time I am for putting them in the front rank of this battle. I would raise a hundred thousand of them to-morrow, and have them drilled. History tells us that they make the best and most docile soldiers in the world. They are not barbarians in nature. They are a people as well calculated to be humanized as any other . . . It is false to say that they are not capable of being made good soldiers and humane soldiers.[23]

On August 10, 1862, however, Major General Hunter disbanded his efforts to organize black troops. Just a scant two weeks later, Secretary of War Stanton authorized the formation of the 1st South Carolina Volunteers, an African-American regiment under the command of Brigadier General Rufus Saxton. Eventually the regiment would be commanded by Massachusetts abolitionist, Colonel Thomas Wentworth Higginson.

In Louisiana, the War Department would eventually authorize the recruiting efforts of Major General Benjamin F. Butler. Despite being the driving force in the "contraband" policy, Butler had not initially favored the organization of black troops and had not supported the efforts of his subordinate, Brigadier General John W. Phelps, a Vermont anti-slavery advocate, who was attempting to organize black regiments in the Department of the Gulf. But the Massachusetts political general, ever sensitive to shifting political winds, now believed that the tide was turning in favor of black troops and quickly adjusted his political opinions. By the end of October 1862, Butler had organized the 1st, 2nd, and 3rd Louisiana Native Guards. Meanwhile in Kansas, radical Republican Senator James H. Lane began organizing blacks without any official sanction of the Lincoln

Sidebar 1.3

Harriet Tubman (1820–1913) was one of the most famous African-American women of the Civil War era. Born as a slave in Bucktown, Maryland, Tubman ran away from her slave master in 1849 and then played an extensive role in the Underground Railroad prior to the Civil War. During the Civil War, Tubman played an important role in the Department of the South, where she organized a network of spies and informants who helped fugitive blacks come across into Union lines, where many could join the ranks of the Union army. In June 1863, she played an important role in the Comhahee River raid in which Union forces led by Colonel James Montgomery moved up the Comhahee River to gather up bands of fugitives whom Tubman and her associates had recruited to runaway under the noses of their slave masters.

Source: Catherine Clinton, *Harriet Tubman: The Road to Freedom* (New York: Back Bay Books, 2004), 163–167.

administration. By the fall of 1862, Lane was sending his 1st Kansas Colored volunteers into Missouri to harass the local residents, despite lack of official authorization from the War department.[24]

Despite these efforts, however, none of these organizing efforts meant that African-American soldiers would be used in combat roles. According to the Militia Act, only the president was authorized to designate blacks for combat roles. Despite the clamoring of radicals in Congress and the efforts of prominent abolitionist and free black leaders in the north, Lincoln was not persuaded to make this step in the fall of 1862, at least no more than the relatively modest efforts that were being carried on by Saxton, Butler, and Lane; moreover, the preliminary Emancipation Proclamation had said nothing about the recruitment of African-Americans. However, the deteriorating war efforts, the lag in recruitment, and the less than enthusiastic support of Republicans in the fall elections all worked on the administration to bring about a change in thinking on the part of Abraham Lincoln. The final Emancipation Proclamation, issued on January 1, 1863, had a specific language that authorized black recruitment. Still many questions remained: How would black soldiers be received by the public? How well would African-Americans fight? How would the Confederacy respond to a full-scale effort to organize former slaves? And, perhaps more fundamentally, what were the social and political implications of black recruitment? Would soldiers become citizens? Did carrying a bayonet mean the right to cast a ballot? As historian Ira Berlin remarks, "The prospect of arming slaves or even free blacks raised fundamental questions about the place of black people in American society, questions that went far beyond the immediate demands of the war."[25]

The thinking of Lincoln on the meaning of black military service was colored by a pessimistic assessment of the white prejudice. Speaking to a delegation of free blacks on August 14, 1862, Lincoln made a forceful argument for the necessity of colonization, the physical removal of African-Americans to a suitable location in Africa or Central America. "You and we are different races," Lincoln told the delegation:

> We have between us a broader difference than exists between
> almost any other two races. Whether it is right or wrong I need
> not discuss, but this physical difference is a great disadvantage
> to us both, as I think your race suffers very greatly, many of them
> by living among us, while ours suffers from your presence.

Clearly Lincoln had little thought at this time of a bi-racial society where black military service might be viewed as the beginning of citizenship. "You are cut off from many of the advantages which the other race enjoy," Lincoln reminded the delegation:

> The aspiration of men is to enjoy equality with the best when free,
> but on this broad continent, not a single man of your race is
> made the equal of a single man of ours. Go where you are treated
> the best, and the ban is still upon you.

Lincoln's advice to this delegation was to support an administration's effort to establish a free black colony in Chiriquí, located on the Isthmus of Panama. Just prior to emancipating and arming black soldiers, the president of the United States had evaded the implications of his decisions by thinking the physical removal of African-Americans might render the debate of the issue unnecessary.[26]

How African-Americans would function in a society where slavery was abolished and blacks served in northern armies would certainly be a topic of intense debate in a post-Civil War American; however, the wisdom of arming African-Americans was itself a controversial issue. Indeed northern citizens, politicians, soldiers, and officers held a variety of opinions about the wisdom of arming blacks. Predictably, African-Americans held their own opinions about their ability to perform military service. Because of the pervasiveness of racial prejudice that permeated the United States during the Civil War era, there was a good deal of skepticism about the efficacy of blacks in combat roles. By late 1862, many northerners, with the exception of hard-bitten Peace Democrats, had become comfortable enough with the notion of using blacks in non-combat roles. Since many believed blacks were innately child-like and indolent, the notion of using blacks in combat roles seemed ill-advised. For many white officers in the Union army, "black soldiers were more akin to children than adults. They were excessively trusting, and lacking initiative." At the same time, the notion of black inferiority could also be used to justify using blacks in combat roles. Crude notions of climate determinism held that blacks were more suited to the warmer, more tropical environment of the south and, therefore, might do well in combat roles. And then, of course, was the pragmatic argument that a black soldier stopping a bullet would save a white soldier from death. This notion was crudely expressed in such racist lyrics as "Sambo's Right to be Kilt," a popular song by Charles Graham Halpine. As Halpine crudely put it:

> Some tell us 'tis burnin' shame
>> To make the naygers fight;
>> And that the thrade of bein' kilt
>> Belongs but to the white:
> But as for me, upon my sowl!
>> So liberal are we here,
>> I'll let Sambo be murthered instead of myself,
>> On ever day in the year.
>> And in every hour of the day;
> The right to be kilt I'll divide with him,
>> And divil a word I'll say.
> In battle's wild commotion
>> I shouldn't at all object
> If Sambo's body should stop a ball
>> That was comin' for me direct;
> And the prod of a Southern bagnet,
>> So generous are we here,
> I'll resign, and let Sambo take it
> On every day in the year.
> On every day in the year, boys,
>> And with none o' your nasty pride,
> All my right in a Southern bagnet prod,
>> Wid Sambo I'll divide!

As one northern politician, Iowa Governor Samuel Kirkwood, related to Major General Henry W. Halleck, expressing a sentiment very similar to that of Halpine, "when this war is over & we have summed up the entire loss of life it has imposed upon the country [,] I shall not have regrets if it is found that a part of the dead are *niggers* and that *all* are not white men." Even anti-slavery radicals such as Pennsylvania congressman, Thaddeus Stevens, would use similar logic when arguing for the use of blacks in combat. "The flower of our people are moldering in the swamps of Virginia," Stevens told the House of Representatives, "because we will not employ those who ought to be fighting this battle. New England in every Hamlet mourns her dead. So do the middle and western states. Am I to stand here and to be told that it will not do to let black men shoot and be shot instead of white men!"[27]

For African-Americans, the chance to don the uniform offered the chance of new opportunities. Many equated military service with a chance to earn citizenship. Black corporal, James H. Gooding, a member of the 54th Massachusetts outlined the "stakes" for black participation in the conflict. "Our people must know that if they are ever to attain to any position in the eyes of the civilized world," stated Gooding, "they must forego comfort, home, fear, and, above all, superstition, and fight for it; make up their minds to become something more than hewers of wood and drawers of water all their lives." As another historian puts it, "Enlistment not only strengthened the bondsman's claim to freedom; it also enhanced the freeman's claim to equality." Another African-American corporal in the 55th Massachusetts put it bluntly, "Give me my rights, the rights that this Government owes me, the same rights that the white has."[28]

With the advent of emancipation, however, on January 1, 1863, the president had given official notice that black recruitment would go forward. In addition to the 1st South Carolina Volunteers, the 1st Kansas Volunteers, and recruitment efforts in Louisiana, the War Department would give permission to Governor John A. Andrew of Massachusetts to raise the 54th Massachusetts and then the 55th Massachusetts. Rhode Island was given the authorization to raise a regiment of heavy artillery. In an effort to standardize recruiting, the

> Almost as popular as Frederick Douglass in nineteenth-century United States, John Mercer Langston was a determined and enthusiastic advocate of African-American rights. Born in 1829 and the son of a white planter and free black mother, Langston grew up in southern Ohio after both his parents died at an early age. A graduate of Oberlin College, Langston practiced law and was admitted to the Ohio bar. During the Civil War, he played an active role in recruiting blacks for the 54th and 55th Massachusetts as well as the 127th Ohio Colored Volunteers. After the war, Langston served as consul to Haiti and, in 1888, served in the U. S. House. He died in 1897.
>
> Source: EEATW:
> 2: 332–333.

War Department sent Adjutant-General Lorenzo Thomas to the Mississippi Valley to assist in the recruitment and organization of black regiments. As historian Dudley Cornish writes, "This [Thomas's assignment] was to be no routine mission. It presaged the full-scale organization and employment of Negro soldiers." In March 1863, there were five black regiments in the Union army. Thomas would organize 20 additional regiments by the end of 1863 and a total of 50 regiments by the end of 1864. All told, Thomas's efforts would lead to the induction of 76,000 African-American soldiers or roughly 41 percent of all blacks who served in northern armies. The efforts of Lorenzo Thomas were supplemented by those of Major General Nathaniel Banks, Benjamin Butler's successor in the Department of the Gulf, who organized nearly 21 regiments of black soldiers during his tenure of command. In addition to these efforts, General Daniel Ullman supplemented the efforts of Banks by raising a brigade in Southeast Louisiana, while in North Carolina, the abolitionist general, Earl A. Wild, organized an African brigade in that Confederate state.[29]

In May 1863, the War Department took steps to regularize the recruitment of African-American troops by creating the Bureau of Colored Troops through General Orders Number 143. Henceforth, instead of state identification, black regiments would now be designated as numerical regiments of the United Stated Colored Troops (USCT). Interestingly, this change in organization identified the cause of black troops with the national government. As historian Cornish notes, "Negro soldiers were not fighting for any particular state; they were fighting for the United States, the government which promised them their freedom."[30]

With black now organized into a substantial fighting force, a number of important questions remained. How would they be treated by white officers and white soldiers? Would they be accorded equality in the service and would this service translate into equality in the post-war United States? How would African-Americans acquit themselves under fire? Would they, as many Copperheads argued, be essentially useless and a burden to white soldiers, or, as abolitionists, blacks, and others argued, would they prove to be the equal of whites in every respect? Finally, how would the southern states of the Confederacy regard black soldiers? Would they accord them the status of prisoners of war under the laws of war as understood in the nineteenth century? Or would they regard them as escaped slaves or criminals subject to harsher and more severe punishments?

African-American recruits faced a number of hardships that were not suffered by white soldiers. Because many white officers did not really believe in the ability of blacks to fight, many black troops were detailed for manual labor, cooking, and other menial tasks. Even after blacks proved time and time again that they were fully cable of performing combat duties, prominent Union generals continued to use blacks in roles as laborers. Even late in the war, for instance, Major General William Tecumseh Sherman, the top Union commander in the western theatre, continued to resist War Department policy to use blacks in combat roles. Sherman considered blacks to be worthless as fighters. "A nigger is not a white man," he stated, "and all the Psalm sing on the earth won't make him so." Blacks were also taken advantage of financially, deprived of bounties, given poorer weapons, and inferior housing. While numerous whites advanced their careers by becoming commissioned officers in black regiments, African-Americans, for the most part, were denied commissioned officer positions. The historian Ira Berlin notes, "Skeptical of the ability of black men to lead and fearful of the reaction of white soldiers to the appointment of black men to superior office, Secretary of War Stanton refused to commission black line officers throughout 1863 and 1864."[31]

After African-Americans were recruited into the Union armies, the initial response of many white soldiers was hostile. Relying on well-established stereotypes of black qualities and behavior, some white soldiers believed that blacks were unsuited to military service and would perform military duties on a substandard basis. One Michigan officer remarked:

> It is true that there are many of the blacks well qualified to take care of themselves, but the masses are lazy and shiftless and would become worthless vagabonds if free. They think to be free is to be free from labor.

Prejudice often led to mistreatment, from somewhat innocent pranks to more serious activities. At the same time, many Union soldiers eventually accepted the pragmatic argument that many made in favor of employing black troops. They could, after all, perform menial duties and spare whites from performing them, or, more significantly, they would take bullets that might otherwise kill white soldiers. This was particularly true as whites saw the seriousness and the determination of blacks in battle and under fire. According to the historian, Bell Irvin Wiley, part of the eventual acceptance of black soldiers by whites in the Union army was simply force of habit. Writes Wiley, "Perhaps the most important influence of all in breaking down opposition to Negroes was the simple fact that Yanks grew accustomed to the sight of black men wearing the Federal uniform." In a more recent study on Union soldiers, another historian believes that white acceptance of black soldiers had more to do with ideology and an identification with freedom and emancipation as Union war goals— something many Union soldiers would not have identified with earlier in the conflict. "By war's last year," notes historian James McPherson, "the example of black soldiers fighting for Union as well as liberty had helped convince white soldiers that they should fight for black liberty as well as the Union." Did this mean that white soldiers openly endorsed black citizenship in terms of voting, jury duty, and other measure of social and political equality? Probably not; however, simply the eventual acceptance of black soldiers in the Union army was a significant step in and of itself.[32]

In many situations, black soldiers found out that family members, still enslaved by slaveholders in loyal Border States such as Kentucky or Missouri, were mistreated by their owners—payback, in effect, for losing the services of the male slave. Probably the greatest injustice, however, was unequal pay. Once President Lincoln had made the determination to use blacks in combat roles, most African-American troops anticipated receiving equal pay. Under the Militia Act of 1862, pay for African-Americans was about half that of white soldiers. Black leaders, northern governors, and anti-slavery advocates lobbied the War Department and Congress to address this inequity. Black soldiers and their families wrote letters of protest to the president and other administration officials. James Henry Gooding of the 54th Massachusetts complained to the president in a September 28, 1863 letter. "Now the main question is. Are we *Soldiers*, or are we *Labourers*." He continued, "the Regt., do pray, that they be assured their service will be fairly appreciated, by paying them as american [*sic*] Soldiers, not as menial hirelings." Massachusetts Governor John Andrew was an avid and determined advocate of equal pay. In fact, to address the inequity, the Massachusetts legislature appropriated the monies to equalize pay for the 54th and 55th Massachusetts regiments. For African-American soldiers,

Sidebar 1.4

Many African-Americans who volunteered for military service left family members who were still enslaved. A common complaint for enslaved wives and children was the abuse they suffered from slaveholders who were upset at having to part with a male slave laborer. One female slave from Mexico, Missouri, Martha Glover, wrote to her enlisted spouse and complained bitterly about the treatment she was receiving from her slave masters: "They abuse me because you went & say that they will not take care of our children & do nothing but quarrel with me all the time and beat me scandalously the day before yesterday . . . Oh I wish you had staid with me & not gone till I could go with you for I do nothing but grieve all the time about you."

Source: Berlin, *Freedom's Soldiers*, 117.

however, this was not enough and members of the aforementioned regiments refused to accept any pay until the situation was rectified. For the soldiers of the 54th and 55th, it was a matter of principle.[33]

Eventually, Congress would weigh in on the matter of equal pay; however, even then, there was uneven progress toward the way all black recruits were treated. In a bill passed on June 15, 1864, black recruits would get equal pay but only retroactive until January 1, 1864; moreover, the bill also discriminated in favor of northern free blacks, while excluding slaves who had come across northern lines and then enlisted. Congressman Thaddeus Stevens, a radical Republican from Gettysburg, Pennsylvania, forcefully criticized these discriminatory provisions in the June 15th bill. "It is due to ourselves, I repeat, that if we accept the services of colored troops," Stevens noted, "they should be paid for their services like any other soldiers." Finally in early 1865, Congress rectified the situation by passing a bill that equalized pay for all black soldiers regardless of whether they had been free or technically runaway slaves at the time of their enlistment. For many blacks and many advocates of black civil rights, the struggle to achieve something as elementary as equal pay certainly foreshadowed the difficulty many African-Americans would face in a post-war struggle for citizenship. Despite opposition to slavery and despite unity on the goal of crushing the Confederacy, white northerners were not of a single mind of the nature of black rights in a post-slavery world.[34]

How did black units perform in combat roles? Even before black troops fought in battle, their proponents spoke favorably of the job they were doing. Colonel Thomas W. Higginson, the commander of the 1st South Carolina Volunteers, told his mother that his black regiment was as useful as any white one. He even overheard one white soldier comment in a dress parade about the superior performance of Higginson's regiment. In a series of engagements in 1863, black soldiers performed well above expectations, demonstrating bravery under fire and putting to rest some of the crude stereotypes about black behavior. At Port Hudson, Louisiana, on May 27, 1863, the 1st and 3rd regiments of the Corps d'Afrique made a favorable impression on Major General Nathaniel Banks when they bravely led the assault on a major Confederate stronghold on the Mississippi river. Just a short time later, a larger Confederate force attacked Union forces, which included the 9th and 11th Louisiana Volunteers of African Descent. After initially being driven back by Confederate forces, the black forces rallied and held their position against superior enemy forces. Similarly, the 54th Massachusetts, one of the first northern regiments mustered into the service, distinguished itself in the assault of Fort Wagner near Charleston, South Carolina on July 16, 1863. The 54th Massachusetts was associated with a number of leading abolitionists and free black

One black soldier who distinguished himself at Port Hudson was Captain Andre Cailloux, Company E, 1st Louisiana Native Guards. Although born a slave on February 28, 1825, Cailloux was emancipated at the age of 21. A free black artisan in New Orleans of Creole descent, Cailloux was killed on May 27, 1863 while leading a charge during the battle of Port Hudson. He was, nevertheless, one of the few blacks in the Union army to receive an officer's commission.

Source: C. Davis, ed., *New Catholic Encyclopedia*, 2nd edn (Detroit: Gale Publishing, 2003), 1: 156; Benjamin Quarles, *The Negro in the Civil War*, 1953 reprint (New York: Da Capo Press, 1989), 218.

leaders including Rochester editor, Frederick Douglass, Martin Delany, and other prominent black leaders as well as white anti-slavery activists. It was led by Colonel Robert Gould Shaw, a member of Boston's aristocratic upper crust, known as the Brahmins. The assault on Fort Wagner was an almost impossible assignment; however, the 54th fulfilled it with courage and valor, suffering heavy casualties while almost gaining the fort's parapet. As historian Dudley Cornish remarks, "After the assault on Fort Wagner on July 18 [1863] there was no longer any doubt about using Negro troops to crush the rebellion."[35]

The assault on Fort Wagner, an attack that claimed the life of Colonel Shaw, revealed an additional hazard for black soldiers. Thirteen black prisoners of war were taken by the Confederates; however, departmental commander Major General Pierre G. T. Beauregard was uncertain on how to deal with black prisoners of war, so he contacted the Davis administration in Richmond for direction. Anticipating the northern recruitment of African-American soldiers, Confederate President, Jefferson Davis, anticipated the possibility of receiving black prisoners of war prisoners. As a result, Davis issued a proclamation in December, 1862 that declared that any black soldier captured would be turned over to state authorities and would be dealt with according to the laws of the state in question. The Confederate Congress confirmed this position in a May 1, 1863 resolution. The taking of prisoners after the attack on Fort Wagner was one of the first occasions to test the policy's application. Since the South has a long history of fear about slave revolts, it was predictable that Jefferson Davis and the Richmond government would not respond well to the recruitment of African-American troops by the Lincoln government; moreover, Confederate authorities also harbored deep resentments against white officers who helped in this process. As early as August 21, 1862, the Confederate War Department had responded to the relatively isolated efforts of John W. Phelps and David Hunter to arm and out the South. By May 1, 1863, the Congress of the Confederacy has taken even stronger actions. According to its provisions, U.S. officers could be put to death for their role in training and leading black troops. As for black soldiers, they would not be regarded as bona fide prisoners of war but as escaped slaves—even northern free blacks who had volunteered for military service. The dispute between the Union and Confederate governments over the status of black soldiers would also have the important consequence of a breakdown of prisoner of war exchanges from May 1863 until January 1865. For both officers leading blacks and black soldiers engaged in combat, the war had additional dangers that other Union soldiers did not always face.[36]

Some African-American leaders were so distraught with the dangers that black soldiers faced they threatened to stop recruiting African-American soldiers. Already distressed and angered at unequal pay, leaders such as Douglass now bitterly complained that black soldiers faced an undue risk in wearing the Union uniform. If the Lincoln administration would not initiate a policy that protected African-Americans from re-enslavement or death, then African-American leaders might end their efforts at recruitment. Eventually, on June 30, 1863, President Lincoln issued an order that directed Union military officials to execute a rebel soldier whenever it came across evidence that an African-American soldier had been put to death by rebel authorities. Although this move satiated critics, the Lincoln administration never followed through on the threat.[37]

Many southerners justified the policies of the Richmond government toward captured black soldiers as just and humanitarian. According to the southern myths about slavery, African-Americans were really content under the slave system, but were beguiled by Yankee abolitionists to run away and enlist in Union armies. By turning them over to state authorities who could put them to work or return them to their masters, the Richmond government was, on this argument, simply restoring the proper hierarchical social order. As would become apparent early on after African-American troops assumed combat roles, many Confederate soldiers did not follow official policy, choosing instead to give no quarter and to take no black prisoners of war. Armed African-Americans, donned in Yankee blue, fueled primal emotions in southern males. "Southern soldiers," writes George Burkhardt, "first killed, wounded, or trapped black Federals as a matter of course, although that practice never became the Confederacy's official policy. However, it became a de facto policy by default because it was condoned, never punished, and always denied."[38]

By the end of the American Civil War, the African-American contribution to the Union war effort was substantial. Nearly 180,000 black men served the Union army, amounting to nearly 10 percent of all Union man power. Since there were approximately 48,000 northern free blacks between the ages of 18–45 at the onset of the war, this meant that the bulk of African-American soldiers had been slaves prior to the war, coming across Union lines from the seceded states or enlisting and gaining emancipation as a resident of a loyal slave state. Nearly one third of these African-American soldiers (68, 178) suffered death, wounds, or was missing in action. Without the contribution of African-Americans, the triumph of northern arms would have been delayed and possibly denied. Many black soldiers viewed military service as a means to acceptance into American society. Before the war was over, however, African-American soldiers would suffer horrific acts of violence by Confederate soldiers. One event transpiring at Fort Pillow, Tennessee gained particular notoriety. With hundreds of black Union soldiers killed, maimed, and tortured, the Fort Pillow Massacre would become a powerful symbol of Confederate opposition to the notion of blacks in uniform, but the massacre would also demonstrate the determination of African-Americans to persevere despite the odds. Even more revealing was the response of the northern government to the massacre at Fort Pillow. Eager to induct blacks into the service by the thousands, the Lincoln administration seemed far more tentative when it came to aggressive actions to protect the rights of its black soldiers. In its halting and hesitating course in protecting the rights of its black soldiers, the Federal government action (or inaction) signaled the continuing division in the north over the status of African-Americans. While African-Americans regarded their military service as sufficient for a seat at the banquet of American life, many white northerners were not as certain.[39]

CHAPTER 2

No Quarter

Located on the Mississippi River about 40 miles north of Memphis, Fort Pillow should have been little more than a footnote in the history of the American Civil War. Established by Confederate General Gideon Pillow at the beginning of the war, the fort was constructed using local slaves. It was abandoned by the Confederacy in 1862 after Union forces drove Confederate armies out of Tennessee. The arrival of Union armies to Memphis and West Tennessee created a complex web of social and political relationships as Tennessee Unionists could now openly express their loyalty to the Union cause and appeal to Federal forces for protection—much to the chagrin of their rebel neighbors. By May of 1863, the Union army occupied Fort Pillow, which it used as a base to recruit African-American soldiers as well as a base to conduct operations against local guerrilla groups in the West Tennessee area. With the passage of much more aggressive federal policies by the northern government, such as the 2nd Confiscation Act and the arming of African-American soldiers as directed by the Emancipation Proclamation, the federal garrison at Fort Pillow became a symbol in the West Tennessee area of a new hard war approach by the Lincoln administration. Local residents, loyal to the Confederacy, worried that their slaves would run away and join the Federal armies—which many did—and they resented Federal foraging expeditions. "Expeditions from the fort," notes historian John Cimprich,

> followed the hard war policies of seizing most weapons and many foodstuffs from civilians. By October 1863, over 300 African-Americans were living at a contraband camp near the fort. Blacks could either enlist in the Union army or work at the contraband camp. The fort became a magnet, drawing many fugitives from great distances. Some came after learning about the

Emancipation Proclamation; others simply sought to take
advantage of war-time conditions.[1]

The coming of 1864 brought about a coordinated movement of Federal armies southward. Major General William T. Sherman, principal Federal commander in the West, was determined to utilize every available soldier for his upcoming campaign into Georgia. Accordingly he ordered Major General Stephen Hurlbut, commanding at Memphis, to abandon Fort Pillow. Hurlbut, however, followed his own ideas and the fort was never abandoned. In early February 1864, Major William Bradford, a Tennessee Unionist, had stationed his 13th Tennessee Cavalry at Fort Pillow. By February 21, a small contingent of the 2nd United States Colored Light Artillery (USCLA) was also present at the fort. By April 1864, Hurlbut had determined Fort Pillow was a strategic position that ought to be occupied, apparently regardless of Sherman's previous order. His thinking was no doubt influenced by the fort's commanding position over the Mississippi River and its usefulness in controlling river traffic as well as guarding the approaches to Memphis from the north. As a result, instead of evacuating Fort Pillow, Hurlbut reinforced it, sending the 6th United Stated Colored Heavy Artillery (USCHA) to reinforce the troops already stationed at the fortress. Between the three different regiments, the garrison had approximately 585–605 troops. The overall command of the garrison would be given to the commander of the 6th USCHA, Major Lionel F. Booth, a young officer who had joined the United States Army in 1858.[2]

Fort Pillow was built on a steep bluff, which overlooked the Mississippi River at the junction where a small stream to the north of the fort, Coal

---

Sidebar 2.1

William F. Bradford (ca. 1832–1864) was from Obion County in the Northwest Corner of Tennessee and the member of a politically well-connected family. While practicing law in Union City, Tennessee, Bradford began recruiting men from West Tennessee for a Union Calvary regiment, which eventually became the 13th Tennessee Cavalry. Hated and distrusted by many of the local residents of West Tennessee, many Confederate soldiers had grudges to settle with both Bradford and his command at the battle of Fort Pillow. Taken prisoner the day of the battle, Bradford would die under suspicious circumstances near Brownsville, Tennessee a few days after the battle at Fort Pillow.

Source: WWWCW: 67.

Sidebar 2.2

Lionel F. Booth (1838–1864) was commander of the 6th United States Colored Heavy Artillery. A Philadelphia native, Booth did not attend West Point, but enlisted in the regular army in 1858. He performed a number of different assignments during the Civil War, which included serving as quartermaster of the 1st Missouri Light Artillery. During 1863, he was given command of the company A, 1st Alabama Siege Artillery, an African-American unit. Promoted to Major, Booth was ordered to Fort Pillow, where he commanded his own battalion, now called the 6th USCHA as well as on section of the Battery D, 2nd USCLA, and a battalion of the 13th Tennessee Cavalry.

Source: WWWCW, 63.

Creek, joined the larger river. The fort consisted of two outer lines of defense and the inner portion of the fort. The innermost portion resembled a large horseshoe, approximately 150 yards wide and with the open end of the horseshoe facing west, toward the Mississippi river. The horseshoe was surrounded by a trench approximately 8 ft deep with dirt thrown up on the interior to form a parapet roughly 6 to 8 ft high and 4 to 6 ft wide. To the south of the fort, a small town had developed that boasted shops, storehouses, and a hotel. Since the fort was equipped with several pieces of artillery and also had a Federal gunboat, the *New Era*, anchored on the Mississippi River, to come to its assistance, Major Booth believed he could hold out against a superior force for quite some time.[3]

In March 1864, Confederate Major General Nathan Bedford Forrest, one of the Confederacy's pre-eminent cavalry commanders, planned a raid into western Kentucky and Tennessee. Forrest was born in 1821, a native of Tennessee and oldest of 11 children. The early death of his father left the future cavalry commander with significant responsibilities early in life. Denied a formal education, Forrest relied on hard work and determination to rise in southern society. Moving to northern Mississippi in 1842, Forrest entered into a business partnership with an uncle. By 1851, the young Forrest had resettled in Memphis and became one of the city's foremost slave traders. His business as a slave trader meant that he had an enormous self-interest in preserving slavery, which was his livelihood. It also meant that he accepted the dominant southern thinking on the status and character of African-Americans. Forrest regarded blacks as inferior and unfortunate beings whose principal role in life was to serve the master class. Typical of many white southerners of his day, Forrest was particularly

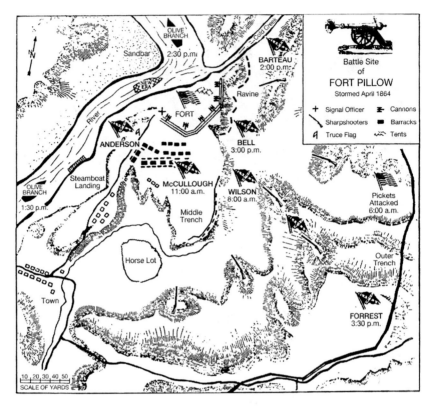

Figure 2.1 Map of Fort Pillow and the surrounding environs.

sensitive to insults or perceived insults to his "honor." During the course of his life, Forrest would not hesitate to use violence to get satisfaction for an insult to his honor. Like many southern planters and aristocrats, the rage and violence that might surface as the result of an attack on personal honor might rage to new heights when an "unruly" slave dared to challenge the "natural" order. A recalcitrant slave, in the eyes of someone like Forrest, was a threat to the very fabric of southern society. Hence, when Forrest and his troops came across a Union garrison, manned, in part, by African-American forces, many who had formerly been slaves, it was no ordinary situation.

Forrest's force consisted of two divisions, one under General James R. Chalmers and another under General Abraham Buford. There were two principal reasons for the raid. As Union Major General William T. Sherman planned an invasion into Georgia with armies of the Tennessee and Cumberland, Forrest believed a Confederate movement into these areas might have the effect of drawing troops away from Sherman's operation. At the same time, as a long time resident of Memphis and the western Tennessee area, Forrest was concerned about the predicament of many Tennessee and Kentucky residents who were loyal to the Confederacy and hoped to exact a measure of revenge against Federal occupiers, particularly those Tennessee residents who had abandoned the Confederacy and enlisted in the Union army. With the inauguration of harsher war measures on the part of the Lincoln administration, it meant more hardships and additional suffering for western Tennessee residents loyal to the Confederacy. Forrest's raid took him as far north as Paducah, Kentucky, where, on March 25, 1864, he surrounded a much smaller Union force under northern commander, Colonel S. G. Hicks and the 40th Illinois. As Hicks' command contained African-American troops, Forrest employed a psychological tactic that he would reintroduce at Fort Pillow. Demanding unconditional surrender, Forrest told his Federal counterpart that he would give no quarter if the surrender were refused. Relying on the threat of no quarter, Forrest hoped to intimidate his Union counterpart into surrender. Just one day prior to the attack on Paducah, one of Forrest's subordinates, Colonel W. L. Duckworth, had used this tactic to gain the surrender of the Union garrison at Union City, Tennessee. At Paducah, however, Forrest's strategy backfired as Hicks refused to surrender and a foolish attack, launched by one of Forrest's subordinates without his approval, was beaten back by outnumbered Union troops. As a result Forrest was forced to abandon the attack on Paducah. According to one historian, the failure at Paducah would have dire consequences for Fort Pillow. "The defeat [at Paducah]," notes historian Ronald K. Huch, "served to intensify the fury felt by the Rebels toward Northern troops in general and black soldiers in particular."[4]

Having made his way back to Jackson, Tennessee in early April, Forrest informed his superiors that he intended to move against Fort Pillow. His official reason for making the attack was the need for supplies, especially horses; however, as several scholars point out, there was a much more primal motive that animated the Confederate commander, who had, after all, made his living in antebellum Memphis, Tennessee as a slave trader. Recent Federal policy, both emancipation and the decision to enlist blacks in the Union cause, undoubtedly offended and angered Forrest, a man who reflected southern beliefs and temperament when it came to the social position of African-Americans. Certainly Forrest would have agreed with the words of one historian, who characterized southern beliefs on emancipation as "a malignant, evil Yankee plot to foment slave revolts and 'servile insurrection.'" Since Forrest had resided in Memphis for many years, he was also naturally sympathetic to the plight of Confederate loyalists in the area as were many of the men in his command. The garrison at Fort Pillow, as he well knew, consisted of black soldiers, many of whom had been the slaves of local residents. On April 8, Forrest made arrangements for the campaign to attack Fort Pillow. Assigning overall command to Brigadier General James R. Chalmers, approximately 1,500 men were designated for the engagement. In addition to two brigades commanded by Chalmers, he would also have the brigades of Colonel Robert "Black Bob" McCulloch as well as the brigade commanded by Colonel Tyree Bell. In order to confuse Federal troops about his real intentions, Forrest also sent a brigade toward Memphis and another toward Paducah.[5]

Following Forrest's orders, Chalmers' Confederate troops arrived on the outskirts of Fort Pillow in the early morning of April 12. While McCulloch's brigade approached from the south, Bell's brigade took up a position along Coal creek, north of the fort. Each brigade quickly drove Federal pickets back from the outer defenses back into the garrison. Confederates had a number of advantages that would allow them to get into favorable position. First there was high ground around the fort with a number of trees, hills, and ravines. This allowed Confederate troops to get into better position without taking an undue risk from the fire of the Union garrison. It also meant Confederate sharpshooters could pour fire on the northern troops within the garrison. Second, at 9:00 a.m., Federal commander, Major Lionel F. Booth, was hit and killed by sharpshooter fire. Booth had already taken a number of actions to improve the defenses of the garrison. He moved troops from company D and E of the 6th USCHA to rifle pits on the south side of the fort and instructed his artillerists to begin a bombardment southward to impede the movement of Confederate troops. He also ordered the evacuation of civilians who resided in the settlement south of the fort to the *New Era*, a federal gunboat attached to the garrison commanded by Captain James Marshall. Now, however, command fell to Major William Bradford of the 13th Tennessee Cavalry. A Tennessee Unionist who was hated by many Confederate soldiers, Bradford was far less experienced than Booth and would make a number of errors in the succeeding hours. To the south of Fort Pillow were also a number of barracks and houses that would afford Confederate attackers protection from artillery fire. Booth had ordered these structures to be burned, but Confederate forces had gotten in position too quickly, and the inexperienced Bradford did not follow through on Booth's directive. Booth had also ordered 20 soldiers of the 6th USCHA to position themselves in rifle pits to the south of the fort. Again, the inexperienced Bradford allowed these rifle pits to be abandoned. By the time Forrest arrived on the scene at approximately 10:00 a.m., Confederate troops were in a favorable position.[6]

After making his own survey of Fort Pillow, Forrest was determined to attack, despite the apparent strength of the fortress and the misgivings of subordinates such as General Chalmers. The Confederate general had little respect for the African-American troops that manned the garrison. A slave trader prior to the war, Forrest's viewed blacks as inferior to whites and as little more than property. Arming a child-like and inferior race, in the opinion of Forrest, was a dangerous and ridiculous experiment, one that Forrest was determined to reveal as foolish with his actions at Fort Pillow. Many of the Confederate enlisted men who served with Forrest had similar thoughts. Indeed, in a culture that feared the slightest hint of slave rebellion, which panicked at the thought of slave uprising along the line of a Nat Turner or Denmark Vesey slave revolt, the appearance of African-Americans in Federal blue conjured up images of "servile war."

The Confederate general and many of his men were also less than enamored with the 13th Tennessee Cavalry regiment. Consisting of many West Tennessee residents who had turned against the Confederacy, Major Bradford and his men were unpopular with many local residents and

---

Sidebar 2.3

Among the most well-known slave revolts in the antebellum South involved Denmark Vesey and Nat Turner. Originally from either Africa or on one of the Caribbean islands, Denmark Vesey (1767–1822) lived in Charleston, South Carolina. After purchasing his freedom, he organized a slave revolt, apparently using a local African Methodist Episcopal Church in Charleston as his cover. Vesey's plan called for slaves to rise up, seize weapons, and then leave for one of the islands in the Caribbean. After being betrayed by slave informants, Vesey was tried, convicted, and put to death on July 3, 1822. Unlike Vesey, Nat Turner (1800–1831) was still a slave at the time he organized his revolt. Residing in Southampton County, Virginia, Turner was also a preacher who learned to read and interpret the Bible. Turner's conspiracy began on August 22, 1831, when Turner and several followers, killed Turner's slave owner, Joseph Travis, and then moved on to other plantations, agreeing that no whites would be spared. Over 50 whites were put to death by Turner's followers, who numbered between 60–80 slaves. Eventually, the United States Army intervened and violently put an end to Turner's rebellion at the town of Jerusalem, Virginia. For his role in the rebellion, Turner was put to death by hanging on November 11, 1831. The impact on the Turner rebellion in many southern states was an increasing paranoia about slave access to education, which led a number of states to pass laws forbidding slaves from becoming ministers or prevent masters from educating slaves.

Source: EEATW, 2: 552–553 and 534–535.

Significant slave revolts in the South:
Stono rebellion, South Carolina, 1739
Gabriel Prosser's revolt, Virginia, 1800
Denmark Vesey revolt, Charleston,
    South Carolina, 1822
Nat Turner revolt, Virginia, 1831

accused of numerous depredations on the local population. One of Forrest's subordinate officers, Colonel Trye Bell, in particular, hated the 13th Tennessee because many of its members had formerly been part of his 7th Tennessee Cavalry and had deserted and went over to the Union side. Ridiculed as "homemade Yankees" and "Tennessee Tories," Forrest and his men would teach these "traitors" the price for their allegiance to the Union and fighting side by side with black troops.[7]

Forrest quickly took action to get his troops in a more favorable situation, ordering Colonel McCulloch to occupy the structures and rifle pits south of the fort and directing Colonel Bell to move his troops into a ravine that was north and east of the fort. With the 18th Mississippi Cavalry under Chalmers' direct command occupying the center, Forrest now had Fort Pillow surrounded on three sides. Sending forward a flag of truce at approximately 3:30 in the afternoon, Forrest demanded unconditional surrender from the garrison, promising to treat all soldiers as prisoners of war, but, if the garrison chose not to surrender, they would be given no quarter. "Your gallant defense of Fort Pillow has entitled you to the treatment of brave men," Forrest told the Union commander:

> I now demand the unconditional surrender of your forces, at the same time assuring you that you will be treated as prisoners of war. I have received a new supply of ammunition and can take your works by assault, and if compelled to do so you must take the consequences.

A repeat of the strategy invoked at Paducah, Kentucky, Major Bradford replied, signing as Booth, asking for one hour to consider Forrest's note. Worried that Bradford's (or Booth as Forrest was led to believe) request was a stalling tactic to allow him to work out some sort of plan with the gunboat *New Era*, Forrest rejected Bradford's request and instead offered him 20 minutes to make up his mind. "Sir, I have the honor to acknowledge receipt of your note, asking for one hour to consider my demand for your surrender," Forrest wrote to Bradford. "Your request cannot be granted. I will allow you twenty minutes from the receipt of this note for consideration; if at the expiration of that time the fort is not surrendered, I shall assault it. I do not demand the surrender of the gunboat."[8]

While the flag of truce was in force, a number of controversial events occurred that have remained part of the debate over Fort Pillow up until the present day. A number of Union witnesses stated that Confederates advanced under the flag of truce to get closer to the parapet so that once the flag of truce was lifted, they would be able to quickly overwhelm the garrison. "I saw the rebels massing and disposing their forces while the flag was under consideration," claimed John F. Ray of the 13th Tennessee Cavalry. "I asked some of them why they came so close while the flag of truce was being canvassed. They only replied that they knew their business there." William Cleary, also of the 13th Tennessee reported, "while the flag of truce was being sent in the rebel officers formed their forces in whatever advantageous positions they were able to select." In fact a larger number of federal witnesses interviewed testified that Forrest's men violated the flag of truce with impunity; however, most historians, whether predisposed to the Confederacy or the Union, are skeptical about the authenticity of such charges. According to Forrest, he did move troops to stop the approach of two federal vessels on the Mississippi river that were moving toward the garrison on the Mississippi River. Both the *Olive Branch* and the *Liberty*, the latter a steamer with reinforcements for the garrison, were traveling northward on the Mississippi. To counter a potential landing, Forrest ordered two companies of McCulloch's men to take up positions on the south side of the bluffs to ward off the federal ships. On the north side of the garrison, Forrest ordered troops under Colonel C. R. Bateau to take up positions on the bluff to ward off a possible landing. Neither ship landed. At the same time, other witnesses claimed that Forrest also used the truce to move troops into closer position to the fort, which would give them an advantage once fighting resumed. While the first instance of troop movement was not a violation of a flag of truce, the second clearly would have been. The evidence for the second violation, however, is mixed and historians have reached no consensus on the matter. As scholar Albert Castel notes, whether the Confederates violated the flag of truce or did not violate it was not material when considering the reasons for Confederate victory that day. ". . . the fort fell," Castel maintains, "before the superior strength and strategy of Forrest, not as the result of a devious ruse."[9]

Approximately 20 minutes after Forrest rejected Bradford's request for additional time, the Union commander—still pretending to be Booth— rejected the Confederate demand for surrender. Bradford may have thought the garrison was strong enough to hold off the Confederates. With good reason, the Union commander may also have distrusted Forrest's promise to treat all captured Federal soldiers as prisoners of war. In the first place, this directly contradicted the official policy of the Richmond government that declared former slaves would not be treated as prisoners of war but instead would be turned over to state authorities and dealt with according to state laws. In effect, Forrest was promising something that directly contradicted official Confederate policy. In the second place, Bradford might also have been concerned with the treatment of the white officers of black troops. Again, according to official Confederate policy, these officers were considered the leaders of slave rebellions and might well be executed for their role in leading black troops. Finally, as a Tennessee Unionist in an area fraught with bitter animosities, Bradford might not have trusted Forrest in his treatment of his own command, the 13th Tennessee Cavalry, reasoning the Forrest and his Confederate cavalrymen would be intent on getting revenge for alleged misdeeds against the Confederate residents of West Tennessee.

For Forrest, there was no second guessing and he gave the order to attack. Answering the command of the bugle, Confederate forces moved in to scale the parapet from the north, the south, and the east. Coming over the wall quickly and in great numbers, the Confederates were in the garrison before Union troops could effectively respond. The panicked defenders quickly concluded that all was lost and began to flee down the

Figure 2.2 This engraving of the Fort Pillow Massacre graphically displays Union soldiers being slaughtered at close range by their Confederate attackers. From *Harper's Pictorial History of the Civil War.* Library of Congress Prints and Photographs Division, LC-USZ62-42018.

steep bluff toward the Mississippi river, hoping to gain the river and possibly escape to the *New Era*. Some witnesses said the black troops panicked first, while others made no distinction. What all agree upon was that once the panic started it became endemic; moreover, once the troops began to flee down the steep bluff, their actions were reinforced by the words of their commander, Major Bradford, who is alleged to have said, "Boys, save yourselves." Some gave up their guns prior to making the descent down the bluff, while other retained their weapons, perhaps hoping to defend themselves during the descent. Because most of the troops had fled the garrison, the United States flag remained flying, a technical indication that the garrison had not surrendered; this fact would be used by Confederates to justify the actions of their troops during the brutal sequence of events that followed. Describing the situation, Lieutenant Mack J. Leaming, the adjutant of the 13th Tennessee, stated:

> Seeing that through a gross violation of the rules of civilized
> warfare the enemy had now gained possession of our works, and
> in consequence that it would be useless to offer further
> resistance, our men through down their arms and surrendered.

What transpired after Union soldiers through down their weapons, in Leaming's words, "beggars all description."[10]

As retreating black and white troops fled down the bluff in chaos and confusion, a brutal and horrific slaughter transpired. For many of the Confederate troops engaged in battle, this was their first encounter with African-American troops. Like Forrest many Confederate troops were eager to prove that black troops were cowardly and inherently unreliable. While many of the enlisted men in the ranks of the Confederate army were not slaveholders, they were products of a southern culture that taught them that the lowest white was superior to the highest African-American. The advent of northern policies arming black troops had all the markings of an organized slave revolt, aided and abetted by white, abolitionist officers. In assessing the attitude of the typical Confederate soldiers, one historian argues that the violation of social norms on the part of armed black troops produced an instinctive, vicious rage on the part of southern whites. "Probably hatred motivated some Confederates," writes historian George Burkhardt, "but for most the emotion was an almost feral rage. They directed that fierce anger at blacks who defied the taboos and social order and who threatened their manhood." Other historians have noted that when the Lincoln administration first decided to arm African-Americans, some Confederate soldiers might take an almost humorous approach to what was considered a social outrage. One soldier described the Union army as "composed of white negroes and black negroes." At Vicksburg, Mississippi, Confederate soldiers asked their Union counterparts "Have you Yanks any nigger wives yet?" Facing black soldiers in battle, however, became a much more serious issue. "Facing black opponents," argues scholar Jason Phillips, "implied parity between former slaves and Confederate soldiers that many Rebels could not stomach." No doubt Confederate troops were also further enraged by the banter between black soldiers and Confederate troops that had transpired prior to the assault. For the first time facing their enslavers and so-called social betters, African-American troops had used the opportunity to sound off to their would-be conquerors with a variety of taunts and insults. Some witnesses recalled that black soldiers had taunted the rebels prior to the assault with words such as "Come on your dirty Rebels!" or "Damn you, what are you here for?" The events that transpired after Confederates overwhelmed the garrison demonstrated that these taunt and insults acted as an accelerant to a fire.[11]

As Union soldiers fled down the bluff to the river, a horrible scene unfolded. Charley Robinson, a civilian photographer from Minnesota who observed the battle, recalled, "As soon as the rebel got to the top of the bank there commenced the most horrible slaughter that could possibly be conceived." Robinson continued:

Our boys saw that they were overpowered [and] threw down their arms and held up, some their handkerchiefs and some their hands in token surrender, but no sooner were they seen than they were shot down, and if one shot failed to kill them the bayonet or revolver did not.

Numerous soldiers were cut down, shot in the head, bayoneted,

Thomas Adison was a black private who belonged to Company C, 6th United States Colored Heavy Artillery. Born a slave in South Carolina, he had migrated to Mississippi at the age of 19. At the time of the Fort Pillow battle, Adison told congressional examiners that he was 40 years old. During the battle, Adison was shot in the face from close range by a Confederate who carried a revolver. Adison testified that after he was shot, he heard the shooter exclaim, "God damn his soul; he is sure dead now; he is a big, old, fat fellow." Adison was among the patients examined by the Joint Committee on the Conduct of the War at Mound City, Illinois. According to physician Stewart Gordon, at the time that Adison testified his condition was listed as "unfavorable," with his sight having been destroyed by wounds to the nose and eye.

Source: Fort Pillow Massacre, House Report No. 65, 38th Congress, 1st session, 20, 54.

and killed in a variety of brutal ways. Although the white soldiers of the 13th Tennessee were not spared in the onslaught, the black members of the 6th USCHA and the 2nd USCLA were special objects of Confederate wrath. One member of the 6th USCHA, Private Arthur Edwards, was shot in the head, shoulder, and right wrist. When he begged for mercy, an enraged Confederate soldier shouted, "God damn you, you are fighting against your master." Private George Shaw, a private in the 6th USCHA, was asked by a rebel soldier what he was doing at Fort Pillow. When Shaw replied, "please don't shoot me," the soldier paid no attention and told him, "'Damn you, you are fighting against your master.' He raised his gun and fired, the bullet went into my mouth and out the back part of my head." The soldier then proceeded to dump Shaw's body in the Mississippi river. After Private Major Williams lay wounded after being shot in the head, he heard a Confederate officer remark, "there's another dead nigger." James Walls of 13th Tennessee testified that after Union soldiers individually surrendered, the Confederates showed them no quarter. While Walls observed whites being shot, it was markedly different for black soldiers. "I saw them make lots of niggers stand up, and then they shot them like hogs." The morning after the battle, Walls recalled,

> the secesh would be prying around there, and would come to a nigger and say, "you ain't dead, are you?" . . . and then the secesh would get down off their horses, prick them in the sides, and say, "Damn you, you ain't dead yet; get up." Then they would make them get up on their knees, when they would shoot them down like hogs.

It seemed like it was almost a sport. James R. Bingham, a Fredonia, New York native, who clerked in a store just south of the fort and witnessed the battle, testified that he overheard Confederate officers who stated that "they would never recognize negroes as prisoners of war, but would kill them whenever taken. Even if they caught a negro with blue clothes on (uniform) they would kill him." Private John Kennedy, a private in the 2nd USCLA claimed that he heard many Union soldiers ask for mercy, "but the rebels did not listen to them but shot some of them through their heads and bodies, knocking others to death with their muskets." As Kennedy ran down the bluff to the river, he was shot in the legs, dragged away, and had all of his belongings taken. While kept as a prisoner, he saw three black soldiers murdered: "They were knocked on their heads with muskets until they expired."

"I was shot after I surrendered," stated John F. Ray, Co. B, 13th Tennessee Cavalry, "and while going down the bluff I saw 12 white soldiers and perhaps 30 negroes shot down after surrender while begging for mercy." When later asked if any Confederate officers were in the vicinity when he was shot by rebel soldiers and if they tried to restrain their soldiers, Private Duncan Harding stated that the only thing he had heard rebel officers say was, "Kill the God damned nigger."[12]

Elias Falls, a private in the 6th USCHA testified that he and many other soldiers continued to be shot even after most of the fighting had ceased. Apparently shot near the Mississippi river, Falls was then forced by his Confederate captors to march back up the bluff toward the fort. "After peace was made some of the secesh soldiers came around cursing the boys that were wounded," Falls recollected:

> They shot one of them in the hand, aimed to shoot him in the
> head, as he lay on the ground, and hit him in the hand; and an
> officer told the secesh soldier if he did that again he would arrest
> him, and he went off.

The warnings of the Confederate officer, however, had little impact on restraining the actions of Confederate soldiers as numerous witnesses attested to similar actions on the part of the Confederate rank and file. The soldiers seemed to be acting on their own, almost as if they could not control their actions and emotions. Another private in the 6th USCHA, Nathan Hunter, recalled how he was shot after the fighting had ceased. With no weapons on his person, he was nevertheless gunned down by Confederate soldiers and left to die. When asked if he had witnessed similar actions to other Union soldiers, he stated, "Yes, sir; they shot down a whole parcel along with me. Their bodies were lying there along the river the next morning. They kicked some of them into the river after they were shot dead." Aaron Fentis witnessed several Union soldiers, both black and white, shot while they were attempting to escape by swimming away in the Mississippi river. "Some were in the river swimming out a piece, when they were shot," Fentis stated, "and they took another man by the arm, and held him up, and shot him in the breast." At least some Confederate soldiers believed Union soldiers had deliberately retreated down the bluff so as to expose Confederate pursuers to the deadly canister of the Union gun boat *New Era*. A Lieutenant Leming overheard a couple of Confederate soldiers berating some wounded black soldiers. "You are trying to get this gunboat back to shell us, are you, God damn you." The wounded soldiers were then shot down. Clearly Confederate actions that day were heightened by the fact that they were facing African-Americans, thought by most southerners to be inferior and incapable of soldiering. Not only would southern actions expose the folly of the northern government for putting trust in the black soldier, it would also punish blacks individually much as runaway slaves were disciplined for the folly of their actions. Unruly slaves must be dealt with harshly so as to set an example for the rest of the servile population. It is certainly also true that the taunting comments that some of the African-American soldiers had hurled at Confederate soldiers who surrounded Fort Pillow on the morning of the 12th accelerated Confederate rage. It was one thing to face a former slave in a blue uniform—that was insulting; however, to face a black soldier in Union blue with an attitude and who seemed to laugh in the face of Confederate privates, that was intolerable.[13]

Several union soldiers claimed that Confederates had set fire to the corpses of dead bodies and attempted to bury other soldiers alive. Jacob Thompson, a black civilian at the fort, claimed to see the charred remains of slain Union soldiers the day after the battle. "They just called them out like dogs," stated Thompson, "and shot them down. I reckon they shot fifty, white and black, right there. They nailed some black sergeants to the logs, and set the logs on fire." On the next day, Thompson described the remains of burned bodies. "I saw them in the morning after the fight," recalled Thompson, "some of them were burned almost in two." Another black private from the 6th USCHA recalled Confederate soldiers deliberately putting wounded soldiers into a building and then setting the structure ablaze. "They told them [the wounded soldiers] that they were going to have the doctor see them, and put them in there and shut them up, and burned them." Rebecca Williams, a female from Obion County Tennessee, visited the Fort Pillow battlefield the day after the battle. "I saw a burned man," she recalled,

> he was lying right where a house was burned. He was a white man, but as I was alone by myself, I felt frightened, and did not look at it. I saw many buried there, some half buried, and negroes lying around there unburied.

Private Daniel Tyler, 6th USCHA, was shot twice and thrown into a hollow with dirt thrown on top of him; however, as Tyler also testified, it was a Confederate soldier that later realized he was alive and pulled him out of the grave. Another member of the 6th USCHA, Corporal Frank Hogan, testified to a live burial. "I also saw them bury 1 of our men alive, being only wounded."[14]

Once the rebels had climbed the wall and gained the interior of the fort, many Union soldiers and civilians heard rebel soldiers shout that they had been ordered by Forrest to slaughter the garrison. And in the aftermath of the battle, one of the most pressing questions was whether Forrest and

Chalmers had in fact ordered a massacre, or were Confederate soldiers simply acting out a primal rage that was stoked by the sight of African-Americans in uniform, challenging their manhood and the southern social order? The clear perception on the part of Union soldiers and civilians who witnessed the Fort Pillow battle was that rebel officers, particularly Forrest, had ordered the massacre and that rebel soldiers were following the directives of the Confederate command. "Voices were heard upon all sides," testified William J. Mays of the 13th Tennessee, "crying, 'Give them no quarter; kill them; kill them; it is General Forrest's orders.'"

Another Union private, Daniel Stamps of the 13th Tennessee Cavalry, testified to hearing similar language: "I heard several of them say it was General Forrest's orders to them to shoot us and give us no quarter at all." George Huston, a private in the 6th USCHA, testified that after many soldiers had run down the bluff and were near the Mississippi river, Confederate soldiers continued to fire on them: "A rebel officer rode up to the bank and said that General Forrest ordered every damned nigger to be shot down. So the enemy kept firing on our defenseless men and killed a great many of them."

Corporal Jerry Stewart of the 6th USCHA claimed that he observed numerous blacks being shot down by Confederates as they gained the parapet. He was told by a Confederate private that "the all colored boys that could escape had best do so by all means, for General Forrest was going to burn or whip them to death after they got farther South." Sergeant Henry F. Weaver of the 6th USCHA testified that some rebel soldiers spared white men so they could focus exclusively on killing blacks. "I saw one of the rebels," Weaver stated,

> and told him I would surrender. He said, "We do not shoot white men." I went up to him and he order me away; he kept on shooting the negroes. There were six or eight around there, and he and another one shot them all down.[15]

Confederate rage, however, also extended to members of the 13th Tennessee. As one member of the regiment remembered, when he asked a Confederate soldier for water after he had surrendered, he was excoriated, "Damn you; I have nothing for you fellows, you Tennesseans claim to be men, and you fight side by side with niggers; I have nothing for you." When Nathan Fulks of the 13th Tennessee Cavalry tried to surrender, he was bluntly told by one Confederate soldier, "'God damn you, you fight with the niggers, and we will kill the last one of you!'" Just as African-American soldiers were shot down as they tried to surrender, Daniel Stamps testified that the same thing happened to members of the 13th Tennessee.

"I saw them shooting the white men there," Stamps recalled, "who were on their knees, holding up their hands to them." Another member of the 13th Tennessee Cavalry, James P. Meador, stated that Confederate soldiers showed little mercy to Tennessee Unionists at Fort Pillow because they fought alongside black soldiers. He recalled hearing one rebel officer say, "Don't show the white men any more quarter than the negroes, because they are no better, and not so good, or they would not fight with the negroes." Major William Bradford tried to surrender by attaching a white handkerchief to the end of his sword. Rebel soldiers, however, informed him that he was not allowed to surrender. Bradford then attempt to swim to safety, but then decided to come back to shore and surrender again—and eventually he was finally allowed to surrender. Later, while a prisoner, Bradford would be killed under suspicious circumstances near the town of Brownsville, Tennessee. Another member of the 13th Tennessee, Isaac Leadbetter told Daniel W. Gooch, a congressional investigator, that he saw the man who shot him. He had surrendered, he recalled, but was still shot twice in the head. When asked if the rebel who shot him had said anything to him, Leadbetter recalled:

> He did not say anything to me until he shot me. He then came down to where I was, and finding that I was not dead, he cursed me, and said he would shoot me again. He was fixing to shoot me again, when one of the boys standing by told him not to shoot me again.

Unlike many others, Leadbetter was fortunate to survive. As Lieutenant Mack J. Leaming put it, "The rebels were very bitter against these loyal Tennesseeans [sic], terming them 'home-made Yankees,' and declaring they would give them no better treatment than they dealt out to the negro troops with whom they were fighting."[16]

Civilians, as well as soldiers, were not immune from Confederate wrath. John Penwell, a civilian from Detroit, Michigan was at Fort Pillow at the time of the battle. While many civilians who worked in the town as sutlers, merchants, or wives of soldiers were actually transported to the *New Era* prior to the final assault on the fort, a few civilians remained behind and fled to the garrison. Penwell lent a hand in the defense of the garrison. When the Confederates began their final assault, like many of the enlisted soldiers, he threw done his musket and tried to surrender. "I threw down my musket," Penwell later recalled. "A fellow who was ahead asked 'if I surrendered.' I said, 'Yes.' He said, 'Die, then, you damned Yankee son of a bitch,' and he shot me and I fell." Battle witnesses also made a number of other accusations against the rebels that day including live burials, the deliberate burning of prisoners, and the shooting of women and children. While the evidence for many of these atrocities is sketchy at best, it would contribute in the days after the massacre to an unflattering portrait of Forrest and his Confederate soldiers. George Shaw, a private in the 6th USCHA, claimed to have seen Confederate soldiers shoot three teenaged boys who were simply helping out in the garrison and were not soldiers. Another member of the 6th USCHA claimed he overheard a Confederate soldier threatening a child, "'Turn around so I can shoot you real good,' and then I heard them fire, and I heard the children fall over." Several witnesses claimed a certain Lieutenant Ackerstrom of the 13th Tennessee Cavalry was wounded, then nailed to the side of a house, and the house was then set aflame. Eli Bangs, a sailor aboard the *New Era*, testified that when he was able to go ashore, he saw the charred remains of a naked black man. Many witnesses claimed to have seen evidence of the same type of activities. One member of the 13th Tennessee recalls observing a Confederate private taunting two black woman and three children who apparently had not been transported from the fort. "'Yes, God damn you, you thought you were free did you?' and shot them all." While historians are justifiably skeptical of the claims that women and children were slaughtered, the testimony of many witnesses that such things transpired would certainly be troubling to northerners when reports of the massacre were circulated.[17]

During the battle, by all accounts, Forrest remained on the heights overlooking the garrison. His principal concern seems to have been making sure no federal gunboats were able to land so as to render assistance to the outnumbered and panicked Union soldiers. To what extent he was aware of the intensity of the slaughter that was transpiring is somewhat unclear. Given the mood of his officers and troops, however, he could not have been completely surprised at their reaction. Participants and some historians sympathetic to the Confederate commander justify Forrest's action that day, in part, because of an alleged pre-existing arrangement between Colonel Bradford and Captain Marshall of the *New Era*. Marshall testified that he and Bradford had an arrangement whereby Union soldiers would escape down the bluff and get aboard the Union vessel. As Confederates pursued escaping Union soldiers down the steep bluff, Marshall would pepper them with canister. Indeed, Marshall later testified that on a prearranged signal from Bradford, the Union soldiers would drop down the bluff and Marshall would break out the canister. The trouble was in the melee that occurred, it was difficult to separate friend from foe. How Marshall would have directed his fire at Confederates without potentially causing Union casualties was not explained. Additionally there was no written correspondence between Bradford and Marshall to corroborate Marshall's testimony. As some historians have observed, what transpired at Fort Pillow once the Confederates gained the parapet and the inner garrison did not resemble anything except confusion and chaos, let alone a prearranged plan.[18]

As previously discussed, numerous witnesses on the battlefield remembered that Confederate soldiers used "Forrest's orders" as justification for killing Union soldiers, even as Union soldiers, both black and white, tried to surrender. At the same time, as the battle and slaughter became apparent, it was Forrest and officers such as James R. Chalmers who finally put an end to the massacre. When Dr. Charles Fitch, a surgeon at Fort Pillow, was captured and felt that his life was threatened, he was allowed to talk to Forrest so as to appeal for protection. Forrest responded harshly to his appeal, "you are the surgeon for that damned Nigger Regiment." When Fitch explained that he was a surgeon, but served for the 13th Tennessee, Forrest's attitude remained equally harsh. Only when Fitch convinced Forrest that he was a northerner, merely serving in Tennessee, did the general agree to give him protection, but then only reluctantly. Given the attitude of Forrest and many of his officers toward blacks, they may not have explicitly ordered a massacre, but they knew it would take place, given the attitudes and prejudices of Confederate soldiers. Although they would eventually put a halt to the massacre, they did not move immediately to stop it. Forrest himself believed that the defeat at Fort Pillow would show northerners the folly of trying to arm blacks. Many Confederate officers, when asked about responsibility for the work of Confederate soldiers that day, made the argument that the common soldiers and many officers would never accept African-Americans as bona fide soldiers; hence, a

One witness to the Fort Pillow Massacre was Edward Benton, a native of Waltham, Vermont. Benton had been involved in providing beef to Union troops in northern Missouri before resettling near Fort Pillow where he purchased approximately 215 acres that bordered the fort. Using the labor of black contrabands, Benton was raising cotton on the land he had recently purchased. While a witness to the events of April 12, 1864, Benton also testified that many Confederate soldiers were upset that he was using black labor provided to him by Union military officials in Memphis. "I might state that that I was inquired after by a large number of officers [Confederate]," Benton stated, "and it was said they would hang me on a flag-pole." When asked why the Confederates were so hostile toward him, Benton replied, "From the fact that I employed government darkeys from Colonel Phillips, at Memphis."

Source: Fort Pillow Massacre, House Report No. 65, 122.

reasonable interpretation of this observation was that additional battles involving black soldiers facing Confederates soldiers would result in a high casualty rates for African-American troops, particularly if Confederate soldiers had the advantage.[19]

The final assault and route of the Union garrison took less than an hour. After the primary fighting was concluded, witnesses to the battle were treated to a gruesome sight. Mangled bodies, both wounded and dead, lie scattered down the steep bluff to the Mississippi. In the river, numerous soldiers, both black and white, floated, having been shot as they attempted to swim to the *New Era*. Even Confederate witnesses, in the immediate aftermath of the battle, realized that something awful and horrific had transpired. As one Confederate soldier testified, "Blood, human blood stood about in pools and brains could have been gathered up in any quantity." Another witness to the battle, Samuel H. Caldwell, confided to his wife, "So you can guess how terrible was the slaughter. It was decidedly the most horrible sight that I have ever witnessed." A correspondent named "Vidette" published a brief report on the Fort Pillow Massacre in the *Mobile Advertiser and Register* shortly after the battle transpired. After describing how the garrison was a given a chance to surrender, the correspondent wrote, "Indiscriminate slaughter followed— about a hundred prisoners were taken, the balance was slain. The fort ran with blood; many jumped in the river and drowned, or [were] shot in the water." "The sight was terrific—the slaughter sickening." Horace Wardner, a Union surgeon stationed at a hospital in Mound City, Illinois, treated a number of wounded soldiers from the Fort Pillow battle. "They [the wounded from Fort Pillow] were the worst butchered men I have ever seen," Wardner testified:

> I have been in several hard battles, but I have never seen men so mangled as they were; and nearly all of them concur in stating that they received all their wounds after they had thrown down their arms, surrendered, and asked for quarter.[20]

During the night, many witnesses said the torture of prisoners and the wounded continued. According to Mack R. Leaming, the adjutant of the 13th Tennessee, Confederate soldiers committed unspeakable acts during the night. "This horrid work of butchery did not cease even with the night of murder, but was continued the next morning, when numbers of our wounded were basely murdered after a long night of pain and suffering where they had fought so bravely," stated Leaming. Some witnesses also testified that wounded soldiers, both black and white, were tortured and killed the next day as they lay in their sickbeds. "We saw several negroes burning up in their quarters on Wednesday morning," noted Francis A. Smith and William Cleary, both lieutenants in the 13th Tennessee Cavalry. "We also saw the rebels come back in the morning and shoot the wounded." Wounded white soldiers were not spared from execution, according to the pair, because they fought with blacks and, therefore, practiced the doctrine of "negro equality."[21]

Although the evidence for this is unclear, with many Confederates stating that the majority of their forces had already withdrawn from the Fort Pillow area, when the sun rose on the morning of April 13, signs that a horrific slaughter had taken place were abundant. Early that morning, in response to the shelling of Union gunboats in the area, Forrest, through his subordinate, Colonel Charles Anderson, arranged a truce with Acting Master William Ferguson of the *Silver Cloud*. Ferguson was given until 5:00 p.m. to transport Union wounded aboard his ship as well as the *Platte Valley*. Ferguson claimed that Union soldiers carried aboard 70 wounded soldiers and counted 150 dead bodies. Ferguson's report confirmed that a brutal massacre had taken place. Not only did he report that the buildings around the fort had been burned with what appeared to be the charred remnants of Union soldiers, he also reported graphic evidence of cruelty and savagery practiced on Union soldiers. "Bodies with gaping wounds, some bayoneted through the eyes, some with skulls beaten through, other with hideous wounds as if their bowels had been ripped open with bowie knives, plainly told that but little quarter shown to our troops." Ferguson concluded, "here was evidence of a massacre carried on long after any resistance could have been offered, with a cold-blooded barbarity and perseverance which nothing can palliate."

Nor was Ferguson the only Union witness to the evidence of atrocity. Captain John G. Woodruff, 113th Illinois infantry, came from Memphis aboard the *Platte Valley* to assist in transporting the wounded and burying the dead:

> We saw the bodies of 15 negroes," noted Woodruff, "most of them having been shot through the head. Some of them were burned as if by power around the holes in their heads, which led me to conclude that they were shot at very close range.

When Woodruff asked Colonel James R. Chalmers to explain these excesses, Chalmers stated, "the men of General Forrest's command had such hatred for the armed negro that they could not be restrained from killing the negroes after they captured them." Chalmers further stated that these atrocities had not been ordered by either him or General Forrest;

however, such slaughters would probably continue "so long as we persisted in arming the negro." [22]

A final indignity transpired the day after the battle during the flag of truce as Union men and officers oversaw the removal of wounded soldiers and the burial of the dead. Several witnesses stated that Confederate officers, General James R. Chalmers most notably, were invited onto the Union boat, *Platte Valley*, and accorded drinks and other amenities. John Penwell, a civilian who was present at Fort Pillow, was aboard the *Platte Valley* the day after the massacre. "I went on board, and took my seat right in front of the saloon. I knew the bartender," Penwell stated, "and wanted to get a chance to get some wine, as I was very weak." Just as Penwell was to go up to the bar, he was pushed aside by a Union officer:

> I was just going to step up to the bar, when one of our officers
> . . . stepped in front of me and almost shoved me away, and
> called up one of the rebel officers and took a drink with him; and
> I saw our officers drinking with the rebel officers several times.

Given the evidence of barbarities that had been committed the day before against Union soldiers, several witnesses who claimed to have observed this treatment, were upset with the apparent hospitality accorded Chalmers and other rebel officers. At the same time, given the fact that Chalmers had stated that the massacre had not been explicitly ordered, Union officers aboard the vessel may have accepted his explanation as accurate, blaming the massacre instead on the enraged common soldier of the Confederacy.[23]

For his part, Forrest was proud of his accomplishments at Fort Pillow and initially had few doubts about his orders and what had transpired during battle. Since he had given the garrison an opportunity to surrender, he could not be blamed for what transpired in the battle that day. Having no intention of occupying the fort, he gathered up supplies, horses, and other war material and moved on to Jackson, Tennessee to the east. In a letter to Confederate president, Jefferson Davis, Forrest claimed that his victory "was complete." Claiming to have killed 450–500 of the 700 estimated Union soldiers at Fort Pillow, Forrest put his own losses at 20 killed and 60 wounded. Writing to his immediate superior, Lieutenant General Leonidas Polk, Forrest stated, "The victory was complete, and the loss of enemy will never be known from the fact that large numbers ran into the river and were shot and drowned." Forrest certainly did not believe that his command had, in fact, been involved in a massacre. Offering a clue as to his motivation in attacking Fort Pillow, Forrest added, "It is hoped that these facts will demonstrate to the Northern people that the negro soldier cannot cope with Southerners." And Forrest's actions were noticed and applauded by other southern soldiers. One soldier was happy "that Forrest had it in his power to execute such swift and summary vengeance upon the negroes and I trust it will have good influence in deterring others from similar acts." Perhaps Forrest and other southerners really believed that brutal treatment of African-Americans in battle would discourage future enlistments. In a similar fashion, Forrest's second in command, Brigadier General James R. Chalmers also basked in the glory of the West Tennessee campaign. Writing an address to the soldiers in his command, Chalmers positively gloated:

> I congratulate you upon your success in the brilliant campaign recently conducted in West Tennessee under the guidance of Major-General Forrest, whose star never shone brighter, and whose relentless activity, untiring energy, and courage baffled the calculations and paralyzed the arms of our enemies.

According to Chalmers, a major accomplishment of the campaign, including the victory at Fort Pillow, was the relief it accorded the rebel residents of West Tennessee. "West Tennessee is redeemed," Chalmers stated, "and our friends who have heretofore been compelled to speak with bated breath now boldly proclaim their sentiments." Relieving the sufferings of the residents of West Tennessee and exposing the folly of arming African-Americans were two of the principal reasons for Forrest's campaign into West Tennessee and his attack on Fort Pillow. In the immediate aftermath of the Fort Pillow Massacre, Forrest and Chalmers believed that they had accomplished their goals.[24]

What were the actual losses at Fort Pillow and do they justify using the term massacre? Historians have debated the actual losses for many years; however, the most thorough research on the topic has been performed by the historians John Cimprich and Robert Mainfort. Since there was no official report filed on Fort Pillow, Cimprich and Mainfort mined national archive records to compile a thorough and convincing account and analysis of the battle's casualties. Pegging the number of men present at Fort Pillow between 585–605, there were between 277–297 deaths, meaning approximately 47–49 percent of Union soldiers were killed—a much higher casualty rate than the typical bloody Civil War battle. However, these numbers do not tell the whole story, for there was a marked difference in black and white casualty rates. Although historians writing from a southern point of view had claimed casualty rates were not that severe, Cimprich and Mainfort demonstrate that blacks were killed at a rate of 64 percent as opposed to 31 percent for white, showing a clear determination on the part of Confederate soldiers to punish blacks for challenging the social order. While Forrest stated a determination to teach the northern public a lesson about the reliability of black soldiers, the motive of the common Confederate soldiers seemed to be intimidation and punishment of African-American soldiers for violating the social norms of the South. By slaughtering black soldiers and refusing to offer quarter, it might convince northern blacks and escaped southern slaves to reconsider enlisting in Union armies. Without the benefit of African-American soldiers, the northern government might lose an important resource in its effort to subdue and defeat the Confederacy. At the same time, Confederate soldiers had little inkling as to how their actions would play to the northern public as well as their impact on African-Americans and potential African-American recruits to the Union armies.[25]

While Forrest and his officers were proud, even boastful, of their complete victory over Union forces at Fort Pillow, they scarcely realized the dilemma facing them and the Confederate government within a few days after the massacre. Indeed, they seriously miscalculated the fallout that events at Fort Pillow would cause. As survivors of the massacre were interviewed and as newspaper correspondents published reports of the atrocities committed at Fort Pillow, a wave of public reaction set in against Forrest and the Confederacy. The published report of the Joint Committee on the Conduct of the War would further inflame northern public opinion, particularly as this report alleged that the actions at Fort Pillow were the result of a deliberate policy pursued by the Confederate government at Richmond. The aftermath of Fort Pillow would implicate the Confederate government in a cover-up of sorts; however, it would also present an enormous challenge to the Union government and the administration of Abraham Lincoln. As African-American leaders and radical Republicans demanded that the administration and the president institute harsh measures of retaliation against the Confederacy, other segments of northern society were not as upset over the events that had transpired at Fort Pillow. For northern peace Democrats, or Copperheads, to take special measures of retaliation against the Confederacy on behalf of black soldiers seemed particularly ill-advised, especially since it might have unpleasant consequences for white Union soldiers. The Lincoln administration, too, had to consider the consequences of any policy that might encourage the Davis administration to retaliate in kind. At the same time, if measures were not taken to protect African-American soldiers, blacks might not be willing to answer the call to Union arms on the grounds that it was too risky, and, furthermore, African-American leaders might not be so willing to speak out on behalf of military service for black males. In the end, President Lincoln was faced with a number of unpleasant alternatives, each with substantial risks. When all was said and done, however, the most important actors in this controversy were the black soldiers themselves. Convinced that they had earned the right to equal protection as legitimate soldiers in arms, they would also take matters into their own hands on the field of battle, regardless of the actions of the Lincoln administration. If the Union government would not ensure their safety and protection as prisoners of war, if the Union government would not initiate retaliation against the Confederacy for its brutal massacre at Fort Pillow, African-American soldiers would be their own advocates and take matters into their own hands.

CHAPTER 3

Controversy

Nathan Bedford Forrest, James R. Chalmers, and other officers in the Confederate high command had little inkling of the reaction that the engagement at Fort Pillow would trigger throughout the northern states. The day immediately following the massacre, during the truce that was negotiated between Confederate and Union officers, a number of eyewitness testimonies were recorded. As historian John Cimprich has detailed, an account of the massacre, published by a correspondent of the *Missouri Democrat* and based on three eyewitness accounts of the battle, was published within days of the battle. By April 14, the story of the Fort Pillow Massacre had spread throughout the north via the Associated Press wire. The basic element of the narrative was that a Confederate force had attacked a much smaller Union force. Confederate soldiers overwhelmed the outnumbered garrison and would give Union soldiers no quarter, even after soldiers tried to surrender individually. While numerous whites were killed, the Confederates displayed a marked prejudice toward black soldiers, who were killed at a much higher percentage than their white counterparts. In addition to these reports, other accusations of grotesque behavior on the part of Confederate soldiers punctuate these accounts including living burials, the killing of women and children, the burning of corpses, and numerous violations of the flag of truce.[1]

In the days that followed the massacre at Fort Pillow, the northern press and individual northerners expressed outrage at alleged rebel atrocities. Press accounts and personal correspondence often expressed an intense, emotional response. "That was a horrible massacre by Forrests [sic] men at Fort Pillow," Grotius R. Giddings wrote to his father, former congressmen Joshua R. Giddings. "It shows a barbarity that I had not dreamed they had."

"The whole civilized world will be shocked by the great atrocity at Fort Pillow," predicted the *Chicago Tribune*. "But in no respect does the act misrepresent the nature and precedents of Slavery."

The abolitionist newspaper, the *Independent*, was equally as harsh in its assessment of the Fort Pillow affair. "Such horrors," it editorialized, "are no greater than those to which four million of blacks have been exposed in slavery before this war began." In another editorial, the paper called for retaliation, stating, "Let the Government at Washington, that shrinks from bloody retaliation, make answer by securing the abolition of slavery and the recognition of the black man as the equal before the law."

A recruiter of African-American troops stationed in Memphis, Brigadier General Augustus L. Chetlain was both shocked and outraged by what had transpired at Fort Pillow. Writing to Illinois congressman, Elihu Washburne, Chetlain stated, "there is a great deal of excitement . . . in consequence of this affair—especially among our colored troops. If this is to be the game of the enemy they will soon learn that it is one *at which two can play*."

Finally, Horace Greeley's *New York Tribune* stated, "It has long been clear to us that the Rebel leaders meant to impress upon this struggle every possible feature of cruelty."[2]

Although a few Democratic papers expressed skepticism over the accounts of Fort Pillow or asked for additional time to evaluate and investigate allegations of brutality, there seemed widespread support throughout the north for retaliation and a demand for the president to respond to the actions at Fort Pillow. For a few weeks after the massacre, it seemed that the central purpose in the American Civil War was to avenge the atrocities at Fort Pillow. "The massacre at Fort Pillow," opined *Harper's*, "is a direct challenge to our Government to prove whether it is in earnest or not in emancipating slaves and employing colored troops." While the *Liberator*, the anti-slavery newspaper established by the abolitionist, William Lloyd Garrison, remarked, "The mass of the rebel force at Fort Pillow, officers and soldiers, did 'with alacrity' the infernal work required of them, and enjoyed the torturing and butchery of prisoners as much as the victory which gave them the opportunity." At the same time, the *Liberator* wondered if retaliation was appropriate and whether it would put the north on the same level as the Confederacy. Other papers had no such doubts. One Indianapolis newspaper wanted an eye for an eye. "Let the fate of the Fort Pillow prisoners overtake a like number of rebel prisoners in our hands, and their blood be upon the heads of the Fort Pillow butchers." The *Independent* asked, "Shall we now have some action by the Government, which will prevent a repetition of these atrocities?" A Buffalo, New York correspondent of Massachusetts

Republican Senator, Henry Wilson, asked the Senator to use his influence with the president. "Please tell him [Lincoln] the *Loyal People demand* from him *retaliation* for the horrible crimes of the 'Fort Pillow' affair . . ."

"The blood of these slaughtered men is on skirts as well as on the skirts of the rebels," opined the *New York Times*. "If we permit them to be killed while we stand by, when it is in our power to protect them; and Heaven and history will hold us responsible."

One black New Yorker, Theodore Hodgkins, wrote to Secretary of War Edwin Stanton and stated the position succinctly. Lincoln had promised earlier in 1863 to retaliate against the Confederacy for the mistreatment of black soldiers, but even when there was evidence that black troops had been murdered, nothing was done. "To be sure there has been sort of a secrecy about many of the slaughters of colored troops that prevented an official declaration to be made" the black New Yorker argued. With the massacre at Fort Pillow transpiring, Confederate brutality was out in the open, but what would the Federal government do in response with the whole world now looking on? "If the murder of the colored troops at Fort Pillow is not followed by prompt action on the part of our government," wrote Hodgkins, "it may as well disband *all its colored troops* for no soldiers whom the government will not protect can be depended upon."[3]

Both the War Department and Congress authorized investigations of the Fort Pillow Massacre with Congress authorizing the controversial Joint Committee on the Conduct of the War to investigation the rumors and allegations surrounding events at Fort Pillow. The War Department's investigation was ordered by Secretary of War, Edwin M. Stanton. The congressional investigation was the outcome of an intense debate that took place in the Senate on April 16, 1864, a scant four days after the massacre took place. Jacob Howard, a Republican senator from Michigan, introduced a resolution, authorizing the Joint Committee on the Conduct of the War to investigate the atrocities at Fort Pillow. Some members of the Senate objected on the grounds that the War department was already conducting its own investigation. In addition, the Joint Committee had already acquired a reputation for rank partisanship in some of its previous investigations, a reputation that might have soured some members of Congress on the resolution. Howard, however, was adamant, claiming that Congress had a responsibility to black recruits. "Without this protection," Howard argued, "we know very well what will be the fate of the black troops." While not disparaging the War department's investigation, Howard believed that it was Congress's responsibility to sort out fact from fiction, especially in light of the lurid details that were circulating. In the end, Howard's resolution was passed and the Committee appointed a subcommittee of two members, Senator Benjamin F. Wade, a well-known radical Republican Senator from Ohio and Representative Daniel W. Gooch, a much lesser known Republican from the Boston area. A few days later, the *New York Herald* reported that Committee members had gone to the White House to meet with both Stanton and President Lincoln and "to consult as to what course should be pursued in the investigation."[4]

Armed with a stenographer and a letter of introduction from War Secretary Stanton, the two congressmen headed west on the evening of April 19, visiting Mound City, Illinois, Columbus, Kentucky, Fort Pillow, and Memphis, Tennessee, interviewing wounded prisoners, civilians, and other relevant personnel—a total of 51 witnesses were eventu-

Created in December 1861, the Joint Committee on the Conduct of the War was a controversial joint select congressional committee charged with investigating all aspects of Union military operations. From Union military defeats and supply contracts to the treatment of Union prisoners of war, the Committee conducted a variety of investigations during the course of the Civil War. Chaired by radical Republican Senator Benjamin F. Wade, the Committee's investigation of the Fort Pillow Massacre was one of its most high profile investigations.

Source: Bruce Tap, *Over Lincoln's Shoulder: The Committee on the Conduct of the War* (Lawrence: University Press of Kansas, 1998).

ally interviewed. The culmination of the subcommittee's efforts was the publication of a report of its findings, which was carried in numerous northern newspapers. Given the Committee's partisan reputation, not everyone accepted the Committee's findings as authoritative. Secretary of the Navy, Gideon Welles, while a Republican and a member of the administration, was skeptical. "There must be something in these terrible reports," Welles reflected, "but I distrust Congressional committees. They exaggerate." Appearing in major daily papers and with 60,000 copies printed and distributed, the report did create a sensation in northern public opinion.[5]

As the subcommittee and War department investigators interviewed witnesses and drafted their statements for publication, reports of the massacre continued in the northern press. The tone of the discourse remained angry, accusatory, and vindictive. Clearly the northern press, particularly those papers in the Republican camp, was out for blood. In an article entitled "The Fort Pillow Butchery," for instance, the *New York Times* reported on April 23, 1864 that "there is now an overwhelming and painfully minute mass of proof of the truth of the first reports of the rebel massacre of our troops, black and white, at Fort Pillow." It continued,

> It now only requires the official statement of the officers appointed to investigate the matter, to furnish irrefragable proof for history . . . Jeff. Davis officially proclaimed this to be his policy, and he was backed up in his ferocious proclamation by the whole rebel press. To deny that the rebels would carry out their measure is preposterous to the perception of all of us who know that, atrocious as rebel threats have been, their deeds have always been more bloody than their threats.[6]

When the Joint Committee on the Conduct of the War official report appeared, it did not disappoint those who had been most outspoken in denouncing rebel actions at Fort Pillow. The Committee's report did not hold Forrest personally or primarily responsible for the massacre. Instead it focused on the brutality of southern culture and the policies of the Confederate government with respect to African-American troops. "It was at Fort Pillow, however," the report stated, "that the brutality and cruelty of the rebels were most fearfully exhibited." According to the Committee, the atrocities at Fort Pillow were not the result of passions of the moment, "but were the result of a policy deliberately decided upon and unhesitatingly announced." Simply put, the actions of Confederate soldiers were the outcome of the decision of Confederate authorities not to recognize black soldiers as bona fide combatants who would be accorded rights as prisoners of war according to commonly understood military practices. Reviewing the allegations of atrocities and providing detailed examples of the brutality of Confederate soldiers at Fort Pillow, the report described Confederate actions in graphic, negative terms. "No cruelty which the most fiendish malignity could device was omitted by these murderers." Accepting the testimony of many Union witnesses at face value, the Committee's report accused Forrest and the Confederates of violating well-established rules of warfare by moving troops into favorable positions under the cover of a flag of truce. Equally upsetting to Wade and Gooch was the allegation of some Union witnesses of the hospitalities extended to Confederate officers the day after the massacre, when a truce was negotiated to allow Union soldiers to bury the dead and transport their wounded. According to these witnesses, Union officers entertained Confederate officers aboard the *Platte Valley* and bestowed:

> civilities and attention upon the rebel officers, even while they were boasting of the murders they had there committed. Your

committee was unable to ascertain the names of the officers who
have thus inflicted so foul a stain upon the honor of our army.
They are assured, however, by military authorities that every effort
will be made to ascertain their names and bring them to the
punishment they so richly deserve.[7]

With reports of the Fort Pillow Massacre and demands for retaliation
rampant in the press and the report of the Joint Committee on the
Conduct of the War creating more pressure for action, President Lincoln
was now forced to consider a response. From the House of Representatives,
radical Republican George Washington Julian, a member of the Joint
Committee on the Conduct of the War, demanded that Congress could
no longer look upon the South as brethren. "The recent massacre at Fort
Pillow," Julian observed, "clearly foreshadows the policy the rebels are to
pursue in the future, and thus necessitates a policy on our part which shall
no longer deal with the rebels as brethren, but as devils." Julian, like other
radical Republicans, looked forward to the end of the war and the
reconstruction of the South. In his opinion, the brutality of the Fort Pillow
Massacre supported his plan for a punishing reconstruction in which
confiscation of the land of wealthy planters was at the forefront. Leading
Republican papers, such as the *Chicago Tribune*, demanded action. "The
report of the Committee on the Conduct of the War," it maintained,
"more than fully confirms previous reports of the Fort Pillow horror." It
demanded that the Lincoln administration adopt a policy of executing a
similar number of Confederate prisoners of war currently held by the
Union army. Of course, the Union government had already confronted
the possibility that the Confederate government would not recognize blacks
as legitimate soldiers and had taken appropriate action. When the Lincoln
administration had taken its first actions toward arming blacks, the
Davis administration had declared that blacks would not be accorded treatment as prisoners of war, instead they would be turned over to state authorities,
where they would be treated according to state laws. Officers of black
regiments would be regarded as fomenting slave rebellions and treated
accordingly. Speaking to a Sanitary Fair in Baltimore on April 18, 1864
and well before the Joint Committee on the Conduct of the War had
reported on its findings, President Lincoln expressed grave concern over
the Fort Pillow Massacre: "Having determined to use the negro as a soldier,
there is no way but to give him all the protection given to any other
soldier." As Lincoln saw it, however, the massacre at Fort Pillow, at that
point in time, was still not an established fact: "We fear it, believe, I may
say, but we do not know it." It was important to establish the reality of
these atrocities before any actions were taken, and only an investigation

of the affair would yield the appropriate knowledge. While Lincoln hinted
at retaliation in his remarks, he was not yet prepared to act. In early May
he laid the issue before his Cabinet, asking them to go on record with a
course of action. Recalling the meeting, Gideon Welles struggled with
coming to a conclusion. He regarded the idea of man for man retaliation
as both repulsive and "barbarous." At the same time, the Federal government was under an obligation to protect its black soldiers. Over the next
couple of days, Cabinet members sent Lincoln their recommendations in
letter form.[8]

Secretary of State William H. Seward believed that the Confederate
leadership should be given a chance to present evidence that disproved
the Fort Pillow Massacre, or at least to disavow the massacre and to pledge
not to allow the repetition of such an event in the future. The commanding
general of the Union army, in Seward's opinion, should communicate to
his counterpart in the Confederate army that a massacre took place after
black troops surrendered, and, additionally, that there was no evidence
that the Confederacy disavowed such actions. While waiting for a response,
a number of Confederate prisoners of war—equal to the number of
soldiers slain at Fort Pillow—should be isolated until a response was
received. The fate of said prisoners would depend on the response of the
Confederate government. Somewhat harsher was the recommendation of
War Secretary Edwin Stanton, who believed Confederate officers currently
confined should be chosen by lots and collected in a number that equaled
the soldiers killed at Fort Pillow. Stanton also recommended that officers
such as Forrest and Chalmers be exempt from any possibility of exchange
if captured and be immediately tried for war crimes. Once the first two
conditions were communicated to the Richmond government, Stanton
recommended that confined officers be offered in exchange for Forrest
and Chalmers. If the Davis government refused, then the Lincoln
administration could retaliate in a way it deemed appropriate. In addition,
Stanton also recommended that the Union government simply stop all
prisoner exchanges and that rebel officers currently in Union prisons be
put on rations that were on a par with those Union prisoners received in
Confederate prison camps. For Stanton a key point was to retaliate only
against Confederate officers, especially as the Richmond government had
made a special point of targeting Union officers of black regiments.[9]

Naval secretary Gideon Welles worried about the impact the Fort
Pillow Massacre would have on African-American troops. In the immediate
aftermath of Fort Pillow, he had counseled caution in order to make sure
that the atrocities reported in the press and by the Joint Committee on
the Conduct of the War were, in fact, true. With the evidence now
providing sufficient confirmation, Welles knew that the Union government

must respond. What initially worried Welles was the impact that the Fort Pillow Massacre might have on African-American troops. "Such a vindictive warfare toward a whole race, will undoubtedly provoke retaliation from the proscribed race." What might follow, Welles believed, was a "war of extermination." Welles believed that Confederate authorities ought to be given information on the massacre with an opportunity to disavow the policy. He then recommended a course of action somewhat different from his colleagues in that he demanded that the Confederate authorities punish guilty officers such as Forrest and Chalmers. If the Richmond government refused to take such a course of action, like Seward and Stanton, Welles recommended that the Lincoln administration hold a number of Confederate officers in close quarters and be held accountable for these actions.[10]

Arguing a slightly more aggressive line was Salmon P. Chase, Secretary of the Treasury. Chase argued that all soldiers were entitled to equal treatment when it came to capture in battle. "To redeem this pledge," Chase argued, "it seems necessary to retaliate the slaughter in violation of the laws of war, of the officers and men at Fort Pillow by the execution of an equal number of rebel officers and soldiers." Chase further stipulated that officers set aside for execution must be high ranking since the Confederacy placed little value of the lives of common soldiers. According to Chase, a group of high ranking Confederate officers should be set aside and then a demand sent to the Richmond government, asking if the Fort Pillow Massacre was authorized as official Confederate policy. If the answer was yes, then the Union government should act decisively by immediately executing an equal number of Confederate prisoners of war.[11]

One Cabinet member who aggressively argued against retaliation was Montgomery Blair, Post-Master General of the United States. Citing scholarly authorities on the laws of warfare, Blair maintained that man for man retaliation was not justified under commonly accepted laws of warfare. Citing examples from past American military campaigns, Blair argued that in the case of Indian massacres, Native-American prisoners were not summarily executed. To retaliate for the Fort Pillow, maintained Blair, would play into the hands of the authorities at Richmond. Knowing that the common whites of the South were beginning to tire in their support of the Confederate cause, Blair believed a policy of retaliation would play into the hands of the rebel leaders by causing an emotional response among the Confederate masses. Instead of retaliating against prisoners in custody, Blair recommended that the perpetrators of the massacre be hunted down and brought to justice. "A proclamation or order, that the guilty individuals are to be hunted down," Blair reasoned, "will have far greater terrors and be far more effectual to prevent the repetition of the crime than punishment

of parties not concerned in that crime." According to Blair, executing
Confederate prisoners of war would lead to retaliation against Union
soldiers and prisoners of war.[12]

Perhaps the most interesting opinion was offered by Attorney General
Edward Bates, particularly because his opinion, as chief law enforcement
officer of the land, might be expected to carry the most weight. Bates
candidly admitted that he had opposed the use of black soldiers because
he expected outrages like those that had transpired at Fort Pillow. "I know
something of the cherished passions and the educated prejudices of the
southern people," Bates told Lincoln, "and I could not but fear that our
employment of negro troops would add fuel to a flame already fiercely
burning, and thus, excite their evil passions to deeds of horror, shocking
to humanity and to Christian civilization." What worried Bates, however,
was the pressure to retaliate, with the northern government getting "drawn
into the vortex, and made, however unwillingly, sharers in their guilt and
punishment." According to Bates, though, the president had the law on
his side, and he should inflict the proper punishment on Confederate
soldiers as he deemed appropriate. Bates then went on to make a number
of recommendations. The president should make no public plan of
retaliation unless he planned "to act it out to the letter, all its consequences,
direct and contingent." In addition, Lincoln should ask the Confederacy,
through military channels, whether what happened at Fort Pillow was
official Confederate policy. If the Davis administration disavowed the
massacre, then Lincoln should ask that Forrest and Chalmers be turned
over to the Lincoln administration and dealt with appropriately. If the
Confederacy avowed the act, then Lincoln should order all officers of the
Union army and navy to immediately execute any soldier, officer or private
that participated in the Fort Pillow Massacre whenever they might be
captured by Union forces. Still, Bates recommended the administration
avoid an official policy of retaliation. The attorney general stated, "I would
have no compact with the enemy for mutual slaughter—no cartel of blood
and murder—no stipulation to the effect that *if you murder one of my men,
I will murder one of yours.*"[13]

Like the rest of the Cabinet members, Secretary of the Interior, John
P. Usher believed the heinous atrocities at Fort Pillow demanded a strong
response. And, moreover, like his Cabinet colleagues, he, too, demanded
that rebel officers be set aside. "I am of the opinion that the government should set apart for execution," reasoned Usher, "an equal number
of prisoners, who, since the massacre, have been or may hereafter, from
time to time, be captured from Forrest's command, designating, in every
instance, as far as practicable, officers instead of privates." Usher's
contention was that before taking extreme action, Lincoln should evaluate

the military situation. With Grant's armies engaged with the Confederate Army of Northern Virginia in the Wilderness campaign, the president should await the outcome of the present campaign. If Union armies suffered a defeat, it might not be appropriate to take such strong actions, which might prove embarrassing to the United States government.[14]

With the public clamoring for revenge and the Cabinet endorsing some type of man-for-man retaliation, Lincoln finally decided upon a course of action. Lincoln instructed War Secretary Stanton to inform rebel authorities that his government possessed convincing proof of the atrocities at Fort Pillow. Furthermore, that the United States government would set aside a group of Confederate prisoners of war in lieu of a response to a demand of the Lincoln administration: namely, that the Richmond government guarantee that all soldiers—including black soldiers—be treated as bona fide soldiers and legitimate prisoners of war. If the United States government did not receive a suitable response by July 1, 1864, it would assume that the Richmond government would not comply and the northern government would take suitable retaliatory action against the Confederate prisoners. ". . . if no satisfactory attention shall be given to this notice, by said insurgents, on or before the first day of July next," Lincoln wrote,

> it will be assumed by the government of the United States, that said captured colored troops shall have been murdered, or subjected to Slavery, and that said government will, upon said assumption, take such action as may then appear expedient and just.[15]

How would Confederates and southerners react to northern outrage, the publication of the Joint Committee on the Conduct of the War's report, and calls for retaliation for the Fort Pillow Massacre? One of the most interesting interpretations of the southern response examines a number of southern primary sources in the days immediately following the massacre and then contrasts the response once southerners were aware of the northern outrage and accusations. Before southerners, particularly those who had witnessed the battle at Fort Pillow, were aware of northern outrage, that something horrible, even monstrous, had happened was admitted. "For ten minutes death reigned in the fortification, and along the river bank," a reporter named "Marion" recalled when reporting on the Fort Pillow battle:

> Our troops maddened by the excitement shot down the ret[r]eating Yankees, and not until they had attained t[h]e water's

> edge and turned and begged for mercy, did any prisoners fall in
> [t] our hands—Thus the whites received quarter, but the negroes
> were shown no mercy.[16]

A marked change in Confederate press reports occurred, however, once northern reports of the massacre circulated and once the Lincoln administration began clamoring for an official explanation of Confederate actions. In June 1864, Brigadier General Mason Brayman, commander of the Cairo, Illinois district, reported to Ben Wade, chair of the Joint Committee on the Conduct of the War, that Confederates were now in complete denial that anything out of the ordinary had occurred at Fort Pillow. Enclosing a clipping from a Cairo, Illinois newspaper, Brayman told Wade that the facts of the Fort Pillow Massacre were being denied outright, and he informed Wade about the Richmond correspondent of the *Times* of London who claimed that the stories circulating about the Fort Pillow atrocities were the equivalent of fables. "The carnage in proportion to those engaged was very great at Fort Pillow," rebel sources would admit according to Brayman, "but the atrocities complained of were never committed—and the idea of burying men alive was but the creation of an ignorance and falsehood, devised to cover transactions scarcely less hideous, and enormities at which humanity shudders." In fact, by early May 1864 few Confederates were willing to admit that a massacre had occurred. Various reasons were given: the garrison's failure to surrender was the cause of the high casualties; the so-called surrender of individual soldiers was not really a surrender since the Union flag was not pulled down and Union troops tried to flee down the bluff and escape to the *New Era*. Additional reasons offered for the high casualty rate were that banter and taunts prior to the battle on the part of black soldiers had enraged Confederate soldiers or that Confederate soldiers were simply compensating for acts of violence, murder and rape committed by black soldiers against the residents of West Tennessee; however, the most original excuse offered by Confederate officers and picked up by southern newspapers was that the majority of Union soldiers, particularly blacks, were drunk. Although there were casks found near the fort, there is no evidence supporting the contention of Confederate officers and writers. As John Cimprich notes, it was nearly a month after the massacre occurred that this reason was picked up in southern newspapers, and then, only after pressure had been exerted on Confederate authorities and Forrest to account for his actions. Indeed, claiming that black soldiers had been drunk played to stereotypes that many whites had regarding black docility and the expected disastrous results the Union could expect when it put an "inferior" and childlike race into the military. While high casualties had taken place at Fort Pillow, Confederate newspapers, officials, and political leaders put most of the blame on the victims.[17]

Forrest's defense of his actions is amply illustrated in a series of letters that were exchanged between himself and Union Major General Cadwallader Washburn, Union commander of the district of Western Tennessee, in June and July 1864. Quite remarkably, Forrest began the exchange of letters when he inquired about an event that was rumored to have taken place in Memphis, where it was reported that black troops had taken an oath to avenge the defeat at Fort Pillow and heretofore would take no Confederate prisoners. "In all my operations since the war began," Forrest explained, "I have conducted the war on civilized principles, and desire to do so, but it is due my command that they should know the position they occupy and the policy you intend to pursue."

On June 19, Washburn answered Forrest's letter, telling him that black soldiers in Memphis had sworn an oath to avenge the Fort Pillow Massacre. "The affair at Fort Pillow," he noted, "fully justified that belief." Washburn added, "Your declaration that you have conducted the war on all occasions on civilized principles cannot be accepted." Noting that Forrest's attempt to intimidate black troops with the "no quarter" threat had been a singular failure, Washburn demanded that Forrest clarify his position on the status of black troops. Would they be killed? Would they be returned to slavery?

Sidebar 3.1

Cadwallader Colder Washburn (1818–1882) was a Maine politician and early member of the Republican Party, who, like many political figures, took an active part in the Union military during the Civil War. The brother of Illinois congressman, Elihu Washburne, the elder Washburn brother used Elihu's influence with General Ulysses Grant to procure a position on Grant's staff as aide-de-camp. Eventually, Washburn earned the rank of Brigadier General and, after the Fort Pillow Massacre, he was ordered to replace Major General Stephen Hurlbut, as commander of the District of West Tennessee. In the aftermath of the Fort Pillow Massacre, Washburn carried on a vigorous, if not contentious, correspondence with Nathan Bedford Forrest over the massacre as well as Confederate policy on the treatment of African-American soldiers in Federal uniform. On August 21, 1864, probably in an effort to punish for his impertinence, Forrest launched a raid on Memphis with one of its objectives being the capture of Washburn. Fleeing in his pyjamas for the safety of Fort Pickering, Washburn narrowly avoided capture.

Source: EACW, 4: 2063–2064.

Would they be treated as prisoners of war? If the latter, then Washburn assured Forrest that his troops would retract their no quarter pledge.[18]

In a second series of letters, Forrest responded to allegations about the massacre at Fort Pillow and clarified his position on black prisoners of war. Accusing Washburn of leveling the charge of massacre based on ex parte testimony, Forrest denied that a massacre had taken place at Fort Pillow: "I answer that I slaughter no man except in open warfare, and that my prisoners, both white and black, are turned over to my Government to be dealt with as it may direct." As for his official position on black prisoners of war, Forrest stated:

> I regard captured negroes as I do other captured property and
> not as captured soldiers, but as to how regarded by my
> Government and the disposition which has been and will
> hereafter be made of them, I respectfully refer you through the
> proper channel to the authorities at Richmond.

Blaming Washburn for inciting black soldiers to take a "no quarter" pledge, Forrest demanded that Washburn inform him whether his soldiers would be slaughtered in the future or treated as prisoners of war. Forrest reminded him that he currently held 2,000 Union prisoners and would hold them hostage until Washburn gave him a satisfactory response. When Washburn replied to Forrest on July 2, he blamed the attitude of black soldiers on Forrest:

> It was your soldiers who at Fort Pillow raised the black flag, and
> while shooting, bayoneting, and otherwise maltreating Federal
> prisoners in their hands, shouted to each other in the hearing of
> their victims that it was done by "Forrest's orders."

Washburn added, "If you depart from the principles, you may expect such retaliation as the laws of war justify." While Forrest had implied that inferior black soldiers were better off as slaves, Washburn testified that blacks were not anxious to return to their masters and would rather face slaughter than return to slavery.[19]

Washburn had no better luck when he initiated a correspondence with Forrest's superior, Major General Stephen D. Lee. Washburn informed Lee that he had evidence of atrocities committed by Confederate soldiers to black troops under the command of Brigadier General Samuel Sturgis at the battle of Brice's Cross Roads: "From the statements that have been made to me by the colored soldiers who were eye-witnesses, it would seem that the massacre of Fort Pillow had been reproduced at the late affair at Brice's Cross Roads." What Washburn demanded from Lee was simply a frank answer as to how the Confederate government planned to proceed on the issue of black prisoners of war. "For the government of the colored troops under my command," Washburn informed Lee:

> I would thank you to inform me, with as little delay as possible, if it is your intention or the intention of the Confederate Government to murder colored soldiers that may fall into your hands, or treat them as prisoners of war and subject to be exchanged as other prisoners.

Much in the fashion of Forrest, Lee dodged most of Washburn's questions, arguing that any claims about the alleged atrocities at Fort Pillow were exaggerated and based on biased, ex parte testimony. Lee did, however, admit that the high casualties at Fort Pillow were the result of the refusal to surrender and, additionally, the laws of warfare justified the subsequent slaughter. With respect to the status of black soldiers, Lee simply denied that his government authorized the slaughter of black soldiers. "As regards the battle of Tishomingo Creek [Brice's Cross Roads], the statements of your negro witnesses are not to be relied on," Lee stated:

> In their panic they acted as might have been expected from their previous impressions. I do not think many of them were killed. They are wandering over the country, attempting to return to their masters. With reference to the status of those captured at Tishomingo Creek and Fort Pillow, I will state that, unless otherwise ordered by my Government, they will not be regarded as prisoners of war, but will be retained and humanely treated, subject to such future instructions as may be indicated.[20]

July 1, 1864 came and went. There was no official response to Lincoln's demand from the Davis administration. Although Lincoln had used bold and firm language in his instructions to Stanton, in the end nothing would come of his threats. To the contemporary student, Lincoln's inaction might appear as spineless, cowardly, and an abandonment of principle. For Lincoln, however, there were several issues that probably played into his decision to simply let the issue rest. First, by the late summer of 1864, the war effort in the east seemed to be at a standstill. Lieutenant General Grant had boldly engaged the Confederate Army of Northern Virginia in the Virginia theatre in a series of bloody battles: The Wilderness, Spotsylvania Court House, Cold Harbor, and Petersburg. Unlike previous Union commanders, Grant had not retreated when he appeared bested or stalemated. However, by the middle of the summer, his Army of the Potomac was settled into a prolonged siege at the city of Petersburg, just south of Richmond. The casualties involved in Grant's campaign had been horrendous (nearly 65,000 dead, missing, or wounded in a seven week period from the beginning of May, 1864), and without the overwhelming victory that the northern public expected, the peace movement in the Democratic Party became invigorated. Lincoln's own re-election in 1864 began to look problematic. To implement an aggressive policy of retaliation for the Fort Pillow Massacre at this time might appear to be unwise. Although African-American soldiers were much more accepted in the army and among many civilian segments, the most aggressive anti-war Democrats were still virulently anti-black and opposed the military deployment of black troops. To take bold actions on behalf of African-American troops at this juncture of the conflict would simply give the Democratic opposition another issue with which to discredit Lincoln and the Republican Party. From a practical standpoint, would retaliation have worked? Would it have prevented the mistreatment of black soldiers and forced recognition of black prisoners of war? Or would it have simply caused a cycle of violent and retaliatory measures on the part of the Union and Confederate governments?

If President Lincoln and his administration hesitated on pulling the trigger when it came to retaliation, black troops took an entirely different approach. It was, after all, black troops who took on additional risks by donning the Union uniform. Parodied as ignorant, incapable of self-direction, and child-like in character, the actions of African-American soldiers after the Fort Pillow Massacre would demonstrate quite the opposite set of qualities. Indeed, as indicated in the exchange of letters between Forrest and C. C. Washburn, the Fort Pillow Massacre changed the attitude and behavior of many blacks serving in the Union army. If the government would not protect them, they would take measures to protect themselves. And in so doing, these black soldiers would build additional justification for a place at the American political table.

If the response of the Lincoln administration was not all it should have been, black soldiers and black leaders were more than capable of taking appropriate action to prove to the Confederacy that black soldiers could not taken lightly. Indeed, in testimony before the Joint Committee on the Conduct of the War in April, Major General Stephen Hurlbut, told Daniel Gooch and Benjamin F. Wade that African-American troops in the aftermath of Fort Pillow would be difficult to control. "I know very well," Hurlbut testified, "that my colored regiments at Memphis, officers and men, will never give quarter." And the general was right. Shortly after the Fort Pillow Massacre, the 2nd United States Colored Heavy

Artillery held a meeting at Fort Pickering in Memphis. Noting the barbarity of the Fort Pillow Massacre, the regiment adopted a number of resolutions in response to the massacre. The resolutions condemned Confederate actions at Fort Pillow, but also promised to embolden black troops and those who led them: "We accept the issue, and adopt, as our significant motto, 'Victory or Death.'" African-American troops in the 55th and 59th USCT, serving under Brigadier General Samuel Sturgis at Memphis, took an oath before going to battle that they would neither give quarter nor except quarter. Although shortly thereafter, Sturgis was bested by Forrest at the battle of Brice's Cross Roads on June 10, 1864 in northern Mississippi, even Forrest noted that determination and grit of the black soldiers who participated in that battle.[21]

The Fort Pillow Massacre became a familiar rallying cry for African-American troops getting ready for battle. They used the cry as something to invigorate and motivate the troops prior to going into action. And it was a cry that was not limited to troops who had intimate knowledge of the massacre, but was used by black troops in a variety of military theatres. Throughout the western theatre, according to historian Dudley Cornish, the cry of Fort Pillow was on the lips of many black soldiers as they went into battle. "In the after-days of the War," remembered Major General John A. Logan, "the cry with which our Union Black regiments went into battle:—'Remember Fort Pillow!'—inspired them to deeds of valor, and struck with terror the heart of the Enemy. On many a bloody field, Fort Pillow was avenged." But it was not only in the western theatre.

Sidebar 3.2

During 1864, there were several battles in which African-American soldiers were killed out of rage or frustration by Confederate soldiers. At Poison Springs, Arkansas on April 18, 1864, Union forces under Colonel James M. Williams were defeated by a Confederate force under Brigadier General John S. Marmaduke. During the fighting, one black regiment, the 1st Kansas Colored, saw the most action and suffered the highest number of casualties. Although the Confederates would triumph on the field of battle, the 1st Kansas Colored fought bravely and only gave way after high casualties and low ammunition sapped their morale. The 1st Kansas also suffered the heaviest casualties, losing 117 men to death and another 65 wounded. The significance of the battle, however, was what happened afterwards when angry Confederate soldiers would not take blacks as prisoners and killed every African-American soldier that they captured.

Source: EACW, 3: 1535–1536.

A sergeant of the 55th Massachusetts, for instance, described the participation of his regiment in fighting on James Island, South Carolina in early July 1864. "I say, could you have seen the old 55th rush in, with the shout of 'Remember Fort Pillow!' you would have thought nothing could have withstood their impetuosity." George W. Reed, a drummer aboard the U.S.S. *Commodore Reed*, interacted with wounded black prisoners that his ship was transporting from the Virginia front to Washington DC. Belonging primarily to Major General Ambrose Burnside's IX Corps, the drummer boy was impressed by the enthusiasm and courage of these wounded black soldiers:

> Whenever they caught a rebel they cry out, No Quarter!
> Remember Fort Pillow! No quarter for the rebs &c . . . and many
> who were slightly wounded have gone back to the front. They are
> all eager to go back to retaliate.

As the famed historian of the Civil War, Bruce Catton, marveled, blacks in the Army of the Potomac, who could not read, nor had access to newspapers, nonetheless knew about what had transpired at Fort Pillow, Tennessee. From the battlefield in Georgia, Private John Brobst, of the 25th Wisconsin, recollected that even white soldiers picked up on the revenge:

> That Fort Pillow Massacre was a horrible thing, but our soldiers
> make them pay for it down here. There was one of the Iowa
> regiments charged on a rifle pit, and twenty-three of the rebs
> surrenders but the boys asked them if they remembered Fort
> Pillow and killed all of them. When there is no officer with us.

Brobst continued, "we take no prisoners. We want revenge and we are bound to have it one way or another. They must pay for their deeds of cruelty. We want revenge for our brother soldiers and will have it." From the Wilderness campaign, a captain in a Louisiana regiment in the Army of Northern Virginia recalled a Union assault on Confederate lines. "A portion of the attacking force," he recalled,

> was composed of negroes, who cried out as they advanced,
> "Remember Fort Pillow." This so exasperated Wright's
> Georgians that jumping over their works, they drove the
> negroes back for a distance of half of a miles, slaughtering
> large numbers and caputurin three strands of colors and *only
> seventy-nine* prisoners.

In this case, apparently the cry "Fort Pillow" motivated both black soldiers and Confederates. From New York City, George Templeton Strong, a diarist, seemed well aware of what actions African-American soldiers were taking on the battlefield in the aftermath of Fort Pillow. He noted that reports were that black soldiers fought well, but never seemed to capture prisoners. "Don't know how it is—we have made no enquiry—somehow they give the Provost Marshal nothing to do," Templeton continued. "I suppose they have to kill their prisoners before they can take them. When they go into action, they yell 'Fort Pillow!' But it is queer they don't take any prisoners, though they fight so well. Very queer indeed."[22]

Interestingly the Fort Pillow Massacre was also a tool used by Union military recruiters to encourage blacks to enlist. Striking a blow for their freedom as well as avenging the perpetrators of Fort Pillow could be a powerful motivational tool. James T. Ayers, a Union military recruiter from Fairbury, Illinois, who spent time recruiting black soldiers in the south, was not bashful about using such a tool. While recruiting potential enlistees in Huntsville, Alabama in early May, 1864, shortly after the Fort Pillow Massacre, Ayers composed a poem to use as a recruiting tool, a poem that incorporated references to Fort Pillow in several of its verses:

> Load up your guns My brave oald Chums
> Well Charge there Ranks once more
> Fort Pillow, Oh the murdered groans
> We will avenge your [gore?]
> Come my brave boys Load up your guns
> Gird on your glittering steel,
> And if we overtake the hounds
> Fort Pillow they shall feel.
> Charge boys Charge, Clean out there Ranks
> Give them your Coald steel
> From Center to Extended flank
> Make them Fort Pillow feel.

Rather than intimidate blacks and force a reduction in recruitment, the Fort Pillow Massacre, and other incidents where black troops were unjustly killed, had the opposite impact as it appeared to motivate African-Americans to come forward and see the war to its completion.[23]

The determination of Forrest and the Confederate government to intimidate blacks through threats of re-enslavement and death was a singular failure. The nearly 180,000 African-American volunteers was a testament to that failure; however, what did the sacrifices of Fort Pillow and other atrocities committed against black troops accomplish? Among white northerners, except for abolitionists and radical Republicans, few expected the sacrifices of blacks to contribute to full civil, social, and political equality. One member of the United States Congress who was a vocal advocate of equality was Pennsylvania Republican Thaddeus Stevens. For Stevens, military service by blacks, in and of itself, entitled them to equal treatment in northern society. "Let it not forth as the opinion of this House," Stevens declared on April 30, 1864, "that the black man or the red man or any other man who bears our arms and fights for our liberty is not to be treated like every other man." Many African-Americans, however, were even more adamant than Stevens in demanding equality in exchange for their military service. "I am not willing to fight for the Government for money alone. Give me my rights, the rights that this Government owes me," demanded John H. B. Payne, "the same rights the white man has." Payne added, "God has not made one man better than another; therefore, one man's rights are no better than another's." Payne closed by stating, "Liberty is what I am fighting for, and what pulse does not beat high at the very mention of the name?" A group of Tennessee African-Americans petitioned the Union Convention of Tennessee to grant black residents of the state equal rights, arguing that slavery was a violation of natural law, whereas freedom was a natural right. "We know the burdens of citizenship," the petition stated, "and are ready to bear them." One Republican opinion journal used the Fort Pillow Massacre to construct a moral argument for equal rights on behalf of African-Americans. "Nor let us forget the damning atrocities of Fort Pillow," the *Continental Monthly* editorialized, "where black men in the United States were massacred in cold blood, because they were willing to die freemen with their white comrades of the United States army, than live slaves to rebel masters." The journal concluded, "The negro is a man, and not a brute animal."[24]

Once the war concluded and the country moved toward restoration and reconciliation, African-Americans believed military service entitled them to full participation in American life. Obviously with the passage of the 13th amendment on January 31, 1865 (ratification December 1865), the institution of slavery was dead; however, exactly what this meant for blacks and their status within American society was unclear. For defeated southerners, the death of slavery certainly did not mean the death of inequality as would become clear when many southern states adopted black codes shortly after the war concluded so as to keep African-Americans, while technically free, substantially subservient. Many northerners, too, were ambivalent about the meaning of freedom. Although African-

American soldiers had impressed many, there was not an overwhelming consensus about the meaning of freedom. When Congress passed the Wade-Davis reconstruction bill in July 1864, a bill that was significantly more punitive toward the South than President Lincoln's plan for Reconstruction, popularly called the 10 percent plan. Although Lincoln would pocket veto the measure so that it never became law, notably missing from the Wade-Davis bill was any provision for black male suffrage; moreover, as the war hastened to a conclusion in the spring of 1865, there was far from a consensus on issues such as extending the elective franchise to black males. President Lincoln, who had throughout the war, negotiated a middle course between radicals and conservatives in his own party as well as the Democratic party, seemed to have adopted a mildly favorable view toward black suffrage already in early 1864. While early on in the conflict, Lincoln was an advocate of colonization, the events of the war, emancipation and the arming of blacks, prompted him to abandon unrealistic plans such as colonization. By the summer of 1863, he was not bashful in defending his policy of emancipation and arming black soldiers. Writing to James Conkling, in a letter to be read at a political gathering in Springfield, Lincoln was both pragmatic and idealistic. "I thought that whatever negroes can be got to do as soldiers," Lincoln stated,

> leaves just so much less for white soldiers to do, in saving the Union. Does it appear otherwise to you? But negroes, like other people, act upon motives. Why should they do anything for us, if we will do nothing for them? If they stake their lives for us, they must be prompted by the strongest motive—even the promise of freedom. And the promise being made, must be kept.

A mere seven months later, the president began to tentatively endorse limited suffrage for black veterans. Writing to Governor Michael Hahn, who had recently been elected governor of Louisiana, a state reconstructed under the President's 10 percent plan, Lincoln suggested that Hahn keep an open mind toward black suffrage. "Now you are about to have a Convention," wrote the president,

> which, among other things, will probably define the elective franchise. I barely suggest for your private consideration, whether some of the colored people may not be let in—as, for instance, the very intelligent, and especially those who have fought gallantly in our ranks. They would probably help, in some trying time to come, to keep the jewel of liberty in the family of freedom.

Although this was a significant step for a president who had hesitated on both emancipation and the arming of black soldiers, it was a step well in advance of most residents of the northern states.[25]

Once the American Civil War had concluded with the surrender of the Confederate armies of Lee and Johnston in April 1864, the process of Reconstruction began in earnest. Two fundamental questions had to be addressed. The first involved the question of the status of former states that had attempted to secede from the Union. What were they? Were they spoils of war to be treated as conquered territories that were subject to the whims and conditions of a conqueror? Or were they wayward states, temporarily held under the sway of rebellious individuals, which would quickly be restored to their status in the Union with full political representation in the government at Washington? The second, and perhaps even more pressing and important question, concerned the status of African-Americans in the post Civil War society. The emancipation proclamation had freed many of the slaves in the Confederacy, while the passage and ratification of the 13th amendment had given that freedom a Constitutional foundation; however, the fact of freedom said nothing about the status of African-Americans in American society. As could be well expected, African-American leaders and military veterans expected the combination of military service and the 13th amendment to begin a new era of freedom and equality. As Frederick Douglass remarked, to free a slave from an individual master was one thing; however, without economic power and political rights, freedom would mean little to the bulk of African-Americans. "He was free from the individual master, but the slave of society. He had neither property, money, nor friends," wrote Douglass. He stated further:

> From the first I saw no chance of bettering the condition of the freedman, until he should cease to be merely a freedman, and should become a citizen. I insisted that there was no safety for him ... that to guard, protect, and maintain his liberty, the freedman should have the ballot; that the liberties of the American people were dependent upon the Ballot-box, the Jury-box, and the Cartridge-box, that without these no class of people could live and flourish in this country ... Hence regarding as I did, the elective franchise as the one great power by which all civil rights are obtained, enjoyed, and maintained under our form of government, and the one without which freedom to any class is delusive if not impossible, I set myself to work with whatever force and energy I possessed to secure this power from the recently emancipated millions.

But would the bulk of Americans agree with this point of view? And would they be willing not only to advocate for black rights, but also force the former slaveholding states to observe a degree of equality with their former charges?[26]

With Lincoln's assassination on April 15, 1865, the Reconstruction of the South took a much different direction with the succession of Andrew Johnson to the presidency. The former Tennessee Senator and governor had been a slaveholder himself prior to the war. Johnson had grown up in humble circumstances. Throughout most of his political career, the new president was an avowed enemy of the slaveholding aristocracy and had accepted the abolition of slavery as a necessary consequence of the war. Indeed, in October 1864, while campaigning for the vice presidency and the re-election of Lincoln, Johnson had even gone so far as to champion the cause of black freedom, telling a group of African-Americans who gathered at the capitol, "I will be your Moses, and lead you through the Red Sea of war and bondage to a fairer future of liberty and peace." The belief that slavery could not and should not survive the war, however, did not signal an amelioration of Johnson's views on race. If blacks were free, they would certainly not be the social and political equals of whites. In fact, Johnson was still bitterly negrophobic in his outlook and temperament. In early 1866, for instance, a delegation of black leaders came to meet with Johnson, led by Frederick Douglass, the abolitionist, journalist, and the most prominent African-American figure in the United States in the Civil War era. The purpose of the meeting was to get Johnson to support black suffrage in the south; however, the president refused to impose black voting on southern states if it was against the will of the people. After the delegation left, Johnson revealed his real feelings to his secretaries, "Those d_____d sons of b____s thought they had me in a trap! I know that d_____d Douglass; he's just like any other nigger, and he would sooner cut a white man's throat than not."[27]

Republican radicals had initially been encouraged that Johnson would take a firmer course against the South than Lincoln including excluding Confederate officers and politicians from participating in reconstructed state governments and including provisions for additional civil and political rights for African-Americans, including the right to vote. "Our new Presdt. Makes a good impression. Of this be sure," Senator Charles Sumner told an English correspondent:

> His chief topic thus far had been that treason is a crime; but I am satisfied that he is the sincere friend of the negro, & ready to act for him decisively. He has conversed with the Chief Justice & myself on this important subject.

This sentiment was shared by many Republicans in Congress; however, as time would shortly reveal, Johnson was more interested in returning the South to the status quo antebellum. Slavery would certainly perish; however, he was prepared to do little to protect the rights of landless African-Americans in the post Civil War South.[28]

Republican radicals like Thaddeus Stevens became skeptical of President Johnson, shortly after the latter assumed office. Part of the problem for Republican congressman such as Stevens was that Johnson had attempted to begin reconstruction on his own without Congress; whereas Stevens and many Republicans believed Reconstruction was primarily a congressional job. On May 29, 1865, Johnson announced his plan for presidential reconstruction in his North Carolina proclamation. Johnson's plan would restore southern states to the Union quickly and with minimal conditions. Only a few members of Confederate society—those owning property in excess of $20,000—would be prohibited from participating in newly constructed state governments. What irritated radical Republicans is that Johnson did not require southern states to allow African-American males to vote as he believed that voting requirements were a matter of state preference. "I see our worthy president fancies himself a sovereign power—His North Carolina Proclamation sickens me," Stevens wrote to a Pennsylvanian friend. A few weeks later, Stevens wrote directly to Johnson, "Among all the leading Union men of the North with whom I have had intercourse," Stevens told Johnson, "I do not find one who approves of your policy. They believe that 'Restoration' as announced by you will destroy our party (which is of but little consequence) and will greatly injure the country." Radical Republican Senator Charles Sumner shared Steven's sentiments. Writing to Senator Benjamin F. Wade, Sumner complained, "The course of the Presdt. Is so absurd that he cannot force it upon Congress. It must fail . . . Meanwhile the rebels are all springing into their old life, and the copperheads also. This is the President's work." Adding to the frustration with Johnson were reports from the south of recently emancipated African-Americans being abused and mistreated by former owners. One Union officer on duty in Louisiana wrote of the mistreatment of the former slave population, where white landowners were constantly abusing their former slaves: "Truly, the colored race are passing through an ordeal that will test every virtue they possess, and it will not be astonishing if, in many cases they fail to meet the expectations of an uncharitable world." "The fact is," continued this officer,

persecution is the order of the day amongst these returned rebels, against the colored race in general, and Soldiers families

in particular. And I am grieved to Say that many wearing the U. S.
uniform are too easily bought body and Soul over to the evil
designs and purposes of these same individuals.[29]

For the balance of the Johnson presidency, the Republican majority in Congress and Johnson battled over policies regarding the readmission of southern states into the Union. When Johnson, for instance, did nothing to counteract the passage in many states of the black codes, a series of laws that gave African-Americans the right to make contracts, get married, and initiate legal proceedings in court, but also discriminated against blacks by forbidding black participation on juries, interracial marriages, and, in some case, imposed segregation at public places. Congress responded by passing the Civil Rights Act of 1866, a law that would eventually gain constitutional status as the 14th amendment, granting all citizens equal protection under the law. In a cynical ploy, the amendment's section two reduced representation in Congress and the Electoral College by proportion the percentage of the black electorate that was not allowed to vote. In other words, northern states, with small numbers of African-Americans could deny blacks the right to vote with little consequence, but southern states, with a much higher percentage of black population, would be punished by losing clout on the nation scene.[30]

When Johnson urged southern states to reject ratification of the 14th amendment and continued a preference for supporting the empowerment of former leaders of the Confederacy in state government, radical Republicans triumphed in the 1866 Congressional elections, effectively ending President Johnson's attempt to manage the Reconstruction process. In fact, the Republican majority in Congress would spend a good deal of time trying to circumvent Johnson's power, ending in an unsuccessful attempt to remove the president from office in 1868. Congress would then pass a series of Military Reconstruction Acts in 1867 that divided the South into five military districts. Existing state governments were not immediately abolished; however, state governments were now subject to the military officials in charge of the military district. New procedures for the organization of state governments were passed including provision for black enfranchisement and ratification of the 14th amendment. After states organized constitutional conventions and complied with congressional directives, they were readmitted back into the Union and could send representatives to Congress. By 1870, each of the southern states had written the proscribed constitution, had said constitution ratified in a popular referendum, and submitted the constitution to the Congress in Washington for approval. The adoption of new state constitutions in the south promised a new era of political activism for African-Americans.

In 1867, the number of registered black voters in the southern states (735,000) actually outnumbered registered white voters (635,000). African-Americans enjoyed unprecedented political opportunities, both voting and holding office. At the national level, for instance, 14 blacks would serve in the House of Representatives from 1868–1876, and there would be two black Senators sent to Washington during the same time period. Although the majority of office holders during the Reconstruction period were white Republicans, the mere participation of ex-slaves in the political system just a few short years after the institution of slavery had perished was remarkable. And, as northern Republicans would find out in the election of 1868, the maintenance of black voting in the south was absolutely fundamental to holding onto power at the national level.[31]

The election of Republican Ulysses S. Grant to the presidency in 1868 by 300,000 popular votes and a substantial majority in the Electoral College suggested that the Republican Party was in a dominant position in national politics. However, a careful analysis of the voting returns revealed a much more fragile hold of power. Although Grant had taken every state in the north save three (New York, New Jersey, and Oregon), his margin of victory was narrow in many states; moreover, the Democratic candidate, former New York governor Horatio Seymour, actually received a majority of white votes. Grant's victory, in other words, was almost entirely the result of 300,000 black votes, primarily the consequence of the Military Reconstruction Acts of 1867. Thus motivated, Congressional Republicans sponsored the final Civil War era amendment, the 15th amendment that specified that the franchise could not be denied on the basis of race or previous condition of servitude. Ratified in early 1870, African-American males in many northern states gained the right to vote for the first time. More importantly, newly enfranchised blacks in the south now had the force of a constitutional amendment securing their right to vote. In five short years, blacks had gained the right to freedom, equal protection under the law, and the right to the elective franchise. But could these rights be maintained in the long term?[32]

During the Reconstruction era a total of 16 African-Americans were elected to Congress. Two of the 16, Hiram Revels and Blanche K. Bruce, both of Mississippi, served in the United States Senate. One African-American, P. B. S. Pinchback served briefly as governor of Louisiana.

Source: Peter Irons,
A People's History of the Supreme Court
(New York: Penguin Books, 1999), 196.

In the years prior to the Civil War, racial prejudice was universal in the United States. Free states that were anti-slavery were just as likely to be as negrophobic as states with legalized slavery. During the Civil War, the cause of the Union was slow to embrace emancipation and slow to advocate the arming of African-Americans. Should blacks be allowed to fight? Would blacks actually fight if given the opportunity? What would their fighting signify? Did military service confer the right to full participation in the political system? Once the decision to arm African-Americans was made, large segments of the northern populace opposed it. As the Fort Pillow Massacre demonstrated, northerners were bold to speak out against atrocities committed against African-American soldiers but unlikely to take concrete steps to protect them. Was this because of the consequences of such actions? In other words, was it the fear of additional retaliation that prevented the Lincoln administration from acting to prevent future atrocities against its black soldiers, or was it because of a fundamental ambiguity regarding the nation's commitment to its black soldiers? African-American soldiers were adamant that their contribution in the war entitled them to full participation in the life of the American nation. Many northern whites were not quite so sure. Old habits die hard. Given white attitudes towards blacks prior to the war, was it realistic that habits, prejudices, and traditions could be fundamentally revolutionized in a few short years?

In the early 1870s, northern enthusiasm for the continued support of reconstructed state governments in the south began to waver, especially as other issues began to compete for the attention of the nation. Despite the actions of Republican radicals in Congress that seemingly advanced the position and status of blacks during the Reconstruction period, the clues to northern attitudes toward a sustained effort to secure the rights of former slaves was tepid and were available for many to see. As radical Republicans in Congress were adamant that southern states be forced to adopt black suffrage as a condition of readmission to the Union, three northern states (Connecticut, Wisconsin, and Minnesota) put the question of black voting directly to the voters in the fall of 1865. Each state rejected the initiative by a comfortable margin. In other words, in forcing southern states to adopt black suffrage as one of the conditions for restoration to the Union, federal lawmakers were asking the south do to something that many of their own constituents were unwilling to do on their own. At the time that the 15th amendment was being proposed and debated in the Congress, black males still were denied the elective franchise in 11 of 21 states. Since the Republican controlled governments in the south were possible only through the disenfranchisement of many white voters and the presence of Federal troops, their condition was precarious at best. Rumors of rampant corruption and of the unfitness of black voters and legislators were rife in many of the nation's newspapers. The commitment

Shall I trust these men?

Figure 3.1 This August 5, 1865 drawing by Thomas Nast presents sympathetic support for African-American suffrage by contrasting the sacrifices of a wounded black veteran with the pleas of former rebels who had been in rebellion against the United States government. *Harper's Weekly.*

And not this man?

Figure 3.1 continued

to the cause of Reconstruction and the rights of African-Americans—precarious and tentative at best—began to waver.[33]

One could see the change in attitude exemplified in some of the editorial cartoons of the era. Two, in particular, present a contrast in the attitude and opinions of Americans. The first consists of two drawings where the United States, represented by the female Columbia, considers two types of persons for citizenship. In the first drawing, one sees Columbia sitting on a throne and a host of former Confederate generals and political leaders bowing before the female, apparently seeking pardons and a full restoration of their former rights. The second drawing shows Columbia with a wounded black veteran. The soldier has lost a limb and stands besides Columbia on crutches. The original caption below the drawings demonstrates a paradox that is supposed to sway the reader towards the acceptance of black political rights. Under the first drawing are the words, "shall I trust these men?" Under the second drawing, the message is, "And not this man?" The point is obvious. African-Americans have, through military sacrifice, earned the right of citizenship and, in many respects, are more deserving and more reliable than former Confederate military officers and office holders. A second drawing, a scant nine years later, demonstrate a profound change in the editorial attitude of the newspaper with respect to black political participation. Entitled "Colored Rule in a Reconstructed (?) State," the drawing takes an almost antithetical approach to the question of black political participation. Depicting a legislative session in a southern state, the drawing shows black politicians wildly gesticulating and engaged in a savage and unruly debate. The cartoon sends an obvious message: Blacks are making a mess of government in the South and perhaps it was premature to have entrusted them with political rights.

The emergence of white supremacist organizations such as the Klu Klux Klan made the job of protecting black rights even more difficult. Formed in Pulaski, Tennessee, in 1866, the initial Klan was led by none other than Nathan Bedford Forrest, the controversial cavalry commander who had presided over the Fort Pillow Massacre. Dedicated to preserving white supremacy, the Klan devoted itself to terrorizing blacks and preventing them from voting. The Republican Congress passed Enforcement Acts to give the president the power to declare martial law and use federal power to counteract the work of the Klan. President Grant, elected in 1868 and re-elected in 1872, did not initially hesitate to use Federal forces to implement the Enforcement laws; however, by the early 1870s, the determination to enforce Republican reconstruction policy was fast fading. In 1872, a number of prominent Republicans including Charles Sumner and Horace Greeley defected from the party, fused with the Democratic Party, and nominated Greeley to oppose Grant. For many

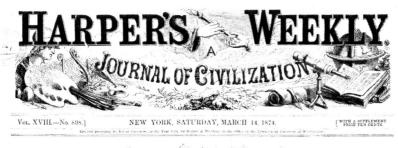

Figure 3.2 By 1874, northern support for the Reconstruction of southern states had begun to wane. This March 14, 1874 editorial cartoon depicts black participation in Democratic institutions in somewhat farcical terms. Cartoon by Thomas Nast, *Harper's Weekly*.

Sidebar 3.3

The original Ku Klux Klan was formed in Pulaski, Tennessee in 1866 and was led by Nathan Bedford Forrest, who functioned as the group's Grand Wizard. Based on secretive rituals and elaborate costumes, the Klan supposedly represented slain Confederates, soldiers with white robes and hoods suggesting a ghost like quality. The primary purpose of the early Klan was the fear that racial integration would lead to miscegenation (the sexual mixing of the races) and the eventual decay of southern society. In addition, those who joined the Klan were determined to prevent African-Americans from voting and exercising political power, and thus would use a variety of intimidation tactics to bring about the suppression of African-American voting, the most extreme of which was lynching. Although the United States Congress did respond with legislation to combat the Klan in early 1870—passing, for instance, the Civil Rights Act of 1871—as the general mood of the country tired of waging battles on behalf of African-Americans, such legislative efforts proved ineffective. With the end of Reconstruction and the disenfranchisement of blacks, the activities of the original Klan subsided. During the twentieth century, the Klan would be reborn on two occasions, just prior to the First World War and just after the Second World War.

Source: EEATW, 2: 325–327.

---

disaffected Republicans, the political corruption that was evident during the Grant presidency was a bigger a concern than a sustained continued effort to maintain the status of blacks. For so-called Liberal Republicans like Greeley, the pre-eminent task before the nation was national reconciliation and restoring sectional harmony between the North and South. As Greeley stated in a speech:

> I tell you friends, that until we have completed this work of National Reconciliation, until
>   We are willing to allow all Americans a fair and equal voice in everything that concerns the
>   well-being and destinies of our country, we cannot have other questions fairly considered
>   at all: wherefore I am for disposing of this, putting out of sight all controversy regarding
>   rebellion, or slaves, or negroes, or the equal rights of man, or anything like this, and having finished this, we will take up other questions in their order and dispose of them likewise.
>   [Applause.] But this stands in the way.

Although Grant managed to win re-election in 1872, the 1874 congressional election registered a decisive defeat to the Republicans and their policies. The contested presidential election of 1876 would signal the formal end of Reconstruction. With electoral delegates contested in the southern states of Louisiana, Florida, and Mississippi, political wire pullers and backroom politicians supposedly worked out an agreement known as the Compromise of 1877. The central agreement in this series of compromises conceded the presidency to the Republican candidate Rutherford B. Hayes; however, in exchange for that concession, Federal troops were to leave southern states, thus ensuring that so-called "home rule" was restored.[34]

Many students of history assume that the Compromise of 1877 signaled the immediate erosion of black civil and political rights. While it is certainly true, that the majority of African-Americans were already involved as tenant farmers in the repressive crop-lien system, voting rights, at least were not immediately curtailed. It is also true that a number of Supreme Court decisions before the Compromise of 1877 and shortly after it greatly circumscribed the rights that African-Americans anticipated due to the ratification of the 14th amendment as well as other Reconstruction era legislation such as the Civil Rights Act of 1875 that guaranteed all persons equal access to public places such as restaurants, hotels, parks, and theatres.

Southern political elites, known as the "Bourbons," had given assurances to the Republican Party that they would be the protectors of black voting. At the same time, as wealthy elites, in some cases planters who owned the lands that blacks sharecropped, the Bourbons held considerable power over African-Americans who were, in many cases,

Sidebar 3.4

In 1883 the Supreme Court took up a series of cases that arose out of individual African-Americans being denied access to public places of accommodation. The suits were filed on the grounds that they violated the equal protection language of the 14th amendment as well as the Civil Rights Act of 1875, the last significant piece of Reconstruction era civil rights legislation. On October 15, 1883, the Supreme Court ruled against the litigants in a decision known as the Civil Rights Cases, arguing that the federal amendment and legislation only protected individuals from state laws that denied equal protection and access; however, where specific individuals chose to discriminate, the Court was powerless to provide a remedy.

Source: Peter Irons, *A People's History of the Supreme Court*
(New York: Penguin Books, 1999), 211–215.

economically beholden to them. In other words, many blacks continued to vote because they could be counted on to support the political choices of the Bourbons. With the rise of agrarian radicalism and Populist movement, however, a new challenge emerged to Bourbon dominance. Poor white and black tenant farmers, united by a common interest of overturning the worst features of the crop-lien system that exploited them, formed alliances that threatened the political power of traditional southern conservative leadership. Led by such charismatic leaders as Thomas Watson, a potential alliance of black and white poor farmers created a crisis among white southern elites. "Alarmed by the success that the Populists were enjoying with their appeal to the Negro voter," writes C. Vann Woodward, "the conservatives themselves raised the cry of 'Negro domination' and white supremacy, and enlisted the Negrophobe element." In other words, having used the black vote to further their own political power, when the Bourbons felt threatened by a black–white alliance in the Populist movement that might challenge their ascendancy, they used the race card to make sure that lower class blacks and whites did not create a powerful political alliance to challenge their political power. The result was passage on a state by state basis of a variety of disenfranchising devices that would drastically reduce the number of eligible African-American voters. The poll tax along with various literacy and constitutional tests were devices that would keep most poor and uneducated whites voting while denying the same rights to African-Americans. By the end of the nineteenth century, African-Americans had experienced an erosion of their 14th amendment rights as well as constriction of their voting rights.[35]

The beginning of the Civil War, the eventual abolition of slavery, and the participation of African-Americans in the military gave hope to abolitionists, anti-slavery elements in the Republican Party, and African-Americans that the United States might be on the verge of moving closer to the ideals expressed in the Declaration of Independence. It was, after all, Abraham Lincoln, as one of the instruments and agents of Union power, who, during his political career, had made so much of the ideals of the Declaration and had often spoken in terms of an ever-expanding and ever-increasing definition of freedom. By the end of the nineteenth century, however, the notion of the expansion of civil rights had given way to fears about immigration and the assimilation of strange and alien cultures. Crude scientific theories were widely in vogue that ranked races and ethnic groups according to "intelligence" and cultural accomplishment. The combination of such scientific theories as well as well-grounded prejudice seemed to justify the exclusion of African-Americans from American political life. Indeed such theories caused many Americans to agree with their southern counterparts who argued that the entire attempt to extend social and political equality to African-Americans was a foolish and dangerous experiment foisted on the country by unbalanced and fanatical New England abolitionists. The consequences for African-Americans who did not accept or who challenged these crude racial stereotypes was evidenced in the rise of lynchings, not only in the south but throughout the United States. Blacks, especially black males, needed to be kept in their place, and if they stepped out of their place, there would be violent and tragic consequences. If the Fort Pillow Massacre represented a collective lynching of blacks, who attempted to break through and challenge southern ideas on their place in society, the experience of African-Americans at the end of the century demonstrated that little had changed. A federal government who had armed them and expected black soldiers to make the ultimate sacrifice failed to provide adequate protection for its black soldiers. Thirty years later, a federal government that had promised rights to a certain segment of its population failed to follow through on those promises. It would be left to a future generation to re-ignite the cause of freedom and equality.

CHAPTER 4

Historians and the Fort Pillow Massacre

Like many controversial historical events, the Fort Pillow Massacre has remained an important topic among historians. In examining the historiography of this event, elements of sectionalism have influenced the interpretations of historians. Southern historians have often seemed partial to interpretations that have shifted the culpability of the massacre onto the actions of Union soldiers or simply denied that a massacre took place altogether; whereas northern historians were influenced by hostile and stereotypical attitudes toward southerners in formulating their interpretation. Historical comments and research have also been influenced by contemporary events. Negative images of African-Americans and other races, popularized by the scientific theories of the late nineteenth and early twentieth centuries, led to interpretations of the Fort Pillow Massacre that were critical of blacks and more supportive of the so-called Southern point of view. The emergence of the modern Civil Rights movement in the middle of the twentieth century, however, seems to have influenced the work of historians and led to the repudiation of many previous interpretations of the Fort Pillow Massacre that has either denied that massacre took place or placed the blame on black Union soldiers.

Immediately after the conclusion of the Civil War, writings about the Fort Pillow Massacre followed along sectional interpretations. Northern writers, influenced by the report and testimony of the Joint Committee on the Conduct of the War, viewed the affairs at Fort Pillow as a brutal massacre perpetrated by a backward and barbarous culture that was the product of the slave system. In many respects, northerners interpreted the Fort Pillow Massacre through interpretive lens of the free labor ideology. According to this viewpoint, the North had produced a culture that was based on free labor. It was a culture that was bold, progressive, innovative, and socially fluid, meaning that the individual that started as a wage earner or a factory operative, through hard work and effort, could become a small farmer or business owner. The south, by contrast, because it was organized primarily on slave labor was static and hierarchical. There was less opportunity for social mobility and, on this interpretation; it was a culture that rewarded sloth and inefficiency. Because it was also an economic system that was based on coercion and associated with violence, many northerners regarded the south as a backward and barbaric social system. Only a culture that was based on the power of the whip could produce an event as brutal and savage as the Fort Pillow Massacre. Indeed, Nathan Bedford Forrest was popularly known as the "Butcher of Fort Pillow" and Republican propagandist used Fort Pillow as a symbol to discredit the south but also the rising Democratic Party, which adopted the mantra of white supremacy.

In the years immediately following the Civil War, the Fort Pillow Massacre was a frequent topic in political campaigns and editorial cartoons. Republican political leaders developed an electoral campaigning strategy known as "waving the bloody shirt," a graphic depiction of the treasonous activities of southerners in fomenting the Civil War along with the active and vigorous support of northern Democrats or "Copperheads." Events like the New York draft riots of 1863 and the Fort Pillow Massacre were obvious candidates for inclusion in speeches where the bloody shirt was waved. In a September 5, 1868 editorial cartoon by Thomas Nast, a popular political cartoonist, entitled "This is a White Man's Government," the Democratic Party's position on race is ridiculed. A black Union veteran, lying upon an American flag, is pinned downed by three individuals, each representing a prominent wing in the Democratic Party: an Irish street brawler, a Confederate veteran, and banker-financier. The Confederate veteran carries a knife that has written upon it "The Lost Cause" and he also sports a button with the inscription "Fort Pillow" upon it. An October 3, 1868 drawing ridicules the Democratic Party in an editorial cartoon entitled "The Modern Sampson" (drawing not included in this book). Here a host of Democratic leaders, including Forrest, are seen cheering on Columbia as she cuts the hair off an African-American male. The hair is labeled "suffrage" and the implication is that without

Thomas A. Nast was one of the foremost political cartoonists of the nineteenth century. A native of Germany, Nast came to the United States in 1846. A supporter of the Republican Party, Nast created political cartoons during the Civil War for such publications as *Frank Leslie's Illustrated Newspaper* and *Harper's Weekly*. His cartoons expressed a pro-Union anti-Southern point of view, both during the war and during the early years of the Reconstruction period.

Figure 4.1 In September 1868, the elective franchise for African-Americans still had considerable support among Republican journalists and newspapers. This Thomas Nast cartoon ridicules the Democratic Party's use of naked racism—This is a White Man's Government—to build electoral support. It depicts three elements of the Democratic Party's base, Irish thugs, Confederate veterans, and Eastern financial interests. *Harper's Weekly*, September 5, 1868.

the vote, the African-American population will not have any power, much like the biblical Samson lost his power when his locks were trimmed. The editorial cartoonist, Thomas Nast, makes the obvious point that many Republicans would have agreed with: that the Democratic Party stood for barbaric and backward ideas. It is no coincidence that Forrest, the butcher of Fort Pillow is included in this cartoon, especially as he sports a button with the words "Fort Pillow" prominently displayed. A September 7, 1871 cartoon entitled "The White Sepulcher" shows Liberal Republican presidential candidate, Horace Greeley trying to cover up a monument that describes all of the misdeeds of the South and the Democratic Party over the years, including slavery, the Ku Klux Klan, political corruption, and so forth. Toward the bottom of the monument, just above the words Ku Klux, is written, "Fort Pillow Massacre, approved by the Congress of the Confederate States of America." The implication was obvious. If you supported the Democratic Party, if you were sympathetic toward the South, one was, in effect, giving one's blessing to the Fort Pillow Massacre.

Although many Union soldiers and generals did not directly address the Fort Pillow Massacre, some did comment on the event. Although not treated extensively in his memoir entitled, *The Great Conspiracy*, Major General John A. Logan, one the Civil War's most skillful political generals, believed the Fort Pillow Massacre was an important event in demonstrating southern character. Prior to the war, Logan had been a member of the Democratic Party from Confederate sympathizing southern Illinois. Early on in the secession crisis, he had even dabbled with going over to the southern side; however, once he answered the call to military service, he became firmly committed to the war, including the abolition of slavery. Becoming a Republican during the course of the war, his position on race and slavery changed dramatically. When Logan reflected on the Fort Pillow Massacre in his memoir, he put the blame squarely on the Confederates and attributed the massacre to a single factor: racism. "And all this murderous malignity," Logan asked, "for what?" Simply, and only, because one-half of the Patriot victims had Black skins, while the other half had dared to fight by the side of the Blacks!" Similarly presidential secretary, John G. Nicolay, in his short biography of the sixteenth president, was critical of Forrest and his Confederates for their actions at Fort Pillow. "It is unnecessary to explain that the bulk of the slain were colored soldiers," Nicolay explained. "Making due allowance for the heat of battle, history can considerably veil closer scrutiny into the realities that wrapped in the exaggerated boast of such a victory."[1]

In the years following the Civil War, many southern writers lived in denial about the outcome of war. First developed by Richmond editor,

This is a white man's
government.
Auction block.
Hunting down with
blood-hounds.
A negro has no rights
which a white man is
bound to respect.
Slavery.
Whipping-post.
New York riots.
Negroes hung at lamp-
posts.
Attempt to introduce
pestilence in the North.
Attempt to burn Northern
cities.
Burning of colored orphan
asylum.
New Orleans and Memphis
massacres.
Belle Isle and Andersonville
atrocities.
Assassination of Lincoln.
Ku-klux outrages to Unionists,
white and black.
Burning of Freedmen's schools.
Whipping and shooting of teach-
ers.
Repudiation.
Fort Pillow massacre, approved
by Congress of Confederate States
of America.

KU-KLUX

THE RULE OF TAMMANY RING.
WHOLESALE FRAUD.
CORRUPTION.
NO CITIZEN HAD ANY RIGHTS THAT A TAMMANY ROUGH
WAS BOUND TO RESPECT.
CORRUPT JUDICIARY—CARDOZO, BARNARD, AND M'CUNN.
FRAUDULENT AND ILLEGAL VOTING.
BRIBERY.
COUNTING OUT THE VOTES OF CITIZENS.
RIOT AND BLOODSHED.

NAMES NOT TO BE FORGOTTEN:
TWEED, SWEENY, CONNOLLY, and HALL.

SLAVERY

Figure 4.2 Horace Greeley was nominated by the so-called "Liberal Republicans" to oppose the re-election of Ulysses Grant in 1872. He was also supported by the Democratic Party. This September 7, 1872 cartoon ridicules Greeley and the Liberal Republicans for the numerous transgressions committed by the South including the assassination of Lincoln, the creation of the Ku Klux Klan, and the Fort Pillow Massacre. Cartoon by Thomas Nast, *Harper's Weekly*.

Edward Pollard, southerners began to interpret the results of the Civil War and the subsequent Reconstruction period through the lens of the "Lost Cause" interpretation of southern history. Embarrassed and humiliated by their defeat at the hands of northerners, southerners needed a reason to explain their defeat as well as maintain the case for their distinctiveness as a culture and a people. According to Pollard and other advocates of the "Lost Cause," the North prevailed in the war exclusively based on its superiority in men, material, and resources. As a region and as a culture, southerners remained unconquered. Southerners continued to believe in hierarchical notions of race and were determined to maintain white supremacy despite the efforts of a Republican Congress to change the status of blacks in the south. Like other Confederate leaders such as Robert E. Lee, Nathan Bedford Forrest became an important symbol of the "Lost Cause." Forrest's leadership of the Ku Klux Klan represented a defiant rejection of Reconstruction and an attempt to restore the southern social order to the antebellum period. Instead of admitting any culpability for Forrest's role at Fort Pillow, writers like Pollard, and even Forrest himself, continued to deny responsibility for the massacre. In the case of Pollard, his argument was built on the premise that Union soldiers had no intent of surrendering, and instead, had a prearranged plan with the crew of the gun boat, *New Era*, to retreat down the bluff and down toward the Mississippi river. By doing this, the Federals hoped to draw rebel soldiers into a trap. Though there were high casualties, the blame for the killings was entirely on the Union garrison. Pollard dismissed the testimony of blacks being savagely cut down as "absurd stories" and stated further:

> Some of the negroes troops, in their cowardice, feigned death, falling to the ground, and were either pricked up by bayonets, or rolled into trenches to excite their alarm—to which circumstance is reduced the whole story of "burying negroes alive."[2]

The first authorized biography of Nathan Bedford Forrest was written by former Confederate officers, Thomas Jordan and John Pryor. Written from a pro-Confederate and pro-Forrest perspective, Jordan and Pryor blamed the Union garrison for the massacre at Fort Pillow. In the first place, the Tennessee Unionists and black soldiers at the garrison were responsible for a number of heinous outrages against the residents of Western Tennessee. These outrages, according to the authors, included pillage, plunder, and, in the case of black troops, rape, the latter charge being made without any credible evidence. Hence, there was already a pent up anger toward the Union forces prior to the confrontation at Fort Pillow. However, according to these historians, a principal reason for the slaughter was simply the availability of whiskey in the fort and the fact the Union troops, particularly African-Americans, had imbibed liberally. Arguing that the Union failure to accept Forrest's demands for surrender justified the slaughter, Jordan and Pryor held Forrest and his confederate soldiers blameless for the events at Fort Pillow. For Jordan and Pryor, Forrest was a larger than life figure, one who was central to the myth of the Lost Cause. Certainly, a man of Forrest's stature could not be responsible for an unchristian and savage massacre.[3]

Like Jordan and Pryor, John Allen Wyeth's *The Life of General Nathan Bedford Forrest* painted a favorable picture of the southern cavalry commander. In addition, Wyeth used a number of affidavits from Fort Pillow survivors—all Confederate—to bolster his justification of Forrest and his Confederate soldiers. Wyeth asserts two primary reasons for the disaster at Fort Pillow. First, Major Bradford and Captain Marshall of the *New Era* secretly formulated a plan whereby the garrison would not surrender, but run down the steep bluff toward the Mississippi river, drawing pursuing Confederate soldiers into a deadly fire. In order to bolster his argument, Wyeth asserted that "No man surrendered above the bluff." In such fashion, pursuing Confederates would then be sprayed with canister from the ship's gun; however, there was really no hard evidence that Marshall and Bradford had fixed upon such a plan. In testimony before the Joint Committee on the Conduct of the War, Marshall had stated such an arrangement was made, but there was no corroboration from any other witnesses; moreover, if there was such a plan it was remarkably unsuccessful and poorly executed. Second, like Jordan and Pryor, Wyeth argued that the garrison was drunk and blamed Bradford's inexperience for allowing free access to liquor prior to the engagement. The drunkenness of the soldiers caused many soldiers to fire at Confederate soldiers when they should have tried to surrender. "But for the insane conduct of their drunken and desperate comrades," Wyeth notes, "a great many of those who perished would have escaped." Additionally, Wyeth maintained that since the flag of the fort was never lowered, this meant no official surrender had transpired. "No marvel the loss of life was terrible," Wyeth remarked. Ridiculing the report of the Joint Committee on the Conduct of the War as based on biased, ex parte testimony, Wyeth admits that the casualties at Fort Pillow were high. "There was never a surrender of the fort," Wyeth notes, "both officers and men claiming they would never surrender or ask for quarter."[4]

By the end of the nineteenth century, the South had completed the process of disenfranchisement of African-Americans begun in the 1880s and 1890s. New "scientific" views of race categorized races and ethnic groups according a rigid hierarchy with western Europeans on top followed by various other groups with African-Americans on the bottom. In the academic historical profession, the negative views about African-Americans helped create new interpretations on the Civil War and Reconstruction period. Columbia historians John Dunning and John W. Burgess, for instance, advanced interpretations that were highly critical of Republican policies during Reconstruction. Starting from the premise the African-Americans were inferior and thus scarcely qualified to participate in democratic institutions, Dunning and a whole school of historians after him pronounced the Reconstruction policies on the South a decisive failure. Writing in 1901, Burgess somewhat skeptically described the result of the decision to arm African-Americans, observing:

> To this it may be answered that the negro race in the South was not exactly a barbarous race. It was an uneducated race, but it did not exhibit the cruel qualities which are generally considered as attaching to barbarism. It was simply a subject race sunken into ignorance, which the President was calling upon to lend a hand in its own enfranchisement.

Burgess then states, "It is to be regretted that the questions at issue between the Union and the Confederacy could not have been fought out, when appealed to the trial of arms, by the whites only."[5]

It is little wonder, as historian John Cimprich points out, that historians might also reinterpret the role of blacks in the Fort Pillow Massacre. James Ford Rhodes was one of the first national historians to retreat from the northern perspective on the Fort Pillow Massacre. While Rhodes did not deny that a large number of black soldiers had been killed, at the same time, he accepted some of the reasons offered by Forrest and his biographers. "It seems clear however that there was not official surrender," Rhodes observes, "and that the United States flag was not hauled down by the garrison or the white flag authoritatively displayed." Rhodes also maintained that the Lincoln administration did not initiate a policy of retaliation because the president did not view the massacre as authorized but "perpetuated in the heat of conflict and had neither been ordered nor suggested by Forrest." Just a few years later, though, Lincoln biographer, Nathaniel Wright Stephenson, described the Fort Pillow Massacre in terms of a wild rumor perpetuated by the radical Republicans, who he described as the "Vindictives." "In April, 1864," Stephenson notes, "the North was swept by a wild rumor of deliberate massacre of prisoners at Fort Pillow.

Here was an opportunity for the President to ingratiate himself with the Vindictives."[6]

In the 1930s, the trend toward skepticism continued. James G. Randall, one of the pre-eminent Civil War historians of the day believed the evidence for Fort Pillow did not allow historians to make a definitive conclusion about what transpired at Fort Pillow. "The Northern investigating committee denounced the affair as a brutal 'massacre' and an act of deliberate savagery," wrote Randall. "On the Confederate side it was pointed out that the slaughter was not ordered by General Forrest, that the 'surrendering' men were resisting capture, and that they were not massacred, but killed in warfare." In the late 1930s and early 1940s, historian T. Harry Williams made detailed studies of the Republican radicals and the Joint Committee on the Conduct of the War. Regarding the radical Republicans as fanatics who did damage to the Union war cause by their harassment of the president and hatred of the South, Williams was skeptical of much of what the radical congressmen did. While Williams did not discount that atrocities had taken place at Fort Pillow, he believed that the two congressmen who conducted the investigation, Benjamin F. Wade and Daniel W. Gooch, grossly exaggerated the atrocities that transpired at Fort Pillow. For Williams, the Committee's report served a principal function as propaganda and must be treated accordingly. Their real goal, according to Williams, was to initiate a vindictive policy towards the Confederacy and they leveraged the Fort Pillow Massacre to force the president's hand. Allan Nevins magisterial, *The Ordeal of the Union*, took a tentative view of the massacre. In most places, when Nevins refers to the affair at Fort Pillow, he put the words massacre in quotation marks, thus indicating to the reader that there might be some doubt about the validity or authenticity to the claim. One historian who bucked the trend toward skepticism was the poet turned historian Carl Sandburg. In his four-volume *The War Years*, Sandburg described the report of the Joint Committee on the Conduct of the War as "a propaganda document intended to emphasize every fact that would infuriate the North for war and to minimize points the South might plead for justification." But, at the same time, Sandburg also called the battle at Fort Pillow for what it was: a massacre, plain and simple. "But a historian," Sandburg contends,

> would have to record that a certain moment arrived when
> Forrest's men were no longer fighting a battle in a war between
> civilized nations. They were from that moment on sharing in a
> race riot, a mass lynching, and the event became an orgy of
> unleashed primitive human animals riding a storm of anger and

vengeance directed at their sworn enemy, who they considered less than human and beyond the laws of civilized war: the Negro.[7]

New southern interpretations emerged in the 1940s that continued to insist that a massacre had not taken place. Writing *"First with the Most" Forrest* in 1944, Ralph Seth Henry argued that part of the reason why the Fort Pillow Massacre was an established fact in the minds of many Civil War northerners was that the Davis administration did not receive Forrest's official report for some time after the battle. Since Forrest's report was first directed to Lieutenant General Leonidas Polk, his immediate superior, and Polk passed away in June 1864, by the time the Richmond government got a copy of the document it was too late to counter northern charges. Northern opinion, according to Henry, was primarily shaped by the report of the Joint Committee on the Conduct of the War. Without an effective refutation to the Committee's report, its interpretation became established facts in the minds of most northerners. Henry repeats many of the assertions of Jordan, Pryor, and Wyeth; namely that Bradford had a secret plan with the commander of the *New Era* to retreat down the bluff and trap the Confederates in deadly canister fire; that the atrocities committed by many of Bradford's 13th Tennessee regiment were the reason why Confederate soldiers were angry. Henry's most significant contention, however, was the claim that the casualty rate was significantly lower than what many had claimed. Arguing that 226 Union soldiers were taken prisoner and 100 were loaded onto Union transport ships, Henry asserts that 336 Union soldiers survived the battle and thus to call the Fort Pillow affair a massacre was inaccurate. Admitting that some Union soldiers were killed after they had tried to surrender, Henry, nonetheless, maintained that this was not due to official policy or the orders of Forrest. For Henry, the fact that Union generals, such as William Tecumseh Sherman, did not ask for retaliation was proof that many Union officers were not convinced that a massacre had taken place at Fort Pillow.[8]

A similar effort was made just a few years later by John J. Jordan, a retired army officer. According to Jordan the publication and circulation of the report of the Joint Committee on the Conduct of the War was primarily responsible for creating the "myth" about the Fort Pillow Massacre. For Jordan a couple of relevant "facts" explain the "massacre." First, Jordan notes that many of the witnesses interviewed by the Committee and by Union military officials were not actually present at Fort Pillow on the day of the alleged massacre; hence, there testimony was hearsay and inherently suspect. Second, the "drunken" garrison never really surrendered. It was only through the efforts of Forrest and Chalmers, who eventually ensured that the garrison's flag was lowered, that the killing ceased. Moreover, as a number of black troops drowned after trying to swim to the *New Era*, Confederate soldiers fired on these fleeing troops. "A number of Negro troops were drowned while they were trying to escape; and it was a proper military act to fire upon these men in the water," argues Jordan, "because there had not been a surrender." Third, the allegations of atrocities committed the night of the battle and the next morning were either lies or were not committed by Confederate troops, since, according to Jordan, most of Forrest's command had left the fort. Since West Tennessee was already filled with irregular forces, Jordan notes that any number of guerrillas could have come into the fort that evening and committed the atrocities. Citing inconsistencies in witness's statements about alleged acts of violence, Jordan dismisses most of the charges as unreliable or downright falsehoods. According to Jordan, there simply was no massacre because, in his estimates of survivors, wounded, and killed, Jordan believed that 398 Union soldiers survived, placing the casualty rate (killed and wounded) at just over 50 percent—something that was exceeded in many other Civil war engagements. The reason Fort Pillow has been known as a massacre was primarily, in Jordan's opinion, due to the biased and unfavorable report of the Joint Committee on the Conduct of the War, which deliberately omitted testimony that was favorable to Forrest. Jordan notes the illiterate blacks gave perfect testimony in terms of grammar and usage. "Yet their statements," notes Jordan, "were couched in perfect language grammatically, and contained many words that were beyond the comprehension of men of this class."[9]

In 1958, the historiography of the Fort Pillow Massacre began to swing back toward a viewpoint that was more sympathetic to African-Americans and more critical of Forrest and his troops. One could argue that this may have been an instance where outside events—namely the beginning of the modern Civil Rights movement—began to influence the interpretations of historians. However, that was not the primary motivation for a newly minted historian from the University of Chicago, Albert Castel, who simply wanted to re-examine the evidence of the Fort Pillow Massacre. Noting that many northern historians believed there had been a massacre and southern historians maintained the opposite, Castel was determined to re-examine the sources and evidence to make a new determination. Castel agreed with southern historians and defenders of Forrest, who maintained that Confederates had not taken advantage of a flag of truce to gain superior position. At the same time, Castel was skeptical of the charge that Major Bradford and Captain Marshall had a plan to entice Confederate soldiers down the bluff so as to ply them with canister. As Castel pointed out, Confederate testimony was contradictory. On the one hand, they claimed Union soldiers had a premeditated plan with the commander of the *New Era*, but, on the other hand, the garrison was supposed to be drunk and disorderly. Both assertions could not be true. Nor did Castel believe that the massacre was deliberately ordered by Forrest. On the contrary, even when Forrest and other officers tried to restrain their soldiers they had difficulty controlling them. According to Castel, Union soldiers probably did keep firing. Why would they not? Not only were they outnumbered, they observed many of their comrades being cut down after they had tried to surrender. "There can be little doubt," Castel observes, "that in a great many cases—many more than Confederates cared to admit—Union soldiers were shot after they personally, at least, had stopped fighting and were trying to surrender." Noting that many of the alleged atrocities—live burials, the killing of women and children—were largely fabrications, Castel maintained that the testimony taken by the Committee on the Conduct of the War still contain many truths that were repeated in duplicate affidavits gathered by the War Department; whereas Confederate testimony was riddled with inconsistencies.[10]

Although Dudley Cornish's study on the arming of black troops appeared in 1956 and certainly accepted the realities of the Fort Pillow Massacre, Castel's article, according to the most prominent scholar of the Fort Pillow Massacre, John Cimprich, was fundamental in changing the direction of subsequent historiography on the Fort Pillow Massacre. From the 1960s onward, the historians have largely accepted the interpretation that a massacre took place at Fort Pillow. Shelby Foote's massive three-volume, *The Civil War: A Narrative*, for instance, acknowledged that a gruesome slaughter had taken place. At the same time, Foote also believed that the North had been whipped into a frenzy by the events of Fort Pillow, largely through the propaganda efforts of the Joint Committee on the Conduct of the War. Certainly blacks had been slaughtered at a much greater rate than whites, as was evidenced by the number of white prisoners taken as opposed to black prisoners; however, Foote contends, many of the other atrocities reported—live burials, burned bodies, slain women and children, were largely fabrications. Despite this tendency toward exaggeration, the casualty figure still showed that something awful had transpired. "Here was discrimination with a vengeance," Foote writes,

> as well as support for a Confederate sergeant's testimony, given in a letter home within a week of the affair, describing how "the poor, deluded negroes would run up to our men, fall upon their knees and with uplifted hands scream for mercy, but were ordered to their feet and then shot down."[11]

In the 1980s two important articles, authored by Robert Mainfort and John Cimprich, appeared in scholarly journals. The first concentrated on publication of primary sources that suggested that a massacre had taken place and was initially acknowledged by southern as well as northern sources. The second was a detailed examination of muster rolls at the National Archive, which shed light on the exact number of Union solders that participated in the Fort Pillow affair and their casualty rates. The first of the co-authored articles focused on primary documents that demonstrated Confederate acknowledgment of the massacre at Fort Pillow. After the publication of the report of the Joint Committee on the Conduct of the War, southerners took a defensive attitude on anything pertaining to Fort Pillow. Mainfort and Cimprich compiled a series of six primary documents that were published or authored prior to the publication of the Joint Committee's report. There were three newspaper accounts, two private letters, and the draft of one Confederate military report. In both of the letters, written by Confederate soldiers, Achilles V. Clark of the 20th Tennessee Cavalry and Samuel H. Caldwell, describe a horrible slaughter that transpired at Fort Pillow. Both letters demonstrate that the failure of the garrison to accept surrender terms was the driving force in fueling the rage of Confederate soldiers. A report from the *Memphis Appeal* also reported a bloody slaughter that had taken place primarily because the garrison refused to surrender: "Indiscriminate slaughter followed— about a hundred prisoners were taken, the balance was slain. The fort ran with blood; many jumped into the river and drowned, or [were] shot in the water." The other documents published in the article made a similar point. The significant point in these primary sources was that until the northern public was aroused about Fort Pillow, many southerners willingly acknowledged that something awful and hideous had transpired on the banks of the Mississippi River that day in April. It was only after charges of slaughter and massacre were made, primarily with the publication of the Joint Committee's report as well as charges of slaughter that filled the northern press that Confederates began to take a defensive posture with regards to the massacre. President Lincoln's threat of retaliation also played a significant role in the way Confederates began to respond to northern accounts of the massacre. Now Confederate papers, officials, and participants in the massacre began to focus on new causes for the slaughter and the charge of the intoxication of the garrison made its first appearance in Confederate papers. "Thus it happened," note the authors, "that a mound of denials and counter charges came to bury the truth about one of the uglier moments in American history."[12]

Seven years later the authors published another short, but essential article on the Fort Pillow Massacre. Noting that much of the controversy on whether Fort Pillow was a legitimate massacre rested on casualty rates, the authors undertook an exhaustive investigation of muster roles, newspapers, pension lists, and National Archive records to compile a definitive estimate of the number of soldiers at the garrison the day of the massacre and the number of killed, wounded, and survivors. As previously noted, the claim that the Fort Pillow battle was a bona fide massacre often rests on the body count, and several southern historians have used numbers to downplay the occurrence of a massacre. Based on their research, Mainfort and Cimprich concluded that the total number of Union soldiers present at Fort Pillow on April 12, 1864 was between 585–605 with deaths of 277–297 or 47–49 percent. "Clearly the death rate was higher than that calculated in any previous study." What was significant, however, was the difference between black and white casualty rates. While whites were killed at a rate of 31 percent, African-American troops experienced an astounding casualty rate of 64 percent, supporting the contention that black soldiers were particularly targeted by Confederate soldiers during the battle. "The new quantitative documentary evidence," the authors maintained, "unequivocally demonstrates that a massacre occurred."[13]

In the early 1990s two important biographies on Nathan Bedford Forrest appeared. Instead of parroting the pro-Confederate sympathies of writers of an earlier generation, both Brian Steel Wills and Jack Hurst incorporated the findings of more recent research on the Fort Pillow Massacre into their biographies. Wills believed that Forrest had little respect for the men who garrisoned Fort Pillow, consisting largely of escaped slaves and Tennessee Unionists. "There was also the opportunity," states Wills, "to expose the fallacy of placing guns in the hands of blacks by demonstrating their inferiority as soldiers." Because of the prevailing attitudes of Forrest and his men, the possibility of a conflict turning into a massacre was high. "Black southerners were commodities to be bought and sold and made to work," Willis comments on Forrest's attitude, "not human beings who might wish to control their lives by carrying weapons and wearing uniforms." Arming blacks was, in the opinion of Forrest, tampering with the social order and the results of such experimentation would not be beneficial. Once Forrest had surrounded the garrison and issued his "no quarter" ultimatum, the fuse was lit. Union soldiers had been hurling taunts at Confederate soldiers for most of the day. According to Wills, Forrest was not prepared for what happened once the order to take the fort was given. Had he formulated a plan for a massacre, he would have undoubtedly led his men into battle as he had done on numerous occasions. In reality, the Confederate general simply lost control of the situation. While he did not object to the high casualty rates for black soldiers, it is an altogether different point to say that he ordered and expected this outcome. In Forrest's personal view, blacks were inferior and should have been captured and returned to their owners. However, Forrest also failed to understand the social dynamics of the situation; how the ordinary Confederate soldier felt about blacks challenging the status quo and, in effect, asserting autonomy and failing to show deference. "For a variety of reasons," Wills concludes, "Fort Pillow became a collective release of pent-up anger and hatred. It became, in clinical terms, a group catharsis."[14]

For the most part, Jack Hurst's biography of Nathan Bedford Forrest also accepts the contention of historians who believe that a significant massacre occurred at Fort Pillow, although he correctly points out that some of the contentions of journalists and congressional committees were exaggerated and even sensationalized. Hurst's biography struggles with the motivation of Forrest. Did he want a massacre? Did he order a massacre? How could Forrest have ordered a massacre and, at the same time as many sources and scholars point out, then be the one who put a stop to the killing? The evidence for Forrest's role in ordering the massacre is mixed according to Hurst; however, since Forrest delivered the ultimatum of surrender or no quarter, he should have reasonably anticipated the reaction of his men in battle. If Forrest did not order a massacre, he should have known that his men intended to initiate one. As some primary sources indicate, one of Forrest's goals was to intimidate black soldiers, but this, as Hurst points out, backfired as well since many African-American soldiers began to reply in kind in subsequent battles.[15]

One striking dissent to the consensus historians have seemed to reach on the Fort Pillow Massacre is the work of Lonnie Maness who, in 1982, published an article attempting to revitalize the pro-southern interpretation of the Fort Pillow Massacre. Offering few original ideas or arguments, Maness essentially revived the argument that was put forward in the 1940s by pro-Confederate historians such as John J. Jordan and Ralph Seth Henry. His principal contention being that casualty rates have been overstated by those historians who believe a massacre took place.[16]

Since the publication of Hurst and Wills' biographies, a number of studies on the Fort Pillow Massacre have been published. There is little doubt now that a massacre did occur; however, there are still numerous points of contention. In 1994, Richard L. Fuchs published *An Unerring Fire: The Massacre at Fort Pillow*. Unlike Wills, who believed a massacre had taken place but Forrest did not officially order the massacre, Fuchs asserts conclusively that Forrest had used the flag of truce to improve the position of his men in the subsequent battle. Forrest himself and many historians have acknowledged troop movement during the flag of truce; however, most have justified it on the grounds that Union vessels were approaching the garrison and Forrest was justified in taking measures to prevent the ships from coming to the aid of the fort. Fuchs, however, believed that Forrest wanted to increase his odds at quickly taking the garrison and even encouraged a massacre to take place. "General Forrest," writes Fuchs,

> participated in the affair through either a deliberate failure to control his forces or by subtly encouraging a result he sought and knew would be the inevitable consequence of a Confederate victory over the garrison. That an intentional massacre occurred at the instigation or with the tacit approval of General Forrest and his command is clearly and convincingly established by the record.

Some of Fuchs points over deliberate violations of the flag of truce have been accepted and incorporated into subsequent studies of the Fort Pillow Massacre, most notably by Andrew Ward in his 2005 monograph, *River Run Red.*[17]

In the last ten years, the Fort Pillow Massacre has continued to draw scholarly attention. Andrew Ward's *River Run Red* (2005) is one of the largest and most comprehensive books written on the Fort Pillow Massacre, devoting several chapters to developing both the context for the massacre as well as a detailed account of its aftermath. At the same time, John Cimprich has continued to refine his 20-plus years of research, culminating in his 2005 *Fort Pillow: A Civil War Memory and Public Memory.* Not only does Cimprich present a comprehensive view of Fort Pillow and massacre, a thorough and interesting chapter on the historiography of the event touches upon the public discussion of how the massacre should be remembered by contemporaries. Cimprich presents a brief discussion over the establishment of the Fort Pillow Historic State Park and how controversial, even in the 1970s and 1980s, telling the story of the Fort Pillow Massacre could be. The movement to establish a historical park at the sight of the Fort Pillow Massacre actually again in the early 1930s. Because of the economic constraints of the Great Depression, according to Cimprich, the early efforts to establish an historical Fort Pillow were stymied. In the early 1970s, the movement for a historic Fort Pillow was reborn and the state of Tennessee eventually purchased 1,628 acres of land. After this purchase, the state could now develop a plan and process for a Fort Pillow Historic State Park, but as Cimprich points out, the controversial nature of Fort Pillow would make this a difficult and controversial task.[18]

In a story that in many ways parallels continuing contemporary debates over public displays of the Confederate flag, in telling the story of the development of Fort Pillow Historic State Park, Cimprich narrates a tale that pits professional historians with their latest interpretation of the Fort Pillow Massacre against public opinion in Tennessee that still clung to scraps of the "Lost Cause" mentality. As Cimprich points out, "The fact that local popular belief ran at odds with the professional consensus created a challenge for park officials." As state archeologist, Robert C. Mainfort began restoration efforts on the physical fort, controversy erupted when educational materials were developed to support interpretations of artifact displays in the Fort's small museum. According to Cimprich, a slide show developed annoyed many southerners because it adopted the viewpoint advanced by Castel and other modern historians that a massacre had indeed taken place at Fort Pillow. The outcry against the slideshow apparently became intense enough that the museum stopped using the slideshow. Despite the revival of pro-Confederate interpretations of the event in the 1980s by such historians as Lonnie Maness, the park eventually was able to put together a video presentation of the Fort Pillow Massacre that supported the modern interpretation of the event, but, at the same time, recognized the contribution of military leaders such as Nathan Bedford Forrest. "Possibly in an effort to reach two conflicting constituencies with a special interest in the park," notes Cimprich, "each highlighted a heroic aspect of one side of the April 12 battle. One praised Forrest's military talents, while the other lauded the contributions of African American soldiers to the Federal war effort."[19]

Two recent studies do not exclusively address the Fort Pillow Massacre; however, by advancing interpretations on Confederate policies toward black Union soldiers, they make the argument that Fort Pillow, like other battles that involved African-American soldiers, involved a deliberate and calculated policy of extermination. Fort Pillow, then, was a massacre that was deliberate and in complete keeping with southern policy with respect to black Union soldiers. According to George H. Burkhardt, the Confederacy had an "official" policy that stated that black soldiers captured in battle should be turned over to state authorities who could then return them to their previous masters or put them to work on suitable public projects. That is not what happened in practice, maintains Burkhardt, who argues that a "de facto" policy of murder and slaughter was often practiced instead of the official policy. "Southern soldiers first killed, wounded, or trapped black Federals as a matter of course," argues Burkhardt, "although that practice never became the Confederacy's official policy. However, it became a de facto policy by default because it was condoned, never punished, and always denied."[20]

Taking a somewhat different approach, Jason Phillips in *Diehard Confederates* seeks to investigate what he terms the southern ethos of "invincibility," the very real sense that many southern soldiers had that made them feel that they could never be defeated by northerners. As Phillips states it, "These soldiers expressed a resilient ethos or culture of invincibility. Throughout the war, diehard Rebels knew that they were not conquered, but even more, they thought they were unconquerable." When the northern government emancipated and subsequently began to train and arm African-American soldiers, however, Confederate soldiers might take a humorous, comical approach, arguing that northern govern-ment were misleading and taking advantage of their former slaves. But, as Phillips notes, "Rebels's pity and ridicule ended, however, when African-Americans entered the fray. Facing black opponents implied parity between former slaves and Confederate soldiers that many Confederates could not stomach." Hence, when Confederate troops confronted blacks in blue uniforms, as they did at Fort Pillow, they showed little doubt or regret about the outright slaughter of African-American troops. "By killing black prisoners," Phillips notes, "Rebels revealed not only racist rage but also a chilling psychological distance from their victims."[21]

The effort to come up with an acceptable "public" interpretation of events at Fort Pillow touches nerves in various parts of American public opinion that still have not reconciled themselves to the events of 1861–1865. The continuing popularity of the Confederate flag along with arguments put forth to justify its public display, the focus on "southern heritage," along with the denial that Confederacy had little to do with racism and the maintenance of the slave system are disturbingly common themes that twenty-first-century Americans are remarkably well acquainted with. In an effort to understand the Fort Pillow Massacre, but, at the same time, be sensitive to other perspectives, historians should not shy away from the consensus that has emerged over the interpretation of the event. A preponderance of evidence makes it obvious that a brutal massacre took place at Fort Pillow on April 12, 1864. None of the reasons put forth by points of view sympathetic to the Confederacy provides a plausible alternative explanation. If African-Americans were drunk, for instance, why did talk of this emerge only after weeks had transpired? Or, as the historian Albert Castel has pointed out, how could African-American soldiers and their white cohorts been drunken and disorderly, but, at the same time, have a secret plan to deceive Confederate attackers? Why didn't Confederate eyewitnesses and military officers who wrote reports of the affair mention this from the beginning? Nor does the explanation that the garrison failed to surrender justify Confederate actions at Fort Pillow. In a strictly technical sense, the failure to lower the flag could have justified a limited amount of killing; however, there came a point late in the afternoon of April 12 that Confederate soldiers knew that all effective resistance on the part of Federal troops had ceased. As individual soldiers, both white and black, knelt before Confederates, threw down their weapons, and tried to surrender, was there a legitimate reason why they continued to be cut down and slaughtered? Was there a secret plan, worked out between Major Bradford and Captain Marshall to lure Confederate troops *down* the bluff to the river and thereby open them up to canister fire from the *New Era*? Perhaps, but only Captain Marshall spoke of it, and, if it was a plan, it was a very poor plan, a plan that would have exposed Union troops to the very same canister fire intended for pursuing Confederate soldiers. The only plausible reason for a massacre and high casualties was the initial refusal of the Union garrison to surrender. After all, they were promised treatment as prisoners of war if they surrendered, but threatened with no quarter if they refused to surrender. Now Union officers could certainly not be blamed if they did not believe Forrest's promise to treat all soldiers as prisoners of war. This was, as Forrest himself would reveal in countless future letters, contrary to official Confederate policy. This policy maintained that blacks were property and not bonafide prisoners of war. They could not be exchanged and would be held by state authorities who would determine how they would be disposed of: imprisoned or returned to their masters. But even if Union troops failed to accept Forrest's demand out of a sense of patriotism or pride, did the laws of warfare really allow for the extermination of the garrison? Perhaps if stubborn and effect resistance hampered the efforts of the Confederates to overwhelm and capture the garrison; however, as most witnesses testify, the Confederates invested and took control of the Fort in a relatively short amount of time. As most Federal soldiers had stopped fighting, the laws of warfare could hardly be supportive of the massacre of unarmed and surrendering soldiers.

Still this is not to say a massacre was deliberately intended or even ordered by Forrest. Most historians do not maintain that the Tennessee general ordered a massacre. At the same time, Forrest and many of his officers were certainly cognizant of the attitude and emotions that surrounded the confrontation with a Federal garrison manned by African-American soldiers. Forrest certainly was sensitive at this blatant attempt to turn the southern way of life topsy-turvy, and he was certainly also aware of how potentially upsetting this might have been to common soldiers enlisted in his command. After all, this was the first time many of them had faced African-American troops. Taught their entire life that blacks were inferior, subordinate, and property, the typical Confederate private must have been enraged as he faced these black artillerymen for the first time, saw them in Federal blue, and listened to their cocky taunts from behind the earthen walls of the fortress. Forrest and James R. Chalmers should have sensed this as well. They should have taken many more precautions to make sure that the blood-letting did not get out of hand. Although they did not order a massacre, Forrest and Chalmers could not have been too upset with the outcome. Forrest bragged to his superiors about the number of dead killed at Fort Pillow as well as talked about how the battle would teach northerners that they could not rely on black soldiers.

With the exception of all but a few contemporary historians, a strong consensus now establishes the fact of a massacre at Fort Pillow. Despite the exaggerations of some witnesses, the sensationalism of press reporting, and the allegations of atrocities that might not have really happened, indeed probably did not happen, most professional historians are convinced that something awful, unspeakable, happened on the banks of the Mississippi river on a spring day in 1864. Whether Confederates were primarily motivated by frustration that they seemed to be losing the war, whether it was primarily their rage at former slaves feigning equality and threatening the social order, at some point a line was crossed, fury was unleashed, and a brutal massacre resulted. Although the emotions and the prejudices of southern soldiers can be understood, what happened on the banks of the Mississippi on April 12, 1864 will always be remembered as a shameful day in American history.

Conclusion

There seems to be little doubt in the minds of most historians that a brutal massacre occurred at Fort Pillow on April 12, 1864. The most compelling reason for that interpretation is the number of eyewitness accounts provided by northerners and southerners; moreover, as some historians have pointed out, northern testimony was remarkable consistent. Many of those who witnessed the events at Fort Pillow testified to seeing the same things. While there may have been some mistakes and exaggerations, the number of things eyewitnesses agreed on was remarkable. Southern accounts, on the contrary, went through various phases as the Fort Pillow Massacre seemed to become bigger and potentially more controversial. With the war in its last phase, with little hope of foreign recognition, the Confederacy had little hope of winning its independence. The brutal massacre of unarmed men, many of whom had individually surrendered—even if former slaves—did not seem to square with the southern ethic of honor. It was a well-established custom in the south for men, particularly men of high social standings, to personally avenge insults or attacks on one's manhood. In order to save face, Confederates involved in the Fort Pillow Massacre had to invent reasons why the garrison's slaughter was justified. The flag over Fort Pillow had not been pulled down; the garrison was drunk; the garrison was retreating in order to make a surprise attack on hard charging Confederates. In the end, with the exception of a few historians, none of these "explanations" have passed the test of historical credulity. A massacre did take place and a bloody one at that. Indeed, the only valid explanation put forth by southern officers such as Forrest and other participants was that the garrison had been given an opportunity to surrender or face a possible massacre. Hence the cause of the massacre was the failure of the garrison to surrender. Yet in many other Civil War engagements—Gettysburg, Shiloh, for instance, troops were allowed to surrender when there was no general surrender by a northern or southern army. The real question is, once it was obvious that northern troops had fled and could no longer effectively resist, why did southerners continue to butcher northern soldiers? That did not seem particularly honorable or manly.

When all the evidence has been examined, it also seems a reasonable conclusion that a massacre was not formally ordered. General Forrest certainly hoped to overwhelm the garrison. He was not afraid to use his men in hard combat as he had proved time and time again; however, as much as Forrest expected a difficult fight, he certainly did not order his men to gun down or maim unarmed Union soldiers, whether black or white. What Forrest and his officers did probably not fully appreciate was the reality of the emotional impact on his soldiers of seeing African-American in arms for the very first time. Forrest's men were, in many cases, from the West Tennessee and the northern Mississippi area. They had grown up in the shadow of the plantation slave system. Although many were probably not slaveholders, many of the soldiers certainly accepted the premise of white supremacy, the mudsill theory, or what one sociologist had termed "herrenvolk" democracy. The basic gist was that as whites in the south, whether rich, middling, or poor, they were, in virtue of their skin color superior to the most intelligent black slave. Their whiteness made them members of the superior race and, therefore, even when poor, every white was a part of the master class. This was the "God-ordained" social order for as long as anyone could remember. How else can one interpret many of the phrases that were reported by eyewitnesses at the battle? Phrases like "God damn you, you are fighting against your master?"[1]

Southerners were also adamant in claiming that only white southerners really understood blacks. Yankee abolitionists and members of the Republican party (Black Republicans as many southerners described members of that party) were not really the friends of slaves at all. In the words of W. J. Cash in his classic *The Mind of the South*, this meant that southerners had to create a portrait of slavery and the old south that was actually idealized and romanticized. "The Old South must be made not only a happy country but the happy country especially for the Negro," wrote Cash. "The lash? A lie, sir; it had never existed. The only bonds were those of tender understanding, trust, and loyalty." While professing sympathy from African-Americans, the freedom and equality that the abolitionists promised plantation slaves would simply lead to life of impoverishment, degradation, and uncertainty. Seduced by wild talk of freedom, the typical slave, reasoned white southerners, would be better off on the plantation than in the northern city. Indeed, all one had to do, wrote many a southern apologist for the peculiar institution, was look to the condition of free blacks in the north. Here, in the land of the Yankee and "free labor," many African-Americans, while free, lived in conditions of abject poverty, the perpetual victims of racial discrimination.[2]

Yet it was April 12, 1864, when confronted with the reality the so-called loyal slaves would make common case with the Yankees, don the blue Union uniform, and become active participants in not only restoring the Union but liberating themselves and potentially altering the social order. For many southern soldiers this reality was perhaps more than could be processed and accepted in such a short period of time. And, as a result, southern soldiers lashed out with a vindictive, vengeful rage, intent on punishing recalcitrant blacks who failed to adequately appreciate the harmonious and kindly nature of the plantation system, but also their white counterparts, the Southern Unionists who encouraged their former slaves in this delusion, but who also betrayed their section and state by making common cause with the Yankees. Then there was also a seething rage against the Yankee officers, the interlopers, and those unbearable abolitionist moralists, who dared to use "ignorant" blacks to carry out their ill-conceived experiments in social engineering. This was not ordinary anger, but rage, a rage fueled by frustration and desperation.

The Fort Pillow Massacre would not be the only engagement that resulted in the indiscriminate slaughter of African-American soldiers. Both before and after the battle at Fort Pillow, there was abundant evidence that Confederate officers and soldiers were implementing a different policy from what the David Administration publicly stipulated. At the battle of Olustee, Florida on February 20, 1864 black soldiers were killed after surrendering. Other Civil War engagements that included the killing of black prisoners included the battle of Poison Springs, Arkansas on April 18, 1864, the battle of Plymouth, North Carolina on April 20, 1864, the battle of Brice's Cross Roads on June 10, 1864, and the battle of Saltville, Virginia on October 2, 1864. And, of course, there were additional battles where African-Americans seemed to vanish into thin air. Despite the official demand from President Lincoln, the Confederate armies, directed by the Davis Administration, paid little attention to the Union government's request for an explanation of the events at Fort Pillow. When it became obvious that the Confederacy intended no official response to Lincoln's demands, the Union government decided that no course of action was the best course of action.

Why did the Lincoln administration decide that the best course of action was the most appropriate course of action? Obviously, one consideration was the impact of retaliation on the Confederacy. If Union military officials initiated a program of man for man retaliation in response to the Fort Pillow Massacre, it might initiate a response from the Davis government that would end up killing more Union soldiers. Yet the lack of response from the Lincoln administration did absolutely nothing to deter the killing of black soldiers that fell into Confederate hands in subsequent battles after the Fort Pillow Massacre. How could the Lincoln administration justify this course of action? The easy response to this question is that northern public opinion was not really all that concerned with the fate of African-American soldiers in some of the smaller Civil War engagements. This is not to say that there were not northerners who did not advocate retaliation on behalf of African-American soldiers. Obviously, in the immediate aftermath of Fort Pillow there was a large public outcry for retaliation and revenge and even the members of Lincoln's cabinet endorsed a course of action that would involve retaliation; however, as the memory of Fort Pillow faded, so did the intensity of northern outrage. Was northern outrage an expression of its compassion for African-American soldiers or was it simply a desire to punish the south? Black soldiers, after all, had only been begrudgingly accepted by the northern public, and when they were accepted, it was more out of a sense of pragmatism and self-preservation than idealism. The Union needed to be saved and black soldiers could help bring that goal about, but would the typical northern whites be willing to risk the lives of white northern soldiers to protest the poor treatment and non-recognition of African-American soldiers? The answer was a fairly obvious "no" for most white northerners. Black military participation was certainly appreciated in the most cynical, pragmatic sense, particularly as a way to spread out war time casualties; however, if blacks believed that the bulk of northerners really intended on making them citizens and making sacrifice on behalf of black soldiers, they were sadly mistaken. What white northerners intended for their African-American brethren once the war was concluded is somewhat mysterious. Slavery was obviously dead, but full citizenship was certainly not on the minds of many white northerners. The war would positively end slavery and inaugurate an era of freedom, but the content of that freedom? That was the rub.

What the northern government failed to do on behalf of its African-American soldiers during the war would be duplicated in the Reconstruction period after the Civil War in how policies advocating civil rights for blacks were abandoned. Again, as during the Civil War, there was always a complicated mixture of idealism and pragmatism at work. The great legislation of the Reconstruction period along with the three critical amendments—the 13th, 14th, and 15th—obviously involved some genuine humanitarian concerns for African-Americans. At the same time, however, it is also true that southern stubbornness also pushed the United

States Congress to enact legislation that was far more aggressive and radical than would have been the case if southern states would have more graciously accepted defeat and have been willing to grant newly freed African-Americans some basic rights and privileges. Was the passage of the great Civil War amendments a signal of a fundamental shift in the attitudes and opinions of Americans? With the complete abandonment of Reconstruction during the 1870s and 1880s, the answer must be no. "Many historians have detected a 'lost moment' during the Reconstruction," notes historian Gary W. Gallagher, "when far more could have been done to achieve true equality for freed people." Gallagher continues:

> If only the white North had followed through on promise of the great Civil War-era amendments, runs his argument, the grim story of the late nineteenth and twentieth centuries could have been much different. Such a view runs aground on the profound prejudice that existed in the United States between 1860 and 1880.[3]

Given the abandonment of African-Americans in the three decades following the Civil War, it is difficult to maintain that racial relations were revolutionized as a result of the Civil War. While the passage of the great Civil War amendments was a tremendous accomplishment, it is also remarkable how the United States Supreme Court during the Gilded Ages began to chip away at these amendments in decision after decision. In the 1883 *Civil Right Cases*, for instance, the court invalidated the Civil Rights Act of 1875. This piece of legislation, based on specific clauses of the 13th and 14th amendments, guaranteed people of color equal access to all places of public accommodation. In a tortured ruling, the Court's majority ruled that the law only applied to state laws that were discriminatory, not the actions of private individuals. Hence, individual black citizens who had been denied access to a restaurant or a concert by a private individual had no recourse. The Federal government could only take action if the state government was discriminating. By the end of the century, aided by additional Supreme Court decisions, the segregation system was well established. *Plessy v. Ferguson* (1896) legalized the doctrine of separate but equal in the area of transportation and decisions such as *Cummins v. Board of Education* (1898) formally extended the separation of the races to education. By the end of the nineteenth century, the idealism and promise of the Civil War era amendments were forgotten by many, and to those who remembered, they must have seemed a cruel joke.[4]

Obviously this does not mean that the legislative accomplishment of the Civil War era were meaningless. When the modern civil rights movement re-emerged in the twentieth century, the fact that such amendments as the 13th, 14th, and 15th amendments were part of the Constitution of the United States was obviously a great legal aid to the movement. At the same time, it is also important to note that many of these same amendments had little lasting impact on the African-Americans of the Civil War generation. Just as the northern government failed to adequately protect its black soldiers after the brutal massacre at Fort Pillow, it also failed to follow through on the dreams of African-American soldiers who help fight to restore the Union and secure their freedom. Black soldiers and black activists believed their contributions to the Union military effort should afford them a seat at the American political banquet. In the end, however, the same society that responded ambivalently to the massacre of its soldiers also responded ambiguously to African-American demands for citizenship after the war for the Union had been successfully concluded. In many ways, the struggle for equal citizenship and equal rights carries on into the twenty-first century.

Documents

DOCUMENT 1: REMARKS TO DEPUTATION OF WESTERN GENTLEMEN,[1] AUGUST 4, 1862

After the passage of the Militia Act of 1862, which allowed African-Americans to serve in the military in non-combat roles, there was pressure on the Lincoln administration from free black leaders, radical Republicans, and abolitionists to allow blacks to perform combat roles. Although the administration would begin some of these efforts in limited ways, the public posture that Lincoln maintained was that such a move would do more harm than good, and, he pointed particularly to the impact it would have on the slaveholding Border States—Delaware, Kentucky, Maryland, and Missouri—states that had remained within the Union but still were committed to the institution of slavery. The following document captures the thinking of the president to the advocates of arming African-Americans and using them in combat roles.

A deputation of Western gentlemen waited upon the President this morning to offer two colored regiments from the State of Indiana. Two members of Congress were in the party. The President received them courteously, but stated to them that he was not prepared to go the length of enlisting negroes as soldiers. He would employ all colored men offered as laborers, but would not promise to make soldiers of them.

The deputation came away satisfied that it is the determination of the Government not to arm negroes unless some new and more pressing emergency arises. The President argued that the nation could not afford to lose Kentucky at this crisis, and gave it as his opinion that to arm the negroes would turn 50,000 bayonets from the loyal Border States against us that were for us.

Upon the policy of using negroes as laborers, the confiscation of Rebel Property, and the feeding the National troops upon the granaries of the enemy, the President said there was no division of sentiment. He did not explain, however, why it is that the Army of the Potomac and the Army of Virginia carry out this policy so differently. The President promised that the war would be prosecuted with all the rigor he could command, but he could not promise to arm slaves or attempt slave insurrections in the Rebel States. The recent enactments of Congress on emancipation and confiscation he expects to carry out.

DOCUMENT 2: LETTER OF ACHILLES V. CLARK[2]

A native of Henry County, Tennessee, Achilles V. Clark was too young to enlist in the Confederate army at the beginning of the conflict and enlisted in the

Confederate Army at the beginning of 1864. Although he began as a private, he was raised to the rank of sergeant in the 20th Tennessee Cavalry. A witness and participant in the battle at Fort Pillow, Clark wrote to his sister shortly after the battle on April 14, 1864. Before the news of Fort Pillow was widely circulated in the North by the press and prior to the publication of the Joint Committee on the Conduct of the War, Clark's account of the battle is regarded by leading historians of the Fort Pillow Massacre as an unvarnished and accurate account of the events that transpired on April 12, 1864.

Camp near Brownsville
April 14th 1864

My Dear Sisters,

I write you a few hurried lines to inform you that I am quite well and have just passed safely through the most terrible ordeal of my whole life. I guess that you know what I mean as you doubtless have before this heard of the taking of Fort Pillow. In as much as I am a member of Forrest's Cavalry modesty would direct that I should say nothing in our praise, nor will I but will tell you in as few words as possible what was done and leave you to judge whether or not we acted well or ill. If you remember we left Paris Wednesday morning from which point we proceeding immediately to Eaton Gibson County where we found Col Bell's camp. Saturday we prepared five days rations in antisipain of a move to some place we knew not where. Sunday evening directly after supper the bugle sounded to saddle. at twelve o'clock we marched off in the direction of Brownsville. We camped just at daybreak on the north side and about two miles from South Forked Deer river where we rested one hour. Mounting our horses we crossed the above mentioned stream and one mile this side took the Fort Pillow road. From this time we rightly supposed that we were going to attack that place. At 10 A.M. (Monday) we stopped to feed and were detained about one hour and a half. At 3 P.M. we stopped again and rested until six. From this time we were on our saddles until we reach a point one and a half miles this side of the Fort where we dismounted to fight (this was about 7 A.M. Tuesday) [;] leaving every fourth man to hold horses, we marched on foot in sight of the fortifications which were said to be manned by about seven hundred renegade Tennesseans and negroes commanded by Major Boothe of the Negro regiment [,] Major Bradford of the 13th Tenn. U. S. V. being second in command. Our brigade filed round to the right of the fort [,] Chalmer's command to the left. Skirmishers were depl[l]oyed and we advanced very slowly it is true but surely toward the enemy. Just here it would be proper to describe the fort which I shall attempt to do. It is a very strong earthwork situated on a high bluff inside the works erected by Gen. Pillow in 1861. It is formed by an irregular trench being dug somewhat in the shape of a half circle the edge of the bluff being the diameter. The fort is quite small just about large enough to hold a thousand men in two ranks. The ditch is eight feet deep and six wide and the dirt thrown from the ditch on the inside formed a bank five feet high making from the bottom of the ditch to the top of the breast work thirteen feet up which we had to climb. By two o'clock P.M. we had approached within fifty yards of the fort on all sides. A part of our regiment was in twenty steps of it. Strange to say after five hours constant firing the Yankees had not killed a single one of our men and wounded only a very few among whom I am sorry to name the gallant Capt. Wilson of our regiment who fell in twenty steps of the fort shot through the lungs dangerously though tis greatly to be hoped not mortally wounded. At 2 P.M. Gen. Forrest demanded a surrender and gave twenty minutes to consider. The Yankees refused threatening that if we charged their breast works to show no quarter. The bulge sounded the charge and in less than ten minutes we were in the fort hurling the cowardly villains howling down the bluff. Our men were so exasperated by the Yankees' threats of no quarter that they gave but little. The slaughter was awful. Words cannot describe the scene. The poor deluded negroes would run up to our men fall upon their knees and with uplifted hands scream for mercy but they were ordered to their feet and then shot down. The whitte men fared but little better. Their fort turned out to be a great slaughter pen. Blood, human blood stood about in pools and brains could have been gathered up in any quantity. I with several others tried to stop the butchery and at one time had partially succeeded. But Gen. Forrest ordered them shot down like dogs, and the carnage continued. Finally our men became sick of blood and the firing ceased. The result. The report kept in the Post Adjutants offices shows the there were seven hundred and ninty men for duty on the morning of the fight. We brought away about one hundred and sixty white men and about seventy five negroes. Two transports came down the morning after the fight and took off the badly wounded Yankees and negroes about thirty or forty in all. The remainder were thrown into the trench before which two hours previous they had stood and bade open defiance to Forrest and all his ragged hounds, and were covered up about two feet deep. We captured seven hundred stands of small arms, six pieces of the finest artillery I ever saw, a large amounts of quarter masters and commissary stores. Our losses as compared to that of the enemy were small yet we deeply mourn the loss of ten or fifteen as brave as men as ever pulled a trigger. Those from our Regt. [included] John Beard of our company [] a bright minded moral young man [who] fell on top of the breast work close to me side.

DOCUMENT 3: LETTER FROM NATHAN BEDFORD FORREST TO JEFFERSON DAVIS[3]

A few days after the battle of Fort Pillow had occurred, Major General Nathan Bedford Forrest wrote a letter to Confederate President Jefferson Davis, where the latter updated the Confederate leader of his operations in Kentucky and Tennessee, including the actions at Fort Pillow. The excerpt from this letter is unique in that it was written before Forrest was aware of the storm of protest that would erupt when stories of the atrocities committed at Fort Pillow were circulated throughout the north by the press. Forrest is blunt and unapologetic in his account of the battle to his political superior.

On Monday last I moved against Fort Pillow and attacked it on Tuesday morning with Chalmers[4] Division, the advance of our troops after getting within the outer works was cautiously and slowly made The Cannading from the Fort and the GunBoats was very heavy and rapids, having gained the desired position, surrounding the Fort with the troops from the River above to its Bluff below a surrender was demanded, which they asked an hour, but were given twenty minutes to consider, it was held by about 700 White and Negro troops, at the expiration of the 20 minutes the fire was renewed . . . the assault was made & the works carried without a halt, the men and officers displaying great gallantry and courage, the Enemy attempted to retreat to the river, either for protection of Gun Boats or to escape, and the slaughter was heavy there were many Union men who had taken shelter in the Fort also, many of whom in their fright leaped into the river and were drowned it is safe to say that in troops Negroes and citizens the Killed Wounded and drowned will range from 450 to 500. My loss is twenty killed and sixty wounded—After securing all the stores we could remove and the Artillery (Six pieces I withdrew my troops and destroyed all the buildings and the works as far as practicable burying the dead and removing the wounded—The Victory was complete and the conduct of my troops and the Officers commanding them shall meet with due attention and a mention in my Official reports—

DOCUMENT 4: STATEMENTS OF EYEWITNESSES TO THE MASSACRE

In addition to the investigation of the Joint Committee on the Conduct of the War, the War Department, under the orders of Secretary Edwin M. Stanton, conducted its own investigation of the Fort Pillow affair. The following six documents consist of statement of eyewitnesses to the massacre. The majority of statements are from soldiers—many African-American privates; however, as there were also civilians present during the battle, a few of their accounts have also been included.

AFFIDAVIT OF HARDY N. REVELLE[5]

Affidavit of Hardy N. Revelle:

I was in business at Fort Pillow previous to the fight on Tuesday last; was engaged as a dry-goods clerk for Messrs. Harris & Co. Went into the fight 6 o'clock on the morning of Tuesday, the 12th of April. Remained outside of the Federal fortification until about 8:30 a. m., acting as a sharpshooter. At this time we were all ordered within the fort. Lieutenant Barr was killed outside the fort; also Lieutenant Wilson, latter of the Thirteenth Tennessee Cavalry. It was not long after 9 o'clock that I took my position behind the fortification and resumed the fight. I was standing not more than 10 paces from Major Booth when he fell, struck in the heart by a musket-bullet. It was but a few minutes past 9. He did not die immediately but was borne from the field. At this time there was continuing fire from both sides. Rebels were not using artillery; our troops were. The next thing I recollect is a flag of truce coming in, the bearer of which, General Forrest, of the rebel army, and some parties of his staff, demanded a surrender of the garrison. Major Bradford was then in command. Forrest did not come within the breast-works, but remained 50 yards outside, and Major Bradford went out to meet him.[6] They conferred in a southeasterly direction from what was known as old headquarters. Bradford is said to have replied that he would not surrender. Forrest told him if he did not there would be no quarter shown. They were in conference about fifteen minutes, during which time there was a cessation of firing. Bradford asked for one hour's time in which to confer with the commander of the gun-boat. Forrest refused it, but I think there was a cessation of hostilities of nearly that length of time. The rebels were busily engaged in plundering our hastily deserted encampment outside the fortifications, as well as robbing some of the stores below the hill. They were also massing their troops and placing them in eligible positions while the flag of truce was being considered. It is my opinion that they could never have gained the positions had they not done so under that flag of truce. They have already consumed seven or eight hours in attempting it, with no success.

At about 2:30[7] in the afternoon a large force of infantry came upon us from the ravine toward the east of where I stood. It seemed to come down Coal Creek. They charged upon our ranks. Another large force of rebel cavalry charged from the south and east, and another force from the northward. They mounted the breast-works at the first charge where I stood. We fired upon them while upon the breast-works. I remember firing two shots while the enemy were upon the walls. The negro troops, frightened by the appearance of such numbers, and knowing they could no longer resist, made a break and ran down the hill, surrendering their arms as the rebels came down our side of the fortifications.

When we found there was no quarter to be shown, and that (white and black) we were to be butchered, we also gave up our arms and passed down the hill. It is stated that at this time Major Bradford put a white handkerchief on his sword-point and waved it in token of submission, but it was not heeded if he did. We were followed closely and fiercely by the advancing rebel forces, their fire never ceasing at all. Our men had given signals themselves that they surrendered, many of them throwing up their hands to show they were unarmed, and submitted to overwhelming odds.

I was about half-way down the hill, partially secreted in a kind of ravine with Dr. Fitch[8], when I saw 2 men (white men) belonging to the Thirteenth Tennessee Cavalry standing behind a stump on which they had fixed a white handkerchief, their hands thrown up. They asked for quarter. When they stood on their feet they were exposed, and I saw them shot down by rebel soldiers and killed.

A captain of the rebel troops then came where we were and ordered all Federals (white and black) to move up the hill or he would "shoot their God-damned brains out." I started up the hill with a number of others in accordance with his order. I was surrendered with our men. While going up I saw a white men fall on both sides of me, who were shot down by rebel soldiers who were stationed upon the brow of the hill. We were at times marching directly toward the men who fired upon us. I do not know how many fell, but I remember of seeing 4 killed that way. I also saw negroes shot down with pistols in the hands of rebels. One was killed at my side. I saw another negro struck on the head with a saber by a rebel soldier. I suppose he was also killed. One more just in front of me was knocked down with the butt of a musket. We kept on up the hill. I expected each moment to meet my fate with the rest.

At the top of the hill I met a man named Cutler, a citizen of Fort Pillow. He spoke to a rebel captain about me, and we then went under orders from the captain to one of the stores under the hill, where the captain got a pair of boots. This was about 4 p. m. on Tuesday.

The captain and Cutler and myself left to find General McCulloch's[9] headquarters, where we were to report and be disposed of. The captain introduced me to a lieutenant and to a surgeon of the rebel army. The surgeon made me show him where goods could be found. The lieutenant got a saddle and bridle and some bits, and then we held them to carry them to where their horses were, outside the fortifications. I also met Mr. Wedlin, a citizen, and he accompanied us. He helped the lieutenant to mount and pack his goods, and he gave Wedlin and myself permission to depart, and instructed us as to the best means of escape.

I am positive that up to the time of the surrender there had not been more than 50 men (black and white) killed and wounded on the Union side. Of these but about 20 had been among the killed. The balance of all killed and wounded on our side were killed and wounded after we had given undoubted evidence of surrender, and contrary to all rules of warfare.

H. N. REVELLE

Sworn to before me at Cairo, Ill., this 17th day of April, 1864.

JNO. H. MUNROE
Captain and Assistant Adjutant-General.

STATEMENT OF SANDY ADDISON[10]

Statement of Sandy Addison, private Company A, Sixth U. S. Heavy Artillery (colored):

I, Sandy Addison, private Company A, Sixth U. S. Heavy Artillery (colored), would on oath state the following:

I was in the battle fought at Fort Pillow, Tenn., on the 12th day of April, A. D. 1864, and that I was taken prisoner about 5 p. m. same day. After the fort had been carried by the enemy the U. S. troops took shelter under the bluff of the hill, the officers all being killed or wounded. The white flag was raised by one of the colored men, but they kept firing upon us. I do not know how many, but a great many were killed under the white flag. I was taken over 2 miles, and camped for the night. There were several prisoners with us. The surgeon dressed their wounds. He sent 3 colored men back to the river under the flag of truce. After they had got a little way off the rebels shot them down while they were going back to the boat; afterward they shot a man (he being wounded he could not go fast enough), and made some plantation hands bury him.

I was a prisoner five day, and made my escape.

SANDY (his x mark) ADDISON

Sworn to and subscribed before me this 30th day of April, 1864, at Fort Pickering, Memphis, Tenn.

MALCOM F. SMITH
First Lieut. and Adjt. 6th U. S. Heavy Artillery (colored).

STATEMENT OF FRANK HOGAN[11]

Statement of Frank Hogan, corporal Company A, Sixth U. S. Heavy Artillery (colored).

I, Frank Hogan, corporal in Company A, of the Sixth Regiment U. S. Heavy Artillery (colored), would on oath state the following:

That I was in the battle fought at Fort Pillow, Tenn., on the 12th day of April A. D. 1864; and that I was taken prisoner by the enemy, and I saw Captain Carson[12] and heard some of the enemy ask him if he belonged to a nigger regiment. He told them he did. They then asked how he came here. He told them he was detailed there. Then they told him they would give him a detail, and immediately shot him dead, after being a prisoner without arms. I also saw two lieutenants, whose names I did not know, but who belonged to the Thirteenth Tennessee Cavalry. I also saw them kill 3 sick men that were lying helpless in their tents. I saw them make our men (colored) pull the artillery, whipping them at the same time in the most shameful manner. I also saw them bury 1 of our men alive, being only wounded. I heard Colonel McCulloch, C. S. Army, ask his adjutant how many men were killed and wounded. The adjutant told he had a list of 300, and that all the reports were not in yet. Colonel McCulloch was commanding a brigade. I also heard a captain, C. S. Army, tell Colonel McCulloch, C. S. Army, that 10 men were killed out of his own company.

FRANK (his x mark) HOGAN

Sworn to and subscribed before me this 30th day of April, 1864, at Fort Pickering, Tennessee, Memphis, Tenn.

MALCOM F. SMITH
First Lieut. and Adjt. 6th U. S. Heavy Artillery (colored).

STATEMENT OF JERRY STEWART[13]

Statement of Jerry Stewart, corporal Company A, Sixth U. S. Heavy Artillery (colored):

I, Jerry Stewart, a corporal of Company A, of the Sixth U. S. Heavy Artillery (colored), would on oath state the following:

That I was in the battle fought at Fort Pillow, Tenn., on the 12th day of April, A. D. 1864, and I was taken prisoner about 4 p. m. of the same day by the Confederates. After the enemy had carried the works I saw them shoot about 100 colored men down when they were without arms. They shot down 1 by my side while we were going up the hill, and he fell against me. They shot at me several times, but I did not get wounded. I saw the sutler[14] (A. Alexander) cruelly murdered by the rebels and his pockets [*sic*]. They asked him first where he belonged. He told them he was a sutler. They then told him he was no better than the rest, and they shot him and buried him with the colored men. I heard a lieutenant in the Confederate army say that Federal tried to get away, and he put five balls through him. I saw Capt. Charles J. Epeneter, Lieut. P. Bischoff, First Sergt. John Thompson, of Company A, Sixth Regiment U. S. Heavy Artillery (colored) taken prisoners. Lieut. D. Hubank [J. J. Eubank?] told me to tell him if there were any nigger officers taken prisoners, and to point them out to him. I told them I did not know of any. A private soldier of the Confederate army told me that all the colored boys that could escape had best to do so by all means, for General Forrest was going to burn or whip them to death after they got farther south.

JERRY (his x mark) STEWART

Sworn and subscribed before me this 30th day of April, 1864, at Fort Pickering, Memphis, Tenn.

MALCOLM F. SMITH
First Lieut. and Adjt. 6th U. S. Heavy Artillery (colored).

STATEMENT OF HENRY F. WEAVER[15]

Fort Pickering, Tennessee, *April 22, 1864*

Statement of Henry F. Weaver, first sergeant Company C, Sixth U. S. Heavy Artillery (colored), of the battle of Fort Pillow, Tenn., on the 12th day of April, 1864.

I called the roll of my company soon after daylight, and had gone to the bank of the river, and was there talking to Second Lieut. T. W. McClure, of my company, and had not been there long when we heard an uncommon noise and commotion around headquarters, and soon the cry that the rebels were coming. We had the company fall in as soon as possible, when we were ordered to take possession of two 10-pounder Parrott guns[16], and soon another order to take them inside the works, which was done immediately and put in battery on the south end of the works. Lieutenant McClure taking command of the right gun and giving me the left gun, for which I had to build a platform before it could be used with any effect; but the platform was soon built and the gun placed on in position, and I was firing at the advancing enemy as they came in sight. In the mean time Company B, Thirteenth Tennessee Cavalry, had left their camp on a hill in front of our main fort and came rushing back in disorder, leaving their horses and all their camp equipage behind. The rebels soon commenced running off the horses under a brisk fire of musketry and a section of artillery of Company D, Second U. S. Light Artillery (colored), commanded by First Lieutenant Hunter. Still farther to the left was a section of light artillery, manned by Company A, Sixth U. S. Heavy Artillery, under the command of Captain Epeneter and Lieutenant Bischoff. By this time (8 o'clock) the enemy's sharpshooters had commenced a brisk fire on the fort, which was kept up with little intermission until about 2 o'clock[17], when a flag of truce was sent in demanding surrender. Early in the action Lieutenant Hill, Company C, Sixth U. S. and post adjutant, was killed while outside the fort setting fire to the quarters of the Thirteenth Cavalry, and it was not long before Major Booth, of the Sixth U. S., and commander of the post, was killed, falling near the trail of my gun, and was carried away. The command devolved upon Major Bradford, of the Thirteenth Tennessee Cavalry. About noon the rebels commenced receiving re-enforcements, and soon advanced close up to the fort, getting into the houses of the cavalry and some rifle pits we had made a few days before, and which proved of more use to them than to us, and kept up such a brisk fire that it was almost impossible to work the guns. The cannoneers were all killed or wounded at my place except one or two, and also at Lieutenant Hunter's gun, and my ammunition was almost gone; and I will here state that not more than one in five of the shells burst, owing to poor fuses. It was near 2 o'clock when a flag of truce was seen advancing, and the firing ceased on both sides, and an officer was sent by Major Bradford to see what was wanted. He returned with a demand for our surrender, stating that our brave defense had entitled us to be treated as prisoners of war; but if we did not surrender they should charge our works, and we would have to take the consequences. All this time the rebels took advantage of the truce and moved up close to our works, and took their positions ready for a charge. The demand to surrender was refused, and up to this time but few had been killed but a good many wounded; but now the charge came, and as they came up they gave their usual yell,[18] and the Thirteenth Cavalry fled for the banks of the river. When the cavalry commenced to break our colored men wavered, and the rebels had by this time succeeded in entering the fort. Lieutenant Van Horn begged and ordered them to stop, but each one sought safety in flight, as the rebels had commenced an indiscriminate slaughter of the black soldiers, and, as far as I could see, every one was shot down as fast as the rebels could shoot their guns and revolvers. Some were shot down so close to me that they would nearly fall on me. I surrendered, the rebel remarking that they did not shoot white men, but wanted to know what in hell I was there fighting with the damned nigger for. I soon got away from him, for he was too intent on murder to mind me; but had gone but a few steps when another rebel met me and demanded my greenbacks, and after robbing me of everything but my clothes he left me as not worthy of his further notice. I then went down the river to the quartermaster's house, where I found Lieutenant Van Horn. We staid there about ten minutes, when a rebel came in and again demanded our surrender. I told him I had done so twice already. He then ordered us to follow him. We did, going up into town and into a store, where he commenced to pillage and I to get on some citizen's clothing, which I soon did, and got out of the store. I now missed Lieutenant Van Horn, and did not see him again until the next Sunday, when I found he had escaped and got back to Fort Pickering before me. . . .

REPORT OF ACTING MASTER WILLIAM FERGUSON, U. S. NAVY, OF THE CAPTURE OF FORT PILLOW.[19]

U. S. Steamer Silver Cloud
Off Memphis, Tenn., April 14, 1864.

Sir: In compliance with your request that I should forward to you a written statement of what I witnessed and learned concerning the treatment of our troops by the rebels at the capture of Fort Pillow by their forced under General Forrest, I have the honor to submit the following report:

Our garrison at Fort Pillow, consisting of some 350 colored troops and 200 of the Thirteenth Tennessee Cavalry, refusing to surrender, and the place was carried by assault about 3 p. m. of the 12th instant.

I arrived off the fort at 6 a. m. on the morning of the 13th instant. Parties of rebel cavalry were picketing the hills around the fort, and shelling those away I made a landing and took board some of the 20 of our troops (some badly wounded), who had concealed themselves along the bank and came out when they saw my vessel. While doing so I was fired upon by rebel sharpshooters posted on the hills, and 1 wounded man limping down to the vessel was shot.

About 8 a. m. the enemy sent in a flag of truce with a proposal from General Forrest that he would put me in possession of the fort and the country around until 5 p. m. for the purpose of burying our dead and removing our wounded, whom he had no means of attending to. I agreed to the terms proposed, and hailing the steamer Platte Valley, which vessel I had conveyed up from Memphis, I brought her alongside and had the wounded brought down from the fort and battle-field and placed on board of her. Details of rebel soldiers assisted us in this duty, and some soldiers and citizens on board the Platte Valley volunteered for the same purpose.

We found about 70 wounded men in the fort and around it, and buried, I should think 150 bodies. All the buildings around the fort and the tents and huts in the fort had been burned by the rebels and amount the embers the charred remains of numbers of our soldiers who had suffered a terrible death in the flames could be seen.

All the wounded who had strength enough to speak agreed that after the fort was taken an indiscriminate slaughter of our troops was carried on by the enemy with a furious and vindictive savageness which was never equaled by the most merciless of the Indian tribes. Around on every side horrible testimony to the truth of this statement could be seen. Bodies with gaping wounds, some bayoneted through the eyes, some with skulls beaten through, others with hideous wounds as if their bowels had been ripped open with bowie-knives, plainly told that but little quarter was shown to our troops. Strewn from the fort to the river bank, in the ravines and hollows, behind the logs and under the brush where they had crept for protection from the assassins who pursued them, we found bodies bayoneted, beaten, and shot to death, showing how cold-blooded and persistent was the slaughter of our unfortunate troops.

Of course, when a work is carried by assault there will always be more or less bloodshed, even when all resistance has ceased; but here were unmistakable evidences of a massacre carried on long after any resistance could have been offered, with a cold-blooded barbarity and perseverance which nothing can palliate.

As near as I can learn, there were about 500 men in the fort when it was stormed. I received about 100 men, including the wounded and those I took on board before the flag of truce was sent in. The rebels, I learned, had few prisoners; so that at least 300 of our troops must have been killed in the affair.

I have the honor to forward a list of the wounded officers and men received from the enemy under flag of truce.

I am, general your obedient servant.

W. FERGUSON

Acting Master, U. S. Navy Comdg. U. S. Steamer Silver Cloud.
Major-General Hurlbut

REPORT OF LIEUTS. FRANCIS A. SMITH AND WILLIAM CLEARY, THIRTEENTH TENNESSEE, CAVALRY, OF THE CAPTURE OF FORT PILLOW.[20]

Cairo, ILL.,
April 18, 1864.

General: We have the honor of reporting to you, as the only survivors of commissioned officers of the Thirteenth Tennessee Cavalry, that on the morning of the 12th day of the present month, at about the hour of daylight, the rebels numbering from 5,000 to 7,000,[21] attacked our garrison at Fort Pillow, Tenn., numbering as it did only about 500 effective men.

They at first sent in a flag of truce demanding surrender, which Major Booth, then commanding the post (Major Booth of the Sixth U. S. Heavy Artillery colored) refused. Shortly after this Major Booth was shot through the heart and fell dead.[22]

Maj. William F. Bradford, then commanding the Thirteenth Tennessee Cavalry, assumed command of the fort, and under his orders a continual fire was kept up until 1 p. m., when our cannon and the rifles of the sharpshooters were mowing the rebels down in such numbers that they could not make an advance. The rebels then hoisted a second flag of truce and sent it in, demanding an unconditional surrender. They also threatened that if the place was not surrendered no quarter would be shown. Major Bradford refused to accept any such terms; would not surrender, and sent back word that if such were their intentions they could try it on. While this flag of truce was being sent in the rebel officers formed their forces in whatever advantageous positions they were able to select. They then formed a hollow square around our garrison, placed their sharpshooters within our deserted barracks, and directed a galling fire upon our men. They also had one brigade in the trenches just outside the fort, which had been cut by our men only a few days before, and which provided them good protection as that held by the garrison in the fort.

Their demand of the flag of truce having been refused, the order was given by General Forrest in person to charge upon the works and to show no quarter. Half an hour after the issuance of the order a scene of terror and massacre ensured. The rebels came pouring in solid masses right over the breast-works. Their numbers were perfectly overwhelming. The moment they reached the top of the walls and commenced firing as they descended, the colored troops were panic-stricken, threw down their arms, and ran down the bluff, pursued sharply, begging for life, but escape was impossible. The Confederates had apprehended such a result, and had placed a regiment of cavalry where it could cut off all effective retreat. This cavalry regiment employed themselves in shooting down negro troops as fast as they could make their appearance.

The whites, as soon as they perceived they were also to be butchered inside the fort, also ran down. They had previously thrown down their arms and submitted. In many instances the men begged for life at the hands of the enemy, even on their knees. They were only made to stand upon their feet, and then summarily shot down.

Capt. Theodore F. Bradford[23], of Company A, Thirteenth Tennessee Cavalry, was signal officer for the gun-boat, and was seen by General Forrest with signal flags. The general in person ordered Captain Bradford to be shot. He was instantly riddled with bullets, nearly a full regiment fired their pieces on him. Lieutenant Wilson of Company A, Thirteenth Tennessee Cavalry, was killed after he had surrendered, he having been previously wounded. Lieut. J. C. Ackerstrom, Company E, Thirteenth Tennessee Cavalry, and acting regimental quartermaster, was severely wounded after he surrendered, and then nailed to the side of the house and the house set on fire, burning him to death. Lieut. Cord Revelle, Company E, Thirteenth Tennessee Cavalry, was shot and killed after surrender.

Maj. William F. Bradford, commanding our forces, was fired upon after he had surrendered the garrison. The rebels told him he could not surrender. He ran into the river and swam out some 50 yards, they all the time firing at him but failing to hit him. He was hailed by an officer and told to return to the shore. He did so, but as he neared the shore the riflemen discharged their pieces at him again. Again they missed. He ran up the hill-side among the enemy with a white handkerchief in his hand in token of his surrender, but still they continued to fire upon him. There were several Confederate officers standing near at the time. None of them would order the firing to cease, but when they found they could not hit him they allowed him to give himself up as a prisoner and paroled him to the limits of the camp. They now claim that he violated his parole the same night and escaped. We have heard from prisoners who got away from the rebels that they took Major Bradford out in the Hatchie Bottom and there dispatched him. We feel confident that the story is true.

We saw several negroes burning up in their quarters on Wednesday morning. We saw the rebels come back that morning and shoot at the wounded. We also saw them at a distance running about, hunting up the wounded, that they might shoot them. There were some whites also burning. The rebels also went to the negro hospital, where about 30 sick were kept, and butchered them with their sabers, hacking their heads open in many instances, and the set fire to the buildings. They killed every negro soldier Wednesday morning upon whom they came. Those who were able they made stand up to be shot. In one case a white soldier was found wounded. He had been lying upon the ground nearly twenty-four hours, without food or drink. He asked a rebel soldier to give him something to drink. The latter turned about upon his heel and fired three deliberate shots at him, saying, "Take that, you negro equality." The poor fellow is alive yet, and in the hospital. He can tell the tale from himself. They ran a great many into the river, and shot them or drowned them there. They immediately killed all the officers who were over the negro troops, excepting one, who has since died from his wounds. They took out from Fort Pillow about one hundred and some odd prisoners (white) and 40 negroes. They hung and shot the negroes as they passed along toward Brownsville until they were rid of them all. Out of 600 troops, convalescents included, which were at the fort, they have only about 100 prisoners, all white, and we have about 50 wounded, who are paroled.

Major Anderson, Forrest's assistant adjutant-general, stated that they did not consider colored men as soldiers, but as property, and as such, being used by our people, they had destroyed them this was concurred in by Forrest, Chalmers, and McCulloch, and other officers.

We respectfully refer you to the accompanying affidavit of Hardy N. Revelle, lettered A, and those of Mr. Rufins, lettered B, and Mrs. Williams, lettered C.

Respectfully submitted,

F. A. SMITH
First Lieutenant Company D, 13th Tennessee Cavalry

WILLIAM CLEARY
Second Lieut. Company B, 13th Tennessee Vol. Cavalry

General M. Brayman

STATEMENT OF DANIEL STAMPS[24]

Statement of Daniel Stamps, Company E, Thirteenth Tennessee Cavalry:

I do hereby certify that I was at Fort Pillow, Tenn., on the 12th day of the present month, when it was attacked by the rebels under Forrest. I was ordered out as a sharpshooter, skirmished with the enemy about one hour, when I was called within the fort. We fired very deliberately while we were outside the fort, and I saw a great many fall dead from the effects of our guns. I staid within the fort perhaps about one hour, when I was again take as a sharpshooter to go down under the bluff to repulse the enemy, reported as coming down Coal Creek. We attained a good position where we could see the enemy very plainly, being ourselves secreted behind some logs. I kept us a steady fire all the time I was in this place, until the flag of truce came up, about 1 p. m., killing one of the enemy at nearly every shot. We were next ordered to cease firing. At the very moment the force of the enemy, which had been kept back by our sharpshooting, made an advance. I looked up and saw large bodies of infantry moving down Coal Creek re-enforcing those previously before us, and whose advance we had prevented. When the rebels had got a good position, where they could pick our men off as they came out of the fort, I saw them break ranks and get water out of the river and make every preparation for a fight, after which they resumed their line of battle. This they did while the flag of truce was being considered and all firing had ceased. The demand of the flag of truce having been refused, the firing resumed, and I discharged my piece several times, bringing one rebel down at every shot; thus for about three-quarters of an hour keeping them from an advance. Afterward, when the negroes had given way on the left, I saw them run out of the fort down the bluff close to my vicinity. Then I saw the white soldiers coming down after them, saying the rebels were showing no quarter. I then threw down my gun and ran down with them, closely pursued by the enemy shooting down every man black and white. They said they had orders from Forrest to show no quarter, but to "kill the last God damn one of them." While I was standing at the bottom of the hill, I heard a rebel officer shout out an order of some kind to the men who had taken us, and saw a rebel soldier standing by me. I asked him what the officer had said. He repeated it to me again. It was, "kill the last damn one of them." The soldier replied to his officer that we had surrendered; that we were prisoners and must not be shot. The officer again replied, seeming crazy with rage that he had not been obeyed, "I tell you to kill the last God damned one of them." He then turned and galloped off. I also certify that I saw 2 men shot down while I was under the bluff. They fell nearly at my feet. They had their hands up; had surrendered, and were begging mercy. I also certify that I saw at least 25 negroes shot down, within 10 or 20 paces from the place where I stood. They had also surrendered, and were begging for mercy. I do also certify that on the ensuing morning I saw negroes who were wounded, and had survived the night, shot and killed as fast as they could be found. One rebel threatened to kill me because I would not tell him where a poor negro was who had been wounded badly, but who had crawled off on his hands and knees and hidden behind a log. I was myself also shot some two hours after I had surrendered.

Mound City, Ill., April 23, 1864.

DANIEL (his x mark) STAMPS

Witness: William Cleary,
Second Lieut. Co. B, 13th Tennessee Cavalry Vols.

Sworn and subscribed to before me on this 25th day of April, 1864 at Mound City, Ill.

WM. STANLEY
Lieutenant and Assistant Provost-Marshal.

DOCUMENT 5: "THE FORT PILLOW BUTCHERY"[25]

Reports of the Fort Pillow Massacre were largely spread throughout the northern states by newspaper reports and editorials. The following selection from the New York Times *is typical of the stories that appeared in many northern newspapers following the Fort Pillow battle.*

"The Fort Pillow Butchery."

There is now an overwhelming and painfully minute mass of proof of the truth of the first reports of the rebel massacre of our troops, black and white, at Fort Pillow. We have had, and have given, evidence the evidence of eye-witnesses, the evidence of victims offered in their last moments, evidence of persons who visited the scene of the butchery immediately after it, and we have had other evidence not less conclusive, such as the arrival at Cairo[26] of some of the bodies, which bore upon them marks of the worst barbarities charged against the rebels. It now only requires an official statement of the officers appointed to investigate the matter, to furnish irrefutable proof for history. It was superserviceable labor on the party of any one to deny the massacre, in behalf of the rebels. JEFF. Davis officially proclaimed this to be his policy, and he was backed up in his ferocious proclamation by the whole rebel press. To deny that the rebels would carry out this measure is preposterous to the perception of all of us who know that, atrocious as rebel threats have been, their deeds have always been more bloody than their threats. We have not yet had the Southern defense of the massacre and their jubilations over it; but their organs[27] in the North have already justified it as a perfectly proper act of war.

DOCUMENT 6: TESTIMONY OF WITNESSES BEFORE THE JOINT COMMITTEE ON THE CONDUCT OF THE WAR

The Joint Committee on the Conduct of the War was authorized by both Houses of Congress to conduct an investigation. Appointing a two person subcommittee consisting of Chair, Senator Benjamin F. Wade and Representative Daniel W. Gooch, Wade and Gooch visited a number of Union hospitals and the battle site in an effort to interview eyewitnesses to the battle as well as to assess the condition of the wounded. The result was a report that scathingly criticized the Confederate government for initiating a barbarous and cruel policy toward African-American soldiers. The following documents are transcripts of some of the interviews with participants in the Fort Pillow Massacre, many of them from African-American soldiers who belonged to the 6th United States Colored Heavy Artillery. The Committee's report was based in a host of eye witnesses transcripts that were similar to the examples that follow.

TESTIMONY OF ELIAS FALLS BEFORE THE JOINT COMMITTEE ON THE CONDUCT OF THE WAR[28]

Mound City Hospital
Illinois, April 22, 1864

Elias Falls, (colored,) private, company A, 6th United States heavy artillery, or 1st Alabama artillery, sworn and examined.

By Mr. Gooch:
    Questions. Were you at Fort Pillow when the battle took place there, and it was captured by the rebels?
    Answer. I was there; I was a cook, and was waiting on the captain and major.
    Question. What did you see done there? What did the rebels do after they came into the fort?
    Answer. They killed all the men after they surrendered, until orders were given to stop; they killed all they came to, white and black, after they had surrendered.

Question. The one the same as the others?

Answer. Yes, sir. Till he gave the orders to stop firing.

Question. Till who gave orders?

Answer. They told me his name was Forrest.

Question. Did you see anybody killed or shot there?

Answer. Yes, sir; I was shot after the surrender, as I was marched up the hill by the rebels.

Question. Where were you wounded?

Answer. In the knee.

Question. Was that the day of the fight?

Answer. The same day.

Question. Did you see any men shot the next day?

Answer. I did not.

Question. What did you see done after the place was taken?

Answer. After peace was made some of the secesh[29] soldiers came around cursing the boys that were wounded. They shot one of them about the hand, aimed to shoot him in the head, as he lay on the ground, and hit him in the hand; and an officer told the secesh soldiers if he did that again he would arrest him, and he went off then.

Question. Did they burn any buildings?

Answer. Yes, sir.

Question. Was anybody burned in the buildings?

Answer. I did not see anybody burned; I saw them burn the buildings; I was not able to walk about; I staid in a building that night with some three or four white men.

Question. Do you know anything about their going into the hospital and killing those who were there sick in bed?

Answer. We had some three or four of our men there, and some of our men came in and said they had killed two women and two children.

TESTIMONY OF SERGEANT BENJAMIN ROBINSON BEFORE THE JOINT COMMITTEE ON THE CONDUCT OF THE WAR[30]

Sergeant Benjamin Robinson, (colored,) 6th United States heavy artillery, sworn and examined.

By Mr. Gooch:

Question. Were you at Fort Pillow in the fight there?

Answer. Yes, sir.

Question. What did you see there?

Answer. I saw them shoot two white men right by the side of me after they had laid their guns down. They shot a black man clear over into the river. Then they hallooed to me to come up the hill, and I came up. They said, "Give me your money, you damned nigger." I told them I did not have any. "Give me your money, or I will blow your brains out." Then they told me to lie down, and I laid down, and they stripped everything off me.

Question. This was the day of the fight?

Answer. Yes, sir.

Question. Go on. Did they shoot you?

Answer. Yes, sir. After they stripped me and took my money away from me they dragged me up the hill a little piece, and laid me down flat on my stomach; I laid there till night, and they took me down to an old house, and said they would kill me the next morning. I got up and commenced crawling down the hill; I could not walk.

Question. When were you shot?

Answer. About 3 o' clock.

Question. Before they stripped you?

Answer. Yes, sir. They shot me before they said, "come up."

Question. After you had surrendered?

Answer. Yes, sir; they shot up pretty nearly all of them after they had surrendered.

Question. Did you see anything of the burning of men?

Answer. No, sir.

Question. Did you see them bury anybody?

Answer. Yes, sir.

Question. Did they bury anybody who was not dead?

Answer. I saw one of them working his hand after he was buried; he was a black man. They had about a hundred in there, black and white. The major[31] was buried on the bank, right side of me. They took his clothes all off but his drawers; I was lying right there looking at them. They had my captain's coat, too; they did not kill my captain; a lieutenant told him to give him his coat, and then they told him to go down and pick up those old rags and put them on.

Question. Did you see anybody shot the day after the battle?

Answer. No, sir.

Question. How did you get away?

Answer. A few men came up from Memphis, and got a piece of plank and put me on it, and took me down to the boat.

Question. Were any rebel officers around when the rebels were killing our men?

Answer. Yes, sir; lots of them.

Question. Did they try to keep their men from killing our men?

Answer. I never heard them say so. I know General Forrest rode his horse over me three or four times. I did not know him until I heard his men call his name. He said to some negro men there that he knew them; that they had been in his nigger yard in Memphis. He said he was not worth five dollars when he started, and he got rich trading in negroes.

Question. Where were you from?

Answer. I came from South Carolina.

Question. Have you been a slave?

Answer. Yes, sir.

TESTIMONY OF DANIEL TYLER BEFORE THE JOINT COMMITTEE OF THE CONDUCT OF THE WAR[32]

Daniel Tyler, (colored,) private, company B, 6th United States heavy artillery, sworn and examined.

By Mr. Gooch:

Question. Where were you raised?

Answer. In Mississippi.

Question. Have you been a slave?

Answer. Yes, sir.

Question. Were you in Fort Pillow at the time it was captured by the rebels?

Answer. Yes, sir.

Question. When were you wounded?

Answer. I was wounded after we all surrendered; not before.

Question. At what time?

Answer. They shot me when we came up the hill from down by the river?

Question. Why did you go up the hill?

Answer. They called me up.

Question. Did you see who shot you?

Answer. Yes, sir; I did not know him.

Question. One of the rebels?

Answer. Yes, sir.

Question. How near was he to you?

Answer. I was right at him; I had my hand on the end of his gun.

Question. What did he say to you?

Answer. He said, "Whose gun are you holding?" I said, "Nobody's." He said, "God damn you, I will shoot you," and then he shot me. I let go, and then another one shot me.

Question. Were many shot at the same time?

Answer. Yes, sir, lots of them; lying all around like hogs.

Question. Did you see any one burned?

Answer. No, sir.

Questions. Did you see anybody buried alive?

Answer. Nobody but me.

Question. Were you buried alive?

Answer. Yes, sir; they thought they had killed me. I lay there till about sundown, when they threw us in a hollow, and commenced throwing dirt on us.

Question. Did you say anything?

Answer. No, sir; I did not want to speak to them. I knew if I said anything they would kill me. They covered me up in a hole; they covered me up, all but one side of my head. I heard them say they ought not to bury a man who was alive. I commenced working the dirt away, and one of the secesh made a young one dig me out. They dug me out, and I was carried not far off to a fire.

Question. How long did you stay there?

Answer. I staid there that night and until the next morning, and then I slipped off. I heard them say the niggers had to go away from there before the gunboat came, and that they would kill the niggers. The gunboat commenced shelling up there, and they commenced moving off. I heard them up there shooting. They wanted me to go with them, but I would not go. I turned around, and came down to the river bank and got on the gunboat.

Question. How did you lose your eye?

Answer: They knocked me down with a carbine, and then they jabbed it out.

Question. Was that before you were shot?

Answer. Yes, sir.

Question. After you surrendered?

Answer. Yes, sir; I was going up the hill, a man came down and met me; he had his gun in his hand, and whirled it around and knocked me down, and then took the end of this carbine and jabbed it in my eye, and shot me.

Question. Were any of their officers about there then?

Answer. I did not see any officers.

Question. Were any white men buried with you?

Answer. Yes, sir.

Question. Were any buried alive?

Answer. I heard that one white man was buried alive; I did not see him.

Question. Who said that?

Answer. A young man; he said they ought not to have done it. He staid in there all night; I do not know as he ever got out.

TESTIMONY OF GEORGE SHAW BEFORE THE JOINT COMMITTEE ON THE CONDUCT OF THE WAR[33]

George Shaw, (colored,) company B, 6th United States heavy artillery, sworn and examined.

By Mr. Gooch:

Question. Where were you raised?

Answer. In Tennessee.

Question. Where did you enlist?

Answer. At Fort Pillow.

Question. Were you there at the fight?

Answer. Yes, sir.

Question. When were you shot?

Answer. About four o'clock in the evening.

Question. After you had surrendered?

Answer. Yes, sir.

Question. Where were you at the time?

Answer. About ten feet from the river bank.

Question. Who shot you?

Answer. A rebel soldier.

Question. How near did he come to you?

Answer. About ten feet.

Question. What did he say to you?

Answer. He said, "Damn you, what are you doing here?" I said, "Please don't shoot me." He said, "Damn you, you are fighting against your master." He raised his gun and fired, and the bullets went into my mouth and out the back part of my head. They threw me into the river, and I swam around and hung on there in the water until night.

Question. Did you see anybody else shot?

Answer. Yes, sir; three young boys, lying in the water, with their heads out; they could not swim. They begged them as long as they could, but they shot them right in the forehead.

Question. How near to them were they?

Answer. As close as that stone, (about eight or ten feet.)

Question. How old were the boys?

Answer. Not more than fifteen or sixteen years old. They were not soldiers, but contraband[34] boys, helping us on the breastworks.

Questions. Did you see any white men shot?

Answer. No, sir. I saw them shoot three men the next day.

Question. How far from the fort?

Answer. About a mile and a half; after they had taken them back as prisoners.

Question. Who shot them?

Answer. Private soldiers. One officer said, "Boys, I will have you arrested, if you don't stop killing them boys." Another officer said, "Damn it, let them go on; it isn't our law to take any nigger prisoners; kill every one of them." Then a white man took me to wait on him a little, and sent me back to a house about two hundred yards, and told me to stay all night. I went back and staid until about half an hour by sun. Another man came along and said, "If you will go home with me I will take good care of you, if you will stay and never leave." I did not know what to do, I was so outdone; so I said, "if you will take good care of me, I will go." He carried me out about three miles to a place called Bob Greene's. The one who me there left me, and two others came up, and said, "Damn you, we will kill you, and not be fooling around any longer." I said, "Don't shoot me." One of them said, "Go out and hold my horse." I took a step or two, and he said, "Turn around; I will hold my horse, and shoot you, too." I no sooner turned around than he shot me in the face. I fell down as if I was dead. He shot me again, and hit my arm, not my head. I laid there until I could hear him no more, and then I started back. I got back into Fort Pillow about sun up, and wandered there until a gunboat came along, and I came up on that with about ten others.

TESTIMONY OF MAJOR WILLIAMS BEFORE THE JOINT COMMITTEE ON THE CONDUCT OF THE WAR[35]

Major Williams, (colored,) private, company B, 6th United States heavy artillery, sworn and examined.

By the chairman [Benjamin F. Wade]:

Question. Where were you raised?

Answer. In Tennessee and North Mississippi.

Question. Where did you enlist?

Answer. In Memphis.

Question. Who was your captain?

Answer. Captain Lamburg.

Question. Were you in the fight at Fort Pillow?

Answer. Yes, sir.

Question. Was your captain with you?

Answer. No, sir; I think he was in Memphis.

Question. Who commanded your company?

Answer. Lieutenant Hunter and Sergeant Fox were all the officers we had.

Question. What did you see done there?

Answer. We fought them right hard during the battle, and killed some of them. After a time they sent in a flag of truce. They said afterwards that they did it to make us stop firing until their re-enforcements could come up. They said that they never could have got in if they had not done that; that we had whipped them; that they had never seen such a fight.

Question. Did you see the flag of truce?

Answer. Yes, sir.

Question. What did they do when the flag of truce was in?

Answer. They kept coming up nearer and nearer, so that they could charge quick. A heap of them came up after we stopped firing.

Question. When did you surrender?

Answer. I did not surrender until they all run.

Question. Were you wounded then?

Answer. Yes, sir; after the surrender.

Question. At what time of the day was that?

Answer. They told me it was about half after one o'clock.[36] I was wounded immediately after we retreated.

Question. Did you have any arms in your hands when they shot you?

Answer. No, sir; I was an artillery man, and had no arms.

Question. Did you see the man who shot you?

Answer. No, sir.

Question: Did you hear him say anything?

Answer. No, sir. I heard nothing. He shot me, and it was bleeding pretty free, and I thought to myself, "I will make out it was a dead shot, and may be I will not get another."

Question. Did you see any others shot?

Answer. No, sir.

Question. Was there anything said about giving quarter?

Answer. Major Bradford brought in a black flag which meant no quarter. I heard some of the rebel officers say: "You damned rascals, if you had not fought so hard, but had stopped when we sent in a flag of truce, we would not have done anything to you." I heard one of the officers say: "Kill all the niggers;" another one said: "No; Forrest says take them and carry them with him to wait upon him and cook for him, and put them in jail and send them to their masters." Still they kept shooting. They shot at me after that, but did not hit me; a rebel officer shot at me.

He took aim at my side; at the crack of his pistol I fell. He went on and said, "There's another dead nigger."

Question. Was there any one shot in the hospital that day?

Answer. Not that I know of. I think they all came away and made a raft and floated across the mouth of the creek, and got into a flat bottom.

Question. Did you see any buildings burned?

Answer. I staid in the woods all day Wednesday. I was there Thursday and looked at the buildings. I saw a great deal left that they did not have a chance to burn up. I saw a white man burned up who was nailed up against the house.

Question. A private or an officer?

Answer. An officer; I think it was a lieutenant in the Tennessee cavalry.[37]

Question. How was he nailed?

Answer. Through his hand and feet right against the house.

Question. Was his body burned?

Answer. Yes, sir; burned all over—I looked at him good.

Question. When did you see that?

Answer. On the Thursday after the battle.

Question. Where was the man?

Answer. Right in front of the fort.

Question. Did any one else that you know see the body nailed up there?

Answer. There was a black man there who came up on the same boat I was on.

Question. Was he with you then?

Answer. Yes, sir; and there were some five or six white people there, too, from out in the country who were walking over the place.

TESTIMONY OF FRANK HOGAN BEFORE THE JOINT COMMITTEE ON THE CONDUCT OF THE WAR[38]

Frank Hogan, (colored), sworn and examined.

By the chairman[Benjamin Wade]:

Question. Were you at Fort Pillow on the day of the fight?

Answer. Yes, sir.

Question. In what company and regiment?

Answer. Company A, 6th United States heavy artillery.

Question. What did you see there that day, especially after the fort was taken?

Answer. I saw them shoot a great many men after the fort was taken, officers, and private soldiers, white and black.

Question. After they had given up?

Answer. Yes, sir. I saw them shoot a captain in our battalion, about a quarter of an hour after he had surrendered. One of the secesh called him up to him, and asked him if he was an officer of a nigger regiment. He said, "Yes," and then they shot him with a revolver.

Question. Did they say anything more at the time they shot him?

Answer. Yes, sir, one of them said, "God damn you, I will give you a nigger officer." They talked with him a little time before they shot him. They asked him how he came to be there, and several other questions, and the asked if he belonged to the nigger regiment, and then they shot him. It was a secesh officer who shot him. I was standing a little behind.

Question. What was the rank of the secesh officer?

Answer. He was a first lieutenant. I do not know his name.

Question. Do you know the name of the officer he shot?

Answer. Yes, sir; Captain Carson, company D.[39]

Question. Why did they not shoot you?

Answer. I do not know why they didn't.

Question. How long did you stay with them?

Answer. I staid with them two nights and one day. They took me on Tuesday evening, and I got away from them Thursday morning, about two hours before daylight. They were going to make an early move that morning and they sent me back for some water, and I left with another boy in the same company as myself.

Question. Do you know anything of the rebels burning any of the tents that had wounded men in them?

Answer. I know they set some on fire on fire that had wounded men in them, but I did not see them burn because they would not let us go around to see.

Question. About what time of the day was that?

Answer. It was when the sun was about an hour or three-quarters on from the day of the battle.

Question. Did you hear the men in there after they set the building on fire?

Answer. Yes, sir; I heard them in there. I knew they were in there. I knew that they were sick. I saw them shoot one or two men who came out of the hospital, and when they went into the tents, and then shot them right in the tents. I saw them shoot two of them right in the head. When they charged the fort they did not look into the tents, but when they came back afterwards they shot those sick men in the head. I knew the men, because they belonged to the company I did. One of them was named Dennis Gibbs, and the other was Alfred Flag.

Question. How long had they been sick?

Answer. They had been sick at the hospital in Memphis, and had got better a little, and been brought up here, but they never did any duty here, and went to the hospital. They came out of the hospital and went into these tents, and were killed there. They were in the hospital the morning of the fight. When the fight commenced, they left the hospital and came into the tents inside the fort.

Question. Did you see them bury any of our men?

Answer. I saw them put them in a ditch. I did not see them cover them up.

Question. Were they all really dead or not?

Answer. I saw them bury one man alive, and heard the secesh speak about it as much as twenty times. He was shot in the side, but he was not dead, and was breathing good right along.

Question. Did you see the man?

Answer. Yes, sir.

Question. How came they did bury him when he was alive?

Answer. They said he would die any how, and they would let him stay. Every once in a while, if they put dirt on him, he would move his hands. I was standing right there, and saw him when they put him in, and saw he was not dead.

Question. Have you seen the three bodies that are now lying over beyond the old hospital?

Answer. Yes, sir.

Question. Did you know them?

Answer. I knew one of them. I helped to take him to the hospital on the Sunday before the fight. There was another man there. I knew the company he belonged to, (Company B) but I did not know his name. He was a colored man, but he had hair nearly straight, like a white man or an Indian. He had been sick a great while.

TESTIMONY OF SURGEON HORACE WARDNER BEFORE THE JOINT COMMITTEE ON THE CONDUCT OF THE WAR[40]

Mound City, Illinois, *April 22, 1864*
Surgeon Horace Wardner sworn and examined.

By the chairman [Benjamin F. Wade]:

Question. Have you been in charge of this hospital, Mound City hospital?

Answer. I have been in charge of this hospital continually since the 25th of April, 1863.

Question. Will you state, if you please, what you know about the persons who escaped from Fort Pillow? And how many have been under your charge?

Answer. I have received thirty-four whites, twenty-seven colored men, and one colored woman, and seven corpses of those who died on the way here.

Question: Did any of those you have mentioned escape from Fort Pillow?

Answer. There were eight or nine men, I forget the number, who did escape and come here, the others were paroled. I learned the following facts about that: The day after the battle a gunboat was coming up and commenced shelling the place; the rebels sent a flag of truce for the purpose of giving over into our hands what wounded remained alive; a transport then landed and sent out details to look about the grounds and pick up the wounded there, and bring them on the boat. They had no previous attention.

Question. They were then brought under your charge?

Answer. They were brought immediately into this hospital.

Question. Who commanded that boat?

Answer. I forget the naval officer's name.

Question. How long after the capture of the place did he come along?

Answer. That was the next day after the capture.

Question. Did all who were paroled in this way come under your charge, or did any them go to other hospitals?

Answer. None went to other hospitals that I am aware of.

Question. Please state their condition.

Answer: They were the worst butchered men I have ever seen. I have been in several hard battles, but I have never seen men so mangled as they were; and nearly all of them concur in stating that they received all of their wounds after they had thrown down their arms, surrendered, and asked for quarters. They state that they ran out of the fort, threw down their arms, and ran down the bank to the edge of the river, and were pursued to the top of the bank and fired on from above.

Question. Were there any females there?

Answer. I found one wounded woman from there.

Question. Were there any wounded children or young persons there?

Answer. I have no wounded children or young persons from there?

Question. Those you have received were most combatants, or had been?

Answer. Yes, sir, soldiers, white and colored.

Question. Were any of the wounded here in the hospital in the fort, and wounded while in the hospital?

Answer. I so understand them.

Question. How many in that condition did you understand?

Answer. I learned from those who came here that nearly all who were in the hospital were killed. I received a young negro boy, probably sixteen years old, who was in the hospital there sick with fever, and unable to get away. The rebels entered the hospital, and with a sabre hacked his head, no doubt with the intention of splitting it open. The boy put up his hand to protect his head, and they cut off one or two of his fingers. He was brought here insensible, and died yesterday. I made a post-mortem examination, and found that the outer table of the skull was incised, the inner table was fractured, and a piece driven into the brain.

Question. This was down while he was sick in the hospital?

Answer. Yes, sir, unable to get off his bed.

Question. Have you any means of knowing how many were murdered in that way?

Answer. No positive means, except the statement of the men.

Question. How many do you suppose from the information you have received?

Answer. I suppose there were about four hundred massacred— murdered there.

Question. What proportion white, and what proportion colored, as near as you could ascertain?

Answer. The impression I have, from what I can learn, is, that all the negroes were massacred except about eighty, and all the white soldiers were killed except about one hundred or one hundred and ten.

Question. We have heard rumors that some of these persons were buried alive; did you hear anything about that?

Answer. I have two in the hospital here who were buried alive.

Question. Both colored men?

Answer. Yes, sir.

Question. How did they escape?

Answer. One of them I have not conversed personally, the other I have. He was thrown into a pit, as he states, with a great many others, white and black, several of whom were alive; they were all buried up together. He lay on the outer edge, but his head was nearer the surface; he had one well hand, and with that hand he was able to work a place through which he could breathe, and in that way he got his head out; he lay there for some twenty-four hours, and was finally taken out by somebody. The others, next to him, were buried so deep that they could not get out, and died.

Question. Did you hear anything about any of them having been thrown into the flames and burned?

Answer. I do not know anything about that myself. These men did not say much, and in fact I did not myself have time to question them very closely.

Question. What is the general condition now of the wounded men from Fort Pillow under your charge?

Answer. They are in as good condition as they can be, probably about one-third of them must die.

Question. Is your hospital divided into wards, and can we go through and take the testimony of these men, ward by ward?

Answer. It is divided into wards. The men from Fort Pillow are scattered through the hospital, and isolated to prevent erysipelas. If I should crowd too many badly wounded men in one ward I would be likely to get the erysipelas among them, and lose a great many of them.

By Mr. Gooch:

Question. Are the wounds of these men such as men usually receive in battle?

Answer. The gunshot wounds are; the sabre cuts are the first I have ever seen in the war yet. They seem to have been shot with the intention of hitting the body. There are more body wounds than in an ordinary battle.

Question. Just as if they were close enough to select the parts of the body to be hit?

Answer. Yes, sir; some of them were shot with pistols by the rebels standing from one foot to ten feet of them.

DOCUMENT 7: FROM THE SOUTH[41]

Once press reports of the Fort Pillow Massacre began to circulate, there was an outcry of public outrage in the North with many citizens calling for harsh retaliatory measures to be taken against Forrest, his officers, and soldiers in Confederate Armies. Predictably and understandably, southerners and the southern press began to answer northern charges with charges of their own, primarily that what had happened at Fort Pillow was being grossly and unfairly distorted by the radical Republicans and the northern press for political gain and to stir up hostile emotions against the Confederacy. The following newspaper report is from the Richmond Enquirer *from April 30, 1864 and was printed in the* New York Times *on May 8, 1864.*

"The Very Violent Indignation of the Yankees."
From the Richmond Enquirer, *April 30 [1864]*

The latest United States papers contain the very violent indignation of the Yankees over the alleged Fort Pillow "massacre." The *World*[42] opposes the slaughter of innocent prisoners, which has been recommended, and advises Mr. Lincoln to make on the Richmond authorities "a demand for the surrender of Forrest, or whatever officers was in immediate command of the soldiers by whom the massacre was committed."

The New-York Times has "A word to the European Admirers of Southern Chivalry," which is intended to be particularly severe upon the effects of Slavery on the People of the Confederate States.

The Times, like all other Yankee journals, labors under the difficulty of *unveraciousness*. A habit of falsehood, long persisted in, has made the assertions of Yankee papers valueless in the eyes of Europeans; and since Minister Adams[43] and Secretary Seward[44] resorted to forgery in the case of Mr. Mallory's[45] report, the European public will be slow to regard the statements of the press of a people whose highest authorities have been detected in such infamous crimes. The "so-called" massacre at Fort Pillow is merely an offset to the damaging truths that have made the names of Butler[46], McNeill[47] and Turchin[48] infamous all over the world. In this light it will be understood and appreciated as merely another falsehood.

If the Yankees desire to aggravate the horrors of this war, why take so indirect a way as going through the useless forms of an idle and silly demand? Why not send off a platoon of soldiers and shoot down three or four hundred prisoners, and send us word? Then we shall execute doubly that number, and thus the difficulties of an exchange be soon removed.

The officer who is charged with this "so-called massacre, Gen. Chalmers, was entertained by some Union officers on board of the steamer *Platte Valley*. This does not look as if there had been any "massacre." The *Journal of Commerce* publishes a rational and probably very correct account of the affair.

We find in the New-York Times that Gen. Patton Anderson[49] has sent to Gen. Hatch[50] a letter giving the names and condition of the Yankee wounded at the battle of Olustee[51], in which we find the colored troops reported to a large extent. If "massacre" were a policy, why would Gen. Anderson adopt a humane and Gen. Forrest a savage course? We have seen no evidence of any "massacre" whatever, but should it become necessary to put a garrison to the sword, under the law of war, we should expect the whites to be shot and the negroes to be sold. A negro at $5,000 is too valuable to be shot.

DOCUMENT 8: CORRESPONDENCE BETWEEN NATHAN BEDFORD FORREST AND UNION MAJ. GEN. C. C. WASHBURN

In the aftermath of the Fort Pillow Massacre, General Nathan Bedford Forrest remained sensitive to the charges that he had perpetuated a massacre at Fort Pillow. In June and July, 1864, Forrest was involved in an extended correspondence with Union Major General Cadwallader Colden Washburn, a Maine Republican who commanded the district of Western Tennessee, headquartered in Memphis. These letters show Forrest attempting to justify his actions at Fort Pillow, while demanding to know if official Union policy was to show "no quarter" to potential Confederate prisoners of war.

Headquarters Forrest's Cavalry[52]
In the Field, June 14, 1864

[Maj. Gen. C. C. Washburn:]

General: I have the honor herewith to inclose a copy of [a] letter received from Brigadier-General Buford,[53] commanding U. S. forces at Helena, Ark., addressed to Col. E. W. Rucker,[54] commanding Sixth Brigade of the command; also a letter from myself to General Buford, which I respectfully request you to read and forward to him.

There is a matter also to which I desire to call your attention, which until now I have not thought proper to make the subject of a communication. Recent events render it necessary, in fact, demand it.

It has been reported to me that all negro troops stationed in Memphis took an oath on their knees, in the presence of Major-General Hurlbut[55] and other officers of your army, to avenge Fort Pillow, and that they would show my troops no quarter. Again, I have it from indisputable authority that the troops under Brigadier-General Sturgis,[56] on their recent march from Memphis, publicly and in various places proclaimed no quarter would be shown to my men. As his troops moved into action on the 11th [10th] the officers commanding exhorted their men to remember Fort Pillow, and a large majority of the prisoners we have captured from that command have voluntarily stated that they expected us to murder them; otherwise they would have surrendered in a body rather than have taken to the bush after the being run down and exhausted. The recent battle of Tishomingo Creek[57] was far more bloody than it would otherwise have been but for the fact that your men evidently expected to be slaughtered when captured, and both sides acted as though neither felt safe in surrendering, even when further resistance was useless. The prisoners captured by us say they felt condemned by the announcement, &c., of their own commanders, and expected no quarter.

In all my operations since the war began I have conducted the war on civilized principles, and desire still to do so, but it is due to my command that they should know the position they occupy and the policy you intend to pursue. I therefore respectfully ask whether my men now in your hands are treated as other Confederate prisoners; also, the course intended to be pursued in regard to those who may hereafter fall into your hands.

I have in my possession quite a number of wounded officers and men of General Sturgis' command, all of whom have been treated as well as we are able to treat them, and are mostly in charge of a surgeon left at Ripley by General Sturgis to look after the wounded. Some of them are too severely wounded to be removed at present. I am willing to exchange them for any men of my command you may have, and as soon as they are able to be removed will give them safe escort through my lines in charge of the surgeon left with them. I made such an arrangement with Major-General Hurlbut when he was in command at Memphis, and am willing to renew it, provided it is desired, as it would be better than to subject them to the long and fatiguing trip necessary to a regular exchange at City Point, Va.

I am, very respectfully, your obedient servant,

N. B. Forrest
Major-General

Headquarters District of West Tennessee[58]
Memphis, Tenn., June 19, 1864

Maj. Gen. N. B. Forrest
Commanding Confederate Forces:

General: Your communication of the 14th instant is received. The letter to Brigadier-Buford will be forwarded to him.

In regard to that part of your letter which relates to the colored troops, I beg to say that I have already sent a communication on the same subject to the officer in command of the Confederate forces at Tupelo. Having understood that Maj. Gen. S. D. Lee[59] was in command there, I directed my letter to him. A copy of it I inclose.

You say in your letter that it has been reported to you 'that all the negro troops stationed at Memphis took an oath on their knees, in the presence of Major-General Hurlbut and other officers of our army, to avenge Fort Pillow, and that they would show your troops no quarter.' I believe it is true that the colored troops did take such an oath, but not in the presence of General Hurlbut. From what I can learn, this act of theirs was not influenced by any white officer, but was the result of their own sense of what was due to themselves and their fellows, who had been mercilessly slaughtered. I have no doubt that they went into the field as you allege, in full belief that they would be murdered in case they fell into your hands. The affair at Fort Pillow fully justified that belief. I am not aware as to what they proclaimed on their late march, and it may be as you say, that they declared that no quarter would be given to any of your men that might fall into their hands. Your declaration that you have conducted the war on all occasions on civilized principles cannot be accepted, but I receive with satisfaction the intimation in your letter that the recent slaughter of colored troops at the battle of Tishomingo Creek resulted rather from the desperation with which they fought than a predetermined intention to give them no quarter. You must have learned by this time that the attempt to intimidate the colored troops by indiscriminate slaughter has signally failed, and that instead of a feeling of terror you have aroused a spirit of courage and desperation that will not down at your bidding.

I am left in doubt by your letter as to the course you and the Confederate Government intend to pursue hereafter in regards to colored troops, and I beg you to advise me with as little delay as possible as to your intentions. If you intend to treat such of them as fall into your hands as prisoners of war, please so state. If you do not so intend, but contemplate either their slaughter or their return to slavery, please state that, so that we may have no misunderstanding hereafter. If the former is your intention, I shall receive the announcement with pleasure, and shall explain the fact to the colored troops at once, and desire that they recall the oath that they have taken. If the latter is the case, then let the oath stand, and upon those who have aroused this spirit by their atrocities, and upon the Government and the people who sanction it, be the consequences.

In regard to your inquiry relating to prisoners of your command in our hands, I state that they have always received the treatment which a great and humane Government extends to its prisoners. What course will be pursued hereafter toward them must of course depend on circumstances that may arise. If your command hereafter do nothing which should properly exclude them from being treated as prisoners of war, they will so be treated. I thank you for your offer to exchange wounded officers and men in your hands. If you will send them in I will exchange, man for man, so far as I have the ability to do so.

Before closing this letter I wish to call your attention to one case of unparalleled outrage and murder that has been brought to my notice, and in regard to which the evidence is overwhelming. Among the prisoners captured at Fort Pillow was Major Bradford, who had charge of the defenses of the fort, after the fall of Major Booth. After being taken prisoner he started with other prisoners in charge of Colonel Duckworth[60] for Jackson. At Brownsville they rested for the night. The following morning two companies were detailed by Colonel Duckworth to proceed to Jackson with the prisoners. After they had started and proceeded a very short distance, 5 soldiers were recalled by Colonel Duckworth and were conferred with by him. They then rejoined the column, and after proceeding about 5 miles from Brownsville the column was halted and Major Bradford taken about 50 yards from the roadside and deliberately shot by the 5 men who had been recalled by Colonel Duckworth, and his body left unburied upon the ground where he fell. He now lies buried near the spot, and if you desire, you can easily satisfy yourself of the truth of what I assert. I beg leave to say to you that this transaction hardly justifies your remark that your operations have been conducted on civilized principles, and until you take some steps to bring the perpetrators of this outrage to justice the world will not fail to believe that it has your sanction.

I am, general, respectfully, your obedient servant,

C. C. Washburn,

Forrest, Washburn, and Forrest's superior, Major General Stephen D. Lee exchanged several more letters during the course of June and July, 1864. The tone of the correspondence became sharper and more critical with each round of letters. While General Forrest continued to assert that treatment of black soldiers was a political decision that was determined by his civilian superiors in Richmond, Washburn continued to confront him with evidence of the charges of atrocities at Fort Pillow.

Headquarters Forrest's Cavalry[61]
In the Field, June 23, 1864

Maj. Gen. C. C. Washburn
Commanding U. S. Forces, Memphis, Tenn.:

General: Your communication of the 19th instant is received, in which you say "you are in doubt as to the course of the Confederate Government intends to pursue hereafter in regard to colored troops."

Allow me to say that this is a subject upon which I did not and do not propose to enlighten you. It is a matter to be settled by our Governments through their proper officers, and I respectfully refer you to them for a solution to your doubts. You ask me to state whether "I contemplate either their slaughter or their return to slavery." I answer that I slaughter no man except in open warfare, and that my prisoners, both white and black, are turned over to my Government to be dealt with as it may direct. My Government is in possession of all the facts as regards my official conduct and the operations of my command since I entered the service, and if you desire a proper discussion and decision, I refer you again to the President of the Confederate States.

I would not have you understand, however, that in the matter of so much importance I am indisposed to place at your command and disposal any facts desired, when applied for in a matter becoming an officers holding your rank and position, for it is certainly desirable to every one occupying a public position to be place right before the world, and there has been no time since the capture of Fort Pillow that I would not have furnished all the facts connected with its capture had they been applied for properly; but now the matter rests between the two Governments. I have, however, for your information, inclosed you copies of the official correspondence between the commanding officers of Fort Pillow and myself; also copies of a statement by Captain Young[62], the senior officer of the garrison together with (sufficient) extracts from a report of the affair by my aide-de-camp, Capt. Charles W. Anderson, which I approve and indorse as correct.

As to the death of Major Bradford, I knew nothing of it until eight or ten days after it is said to have occurred. On the 13th (the day after the capture of Fort Pillow) I went to Jackson, and the report that I had of the affair was this: Major Bradford was with other officers sent to the headquarters of Colonel McCulloch, and all the prisoners were in charge of one of McCulloch's regiments. Bradford requested the privilege of attending the burial of his brother, which was granted, he giving his parole to return; instead of returning he changed his clothing and started for Memphis. Some of my men were hunting deserters, and came on Bradford just as he had landed on the south bank of Hatchie, and arrested him. When arrested he claimed to be a Confederate soldier belong to Bragg's army[63]; that he had been [home] on furlough, and was then on his way to join his command. As he could show no papers he was believed to be a deserter and was taken to Covington, and not until he was recognized and spoken to by citizens did the guards know that he was Bradford. He was sent by Colonel Duckworth, or taken by him, to Brownsville. All of Chalmers' command were [south] from Brownsville via LaGrange, and as all the other prisoners had been gone some time, there was no chance for them to catch up and place Bradford with them, he was ordered by Colonel Duckworth or General Chalmers to be sent to me at Jackson. I knew nothing of the matter until eight or ten days afterward. I heard that his body was found near Brownsville. I understand that he attempted to escape, and was shot. If he was improperly killed nothing would afford me more pleasure than to punish the perpetrators to the full extent of the law, and to show you how I regard such transactions I can refer you to my demand upon Major-General Hurlbut (no doubt upon file in your office) for the delivery to Confederate authorities of one Col. Fielding Hurst[64] and others of his regiment, who deliberately took out and killed 7 Confederate soldiers, one of whom they left to die after cutting off his tongue, punching out his eyes, splitting his mouth on each side to his ears, and cutting off his privates.

I have mentioned and given you these facts in order that you may have no further excuse or apology for referring to these matters in connection with myself, and to evince to you my determination to do all in my power to avoid the responsibility of causing the adoption of the policy which you seemed determined to press.

In your letter you acknowledge the fact that the negro troops did take an oath on bended knee to show no quarter to my men; and you say further, "you have no doubt they went to the battle-field expecting to be slaughtered," and admit also the probability of their having proclaimed on their [line of] march that no quarter would be shown us. Such being the case, why do you ask for the disavowal on the part of the commanding general of this department or the Government in regard to the loss of life at Tishomingo Creek? That your troops expected to be slaughtered, appears to me, after the oath they took, to be very reasonable and natural expectation. Yet you, who sent them out, knowing and now admitting that they had sworn to such a policy, are complaining of atrocities, and demanding acknowledgements and disavowals on the part of the very men you went forth sworn to slay whenever in your power. I will in all candor and truth say to you that I had only heard these things, but did not believe them to be true; at any rate, to the extent of your admission; indeed, I did not attach to them the importance they deserved, nor did I know of the threatened vengeance, as proclaimed along their lines of march, until the contest was over. Had I and my men known it as you admit it, the battle of Tishomingo Creek would have been noted as the bloodiest battle of the war. That you sanctioned this policy is plain, for you say now "that if the negro is treated as a prisoner of war you will receive with pleasure the announcement, and will explain the fact to your colored troops at once, and desire (not order) that they recall the oath; but if they are either to be slaughtered or returned to slavery, let the oath stand."

Your rank forbids a doubt as to the fact that you and every officer and man of your department is identified with this policy and responsible for it, and I shall not permit you notwithstanding, by your studied language in both your communications, you seek to limit the operations of your unholy scheme and visit its terrible consequences along upon that ignorant, deluded, but unfortunate people, the negro, whose destruction you are planning in order to accomplish ours. The negroes have our sympathy, and so far as consistent with safety will spare them at the expense of those who are alone responsible for the inauguration of worse than savage warfare.

Now, in conclusion, I demand a plain, unqualified answer to two questions, and then I have done with further correspondence with you on this subject. This matter must be settled. In battle and on the battle-field, do you intend to slaughter my men who fall into your hands? If you do not intend to do so, will they be treated as prisoners of war? I have over 2,000 of Sturgis's command prisoners, and will hold every officer and private as hostage until I received your declarations and am satisfied that you carry out in good faith the answers you make, and until I am assured that no Confederate soldier has been foully dealt with from the day of the battle of Tishomingo Creek to this time. It is not yet too late for you to retrace your steps and arrest the storm.

Relying as I do upon that Divine Power which in wisdom disposes of all things; relying also upon the support and approval of my Government and countrymen, and the unflinching bravery and endurance of my troops, and with a consciousness that I have done nothing to produce, but all in my power consistent with honor and the personal safety of myself and command to prevent it, I leave with you the responsibility of bringing about, to use your own language, "a state of affairs to fearful for contemplation."

I am, general, very respectfully, yours, &c.,
N. B. Forrest,
Major-General

Hdqrs. Department of ALA., MISS., And EAST LA.[65]
Meridian, June 28, 1864.

Maj. Gen. C. C. Washburn,
Commanding U. S. Forces, Memphis, Tenn.:

General: I am in receipt of your letter of the 17th instant, and have also before me the reply of Major-General Forrest thereto. Though that reply is full and is approved by me, yet I deem it proper to communicated with you upon a subject so seriously affecting our future conduct and that of the troops under our perspective commands.

Your communication is by no means respectful to me, and is, by implication, insulting to Major-General Forrest. This, however, is overlooked in consideration of the important character of its contents. You assume as correct the exaggerated statement of the circumstances attending the capture of Fort Pillow, relying solely upon the evidence of those who would naturally give a distorted history of the affair. No demand for an explanation has ever been made either by yourself or your Government, a course which would have certainly recommended itself to every one desirous of hearing truth, but on the contrary, you seem to have been perfectly willing to allow your soldiers to labor under false impressions upon a subject involving such terrible consequences. Even the formality of parades and oaths have been resorted to for the purpose of inciting your colored troops to the perpetration of deeds of which you say "will lead to consequences too fearful to contemplate."

As commanding officer of this department I desire to make the following statement concerning the capture of Fort Pillow, a statement supported in great measure by the evidence of one of your own officers captured at that place.

The version given by you and your Government is untrue, and not sustained by the facts to the extent that you indicate. The garrison was summoned in the usual manner, and its commanding officer assumed the responsibility of refusing the surrender, after having been informed by General Forrest of his ability to take the fort, and of his fears as to what the result would be in case the demand was not complied with. The assault was made under heavy fire and with considerable loss to the attacking party. Your colors were never lowered, and your garrison never surrendered, but retreated from the fort to the cover of the gun-boats with arms in their hands, and instantly using them. This was true, particularly of your colored troops, who had been firmly convinced by your teachings of the certainty of their slaughter in case of capture. Even under these circumstances many of your men, white and black, were taken prisoners.

I respectfully refer you to history for numerous cases of indiscriminate slaughter [after successful assault], even under less aggravated circumstances. It is generally conceded by all military precedent that where the issue has been fairly presented and the ability displayed, fearful results are expected to follow a refusal to surrender. The case under consideration is almost an extreme one. You had a servile race, armed against their masters and in a country which had been desolated by almost unprecedented outrages. I assert that our officers, with all these circumstances against them, endeavored to prevent the effusion of blood, and as an evidence of this I refer you to the fact that both white and colored prisoners were taken, and are now in our hands. As regards the battle of Tishomingo Creek, the statements of your negro witnesses are not to be relied on. In their panic they acted as ought have to be expected from their previous impressions. I do not think many of them were killed. They are yet wandering over the country, attempting to return to their masters.[66] With reference to the status of those captured at Tishomingo Creek and Fort Pillow, I will state that, unless otherwise ordered by my Government, they will not be regarded as prisoners of war, but will be retained and humanely treated, subject to such future instructions as may be indicated.

Your letter contains many implied threats. These you can of course make, and your are fully entitled to any satisfaction that you may feel from having made them. It is my intention, and that also of my subordinate officers, to conduct war upon civilized principles, provided you permit us to do so, and I take this occasion to state that we will not shrink from any responsibilities that your actions may force upon us. We are engaged in the struggle for the protection of our homes and firesides, for the maintenance of our national existence and liberty. We have counted the cost and are prepared to go to any extremes, and although it is far from our wish to fight under the black flag, still if you drive us to it we will accept the issue. Your troops virtually fought under it at the battle of Tishomingo Creek, and prisoners taken there state that they went into the battle under the impression that they were to [would] receive no quarter, and, I suppose, with the determination to give none. I will further remark that if it is raised, so far as your soldiers are concerned, there can be no distinction for the unfortunate people whom you pretend to be aiding are not considered entirely responsible for their acts, influenced as they are by the superior intellect of their white brothers.

I inclose for your consideration certain papers touching the Fort Pillow affair, which were procured from the writer after exaggerated statements of your press were seen.[67]

I am, general. yours, respectfully,

S. D. LEE
Lieutenant-General

Headquarters District of West Tennessee[68]
Memphis, Tenn., July 2, 1864

Maj. Gen. N. B. Forrest
Commanding Confederate Forces, near Tupelo:

General: Your communications of the 20th and 23d ultimo are received. Of the tone and temper of both I do not complain. The desperate fortunes of a bad cause excuse much irritations of temper, and I pass by it. Indeed, I receive it as a favorable augury and as evidence that you are not indifferent to the opinions of the civilized world.

In regard to the Fort Pillow affair, it is useless to prolong the discussion. I shall forward your report, which you did me the favor to inclose, to my Government, and you will receive the full benefit of it. The record is now made up, and a candid world will judge of it. I beg leave to send you, herewith, a copy of the report of the investigating committee of the U. S. Congress on the affair.[69]

In regard to the treatment of Major Bradford, I refer you to the testimony contained in the report from which you will see that he was not attempting to escape when shot. It will be easy to bring the perpetrators of the outrage to justice if you so desire. I will add what I have heretofore said, that I have it from responsible and truthful citizens of Brownsville, that when Major Bradford was started under an escort for your headquarters at Jackson, General Chalmers remarked that "he would never reach there." You call attention apparently as an offset to this affair of Major Bradford to outrages said to have been committed by Col. Fielding Hurst and others of his regiment (Sixth Tennessee Cavalry). The outrages, if committed as stated by you, are disgraceful and abhorrent to every brave and sensitive mind. On receiving your letter, I sent at once for Colonel Hurst, and read him the extract pertaining to him. He indignantly denies the charge against him, and until you furnish me the names of the parties murdered, and the time when, and the place where, the offense was committed, with the names of witnesses, it is impossible for me to act. When you do that, you may rest assured that I shall use every effort in my power to have the parties accused tried, and, if found guilty, properly punished.

In regard to the treatment of colored soldiers, it is evidently useless to discuss the question further. Your attempt to shift from yourself upon me the responsibility of the inauguration of a "worse than savage warfare," is too strained and far-fetched to require any response. The full and cumulative evidence contained in the Congressional report I herewith forward, points to you as the person responsible for the barbarisms already committed. It was your soldiers who at Fort Pillow raised the black flag, and while shooting, bayoneting, and otherwise maltreating the Federal prisoners in their hands, shouted to each other in hearing of their victims that was done by "Forrest's orders." Thus far, I cannot learn that you have made any disavowal of these barbarities. Your letters to me inform me confidently that you have always treated our prisoners according to the rules of civilized warfare, but your disavowal of the Fort Pillow barbarities, if you intend to make any, should be full, clear, explicit, and published to the world. The United States Government is, as it always has been, lenient and forbearing, and it is not yet too late for you to secure yourself and soldiers a continuance of treatment due to honorable warriors, by a public disclaimer of the barbarities already committed, and a vigorous effort to punish the wretches who committed them. But I say to you now, clearly and unequivocally, that such measure of treatment as you mete out to Federal soldiers will be measured to you again. If you give no quarter, you must expect none; if you observe the rules of civilized warfare, and treat our prisoners in accordance with the laws of war, your prisoners will be treated, as they ever have been, with kindness. If you depart from these principles, you may expect such retaliation as the laws of war justify. That you may know what the laws of war are, as understood by my Government, I beg leave to inclose a copy of General Orders, No. 100, from the War Department, Adjutant-General's Office, Washington, April 24, 1863.[70]

I have the honor to be, sir, very respectfully yours,

C. C. WASHBURN,
Major-General

Memphis, Tenn.[71]
September 13, 1864

Maj. Gen. C. C. Washburn,
Commanding District West Tennessee:

General: I have the honor to address you in regards to certain papers forwarded you by Major-General Forrest, of the so-called Confederate army signed by me under protest while a prisoner of war at Cahaba, Ala.:

I would call your attention to the manner in which those papers were procured about April 27th last. All Federal prisoners (except colored soldiers) were sent to Andersonville and Macon, Ga., myself among the number. About ten days after my arrival at Macon prison, a Confederate captain, with 2 men as guard, came to that prison with an order for me to return to Cahaba. I appealed to the officer in command to know why I was taken from the other officers, but received no explanation. Many of my friends among the Federal officers who had been prisoners longer than myself felt uneasy at the proceeding, and advised me to make my escape going back, as it was likely a subject of retaliation. Consequently I felt considerable uneasiness of mind. On returning to Cahaba, being quite unwell, I was placed in hospital under guard, with still no explanation from the military authorities. On the day following I was informed by a sick Federal officer, also in the hospital, that he had learned that I had been recognized by some Confederate as a deserter from the Confederate army, and that I was to be court-martialed and shot. The colored waiters about the hospital told me the same thing, and although I knew that the muster-rolls of my country would show that I had been in the volunteer service since 1st of May, 1861, I still felt uneasy, having fresh in my mind Fort Pillow, and the summary manner the Confederate officers have of disposing of men on some occasions.

With the above impressions on my mind, about three days after my return to Cahaba I was sent for by the provost-marshal, and certain papers handed me, made out by General Forrest, for my signature. Looking over the papers I found that signing them would be an indorsement of General Forrest's official report of the Fort Pillow affair. I, of course, returned the papers, positively refusing to have anything to do with them. I was sent for again the same day with request to sign other papers of the same tendency, but modified. I again refused to sign the papers but sent General Forrest a statement, that although I considered some of the versions of the Fort Pillow affair which I had read in their own papers exaggerated (said to be copies of Federal papers), I also thought that his own official report was equally so in some particulars. Here the matter rested about one week, when I was sent for by Col. H. C. Davis, commander of post at Cahaba, who informed me that General Forrest had sent Judge P. T. Scruggs[72] to see me and have a talk with me about the Fort Pillow fight. I found the judge very affable, and rather disposed to flatter me. He said that General Forrest thought that I was a gentleman and a soldier, and that the general had sent him (the judge) down to see me and talk to me about the Fort Pillow fight. He then went on to tell over a great many things that were testified to before the military commission which I was perfectly ignorant of, never having seen the testimony. He then produced papers which General Forrest wished me to sign. Upon examination I found them about the same as those previously show me, and refused again to sign them; but the judge was very importunate finally prevailed upon me to sign the papers you have in your possession, pledging himself that if I wished it they should only be seen by General Forrest himself; they were not intended to be used by him as testimony, but merely for his own satisfaction.

I hope, general, that these papers signed by me, or rather extorted from me while under duress, will not be used by my Government to my disparagement, for my only wish now is, after over three years' service, to recruit my health, which has suffered badly by imprisonment, and go in for the war.

I have the honor, general, to be your obedient servant,

JOHN T. YOUNG
Captain Company A, Twenty-fourth Missouri Infantry.

Notes

Introduction

1 George Fitzhugh, *Cannibals All! or Slaves Without Masters*, ed. C. Vann Woodward (Cambridge, MA: Belknap Press, 1960).

2 Debow quotation from Robert W. Johannsen, ed. *Democracy on Trial: A Documentary History of the American Life, 1845–1877*, Second edition (Urbana, IL: University of Illinois Press, 1988), 52; Ulrich B. Phillips, "The Central Theme of Southern History," *American Historical Review* 34 (1928): 30–43 (quote, 31).

3 Lincoln quote is from *The Political Thought of Abraham Lincoln*, Richard Current, ed. (New York: Macmillan Publishing, Co., 1967), 133–134. On the free labor argument, see Eric Foner, *Free Soil, Free Labor Free Men: The Ideology of the Republican Party Before the Civil War* (New York: Oxford University Press, 1970).

4 Seward quote from Johannsen, ed., *Democracy on Trial*, 138.

1 Means to an End

1 James McPherson, *Battle Cry of Freedom: The Civil War Era* (New York: Oxford University Press, 1988), 252–257.

2 The other candidates in the presidential election were Stephen A. Douglas of the northern Democratic party, John C. Breckinridge of the southern Democratic party, and John Bell of the Constitutional Union party. After the firing on Fort Sumter and Lincoln's call for 75,000 volunteers, the Border States of Arkansas, North Carolina, Tennessee, and Virginia seceded from the Union. The slave states of Delaware, Kentucky, Maryland, and Missouri stayed in the Union; however, their support for the Union was tepid and precarious at times, particularly in the early phases of the conflict.

3 Robert W. Johannsen, ed. *The Lincoln–Douglas Debates of 1858* (New York: Oxford University Press, 1965), 254, 316.

4 Ibid., 162. For a comprehensive summary and analysis of the Lincoln-Douglas debates, see Allen C. Guelzo, *Lincoln and Douglas: The Debates that Defined America* (New York: Simon & Schuster, 2008).

5   Jean H. Baker, *Affairs of Party: The Political Culture of Northern Democrats in the Mid-Nineteenth Century* (Ithaca, NY: Cornell University Press, 1983), 213–258; Dan Monroe and Bruce Tap, *Shapers of the Great Debates on the Civil War: A Biographical Dictionary* (Westport, CT: Greenwood Press, 2005), 108–111.

6   V. Jacque Voegeli, *Free But Not Equal: The Midwest and the Negro During the Civil War* (Chicago: University of Chicago Press, 1967), 1–4; Leon F. Litwack, *North of Slavery: The Negro in the Free States, 1790–1860* (Chicago: University of Chicago Press, 1961), 15–78, passim; Joanna D. Cowden, *"Heaven Will Frown upon Such a Cause as This": Six Democrats Who Opposed Lincoln's War* (Lanham, MD: University Press of Maryland, 2001), 162; Gary W. Gallagher, *The Union War* (Cambridge, MA: Harvard University Press, 2011), 43–44; Eugene Berwanger, *The Frontier Against Slavery: Western Anti-Negro Prejudice and the Slavery Extension Controversy* (Urbana, IL: University of Illinois Press, 1964), 1–4, 44–49.

7   Litwack, *North of Slavery*, 20–25. A more recent article that takes a more positive view of colonization is Douglas R. Edgerton, "Averting a Crisis: The Proslavery Critique of the American Colonization Society," *Civil War History* 43 (1997): 142–156.

8   Burrus M. Carnahan, *Act of Justice: Lincoln's Emancipation Proclamation and the Law of War* (Lexington, KY: University of Kentucky Press, 2007), 5–23 (quote, 23).

9   Carnahan, *Act of Justice*, 48–49; Mark Grimsely, *The Hard Hand of War: Union Military Policy Toward Southern Civilians, 1861–1865* (Cambridge, MA: Harvard University Press, 1995), 23–35; McPherson, *Battle Cry of Freedom*, 312.

10   Gallagher, *Union War*, 34, passim.

11   Eric Foner, *Fiery Trial: Abraham Lincoln and American Slavery* (New York: W. W. Norton & Company, 2010), 176–180; Carnahan, *Act of Justice*, 76–79; Lincoln to O. H. Browning, September 22, 1861, in Roy P. Basler, ed. *The Collected Works of Abraham Lincoln* (New Brunswick, NJ: Rutgers University Press, 1953), Bruce Tap, *Over Lincoln's Shoulder: The Committee on the Conduct of the War* (Lawrence, KS: University Press of Kansas, 1998), 81–82.

12   Foner, *Fiery Trial*, 206–207.

13   Sumner to Wendell Phillips, August 8, 1861, in Beverly Wilson Palmer, ed., *The Selected Letters of Charles Sumner* (Boston: Northeastern University Press, 1990), 2: 75; Catherine Clinton, *Harriet Tubman: The Road To Freedom* (New York: Back Bay Books, 2004), 162 (quote); Dudley Taylor Cornish, *The Sable Arm: Negro Troops in the Union Army* (New York: W. W. Norton & Company, 1956), 4–5.

14   Foner, *Fiery Trial*, 169–170; Ira Berlin, Joseph P. Reidy, and Leslie S. Rowland, eds., *Freedom's Soldiers: The Black Military Experience in the Civil War* (Cambridge: Cambridge University Press, 1998), 3–4.

15   Foner, *Fiery Trial*, 174; Carnahan, *Act of Justice*, 88–90.

16   Foner, *Fiery Trial*, 194–202; Richard Carwadine, *Lincoln: A Life of Purpose and Power* (New York: Vintage Books, 2007), 201–203.

17   George B. McClellan to Abraham Lincoln, July 7, 1862, in Stephen W. Sears, ed., *The Civil War Papers of George B. McClellan: Selected Correspondence 1860–1865* (New York: Da Capo Press, 1992), 344.

18   Cornish, *The Sable Arm*, 46; Lincoln to Horace Greeley, August 22, 1862 in Roy P. Basler, ed., *The Collected Works of Abraham Lincoln* (New Brunswick, NJ: Rutgers University Press, 1953), 5: 388–389.

19   Carnahan, *Act of Justice*, 107–109 (quote, 109).

20   McPherson, *Battle Cry of Freedom*, 557–558; Carnahan, *Act of Justice*, 108–110.

21   On the Copperhead opposition to emancipation, see Jennifer L. Weber, *Copperheads: The Rise and Fall of Lincoln's Opponents* (New York: Oxford University Press, 2006), 5–7, passim; Frank L. Klement, *The Copperheads of the MiddleWest* (Chicago, IL: University of Chicago Press, 1960), 13–17, passim; idem., "Midwestern Opposition to Lincoln's Emancipation Policy," *Journal of Negro History* 49 (July, 1964): 169–183; Bruce Tap, "Race, Rhetoric, and Emancipation: The Election of 1862 in Illinois," *Civil War History* 39 (June, 1993): 101–125; John David Smith, "'Let us All Be Grateful That We Have Colored Troops that Will Fight,'" in John David Smith, ed., *Black Soldiers in Blue* (Chapel Hill, NC: University of North Carolina Press, 2002), 7 (quote); *Macomb Eagle* (Illinois), September 27, 1862.

22   *Chicago Times* quotes from Tap, "Race, Rhetoric, and Emancipation," 106; "Remarks to Deputation of Western Gentlemen," August 4, 1862, in Basler, ed., The *Collected Works of Abraham Lincoln*, 5: 356–357; Cornish, *Sable Arm*, 18–24; Benjamin Quarles, *The Negro in the Civil War*, 1953 reprint (New York: Da Capo Press, 1989), 108–109.

23   "Attack on General Hunter," July 5, 1862, in *The Selected Papers of Thaddeus Stevens*, Beverly Wilson Palmer, ed., (Pittsburgh, PA: University of Pittsburgh Press, 1997), 1: 309–317 (quotes, 314–315.

24   Cornish, *Sable Arm*, 56–86; Joseph T. Glatthaar, *Forged in Battle: The Civil War Alliance Between Black Soldiers and White Officers* (New York: The Free Press, 1990), 6–7.

25   Berlin, *Freedom's Soldiers*, 7.

26   "Address on Colonization to a Deputation of Negroes," August 14, 1862, in Basler, ed., *Collected Works*, 5: 370–375.

27   Glatthaar, *Forged in Battle*, 31–35, 83–85 (quote, 83); "Sambo's Right to be Kilt," in Charles Halpine, *The Life and Adventures, Songs, Services, and Speeches of Private Miles O'Reilly* (New York: Carlton, 1864), 55; Samuel Kirkwood to Henry Halleck, August 5, 1862, in Berlin, *Freedom's Soldiers*, 88; "Attack on General Hunter," July 5, 1862, in *The Selected Papers of Thaddeus Stevens*, 1: 315.

28   "G" to *Mercury*, March 3, 1863 in Virginia Matzke Adams, ed., *On the Altar of Freedom: A Black Soldier's Civil War Letters from the Front* (Amherst, MA: University of Massachusetts Press, 1991), 4; Berlin, *Freedom's Soldiers*, 22; Letter of Corporal John H. B. Payne to *Christian Recorder*, May 24, 1864 (printed June 11, 1864), in Edwin S. Redkey, ed., *A Grand Army of Black Men: Letters from African-American Soldiers in the Union Army, 1861–1865* (Cambridge: Cambridge University Press, 1992), 208.

29   Cornish, *Sable Arm*, 105–126 (quote, 110); Michael T. Meier, "Lorenzo Thomas and the Recruitment of Blacks in the Mississippi Valley, 1863–1865," in John David Smith, ed., *Black Soldiers in Blue*, 249–268; Berlin, *Freedom's Soldiers*, 13.

30   Cornish, *Sable Arm*, 130–131 (quote, 131).

31   Glathaar, *Forged in Battle*, 66–67; Berlin, *Freedom's Soldiers*, 24–28, (quote, 28). Sherman quote from John F. Marszalek, *Sherman: A Soldier's Passion for Order* (New York: The Free Press, 1993), 271. On Sherman's position, see also Anne J. Bailey, "The USCT in the Confederate Heartland, 1864," In John David Smith ed., *Black Soldiers in Blue*, 227–232.

32 Bell Irvin Wiley, *The Life of Billy Yank: The Common Soldier of the Union Army*, 1952 rpt. (Baton Rouge, LA: Louisiana State University Press, 1998), 109–123 (quote, 111); James M. McPherson, *For Cause and Comrades: Why Men Fought in the Civil War* (New York: Oxford University Press, 1997), 125–130 (quote, 128).

33 Berlin, *Freedom's Soldiers*, 42–44; Gooding to Abraham Lincoln, September 28, 1863, in ibid., 114–116.

34 Smith, "'Let us All be Grateful,'" 49–51; "Remarks on Black Soldiers, May 25, 1864, in Congress," Beverly Wilson Palmer and Holly Byers Ochoa, eds., *The Selected Papers of Thaddeus Stevens* (Pittsburgh, PA: University of Pittsburgh Press, 1997), 1: 478–480 (quote, 479).

35 T. W. Higginson to Louisa Storrow Higginson, December 10, 1862, in Christopher Looby, ed., *The Complete Civil War Journal of Thomas Wentworth Higginson* (Chicago: University of Chicago Press, 2000), 252; Cornish, *Sable Arm*, 142–156 (quote, 156).

36 Cornish, *Sable Arm*, 159–164; Walter L. Williams, "Again in Chains: The Grisly Fate of Black Prisoners," *Civil War Times Illustrated* 20 (1981): 36–37.

37 William S. McFeely, *Frederick Douglass* (New York: W. W. Norton & Company), 227–228.

38 George S. Burkhardt, *Confederate Rage, Yankee Wrath: No Quarter in the Civil War* (Carbondale, IL: Southern University Press, 2007), 1; Williams, "Again in Chains," 38–39.

39 Cornish, *Sable Arm*, 255, 288–289.

2 No Quarter

1 John Cimprich, *Fort Pillow, a Civil War Massacre, and Public Memory* (Baton Rouge, LA: Louisiana State University Press, 2005), 15–80 (quotes, 68, 80).

2 Cimprich, *Fort Pillow*, 85–87; Andrew Ward, *River Run Red: The Fort Pillow Massacre in the American Civil War* (New York: Viking, 2005), 1–2, 54–55.

3 Ward, *River Run Red*, 128–129; Brian Steel Wills, *The Confederacy's Greatest Cavalryman: Nathan Bedford Forrest* (Lawrence, KS: University Press of Kansas, 1992), 178–180.

4 Wills, *Forrest*, 171–177; Ronald K. Huch, "Fort Pillow Massacre: the Aftermath of Paducah," *Journal of the Illinois State Historical Society* 66 (1973): 62–70 (quote, 68–69).

5 Cimprich, *Fort Pillow*, 92; George Burkhardt, *Confederate Rage*, 28.

6 Wills, *Forrest*, 181–183; Ward, *River Run Red*, 141–145, 156–162.

7 Ward, *River Run Red*, 151–153; Ralph Seth Henry, *"First With the Most" Forrest* (Indianapolis, IN: The Bobbs-Merrill Company, 1944), 250.

8 N. B. Forrest to Lionel F. Booth, April 12, 1864, Booth to Forrest, April 12, 1864, and Forrest to Booth, April 12, 1864 in *The War of Rebellion: A Compilation of the Official Records of the Union and Confederate Armies*, Series I, volume 32, part 1 (Washington, DC: Government Printing Office, 1891), 560–561 (hereafter cited as O. R.); Ward, *River Run Red*, 171–176.

9 "Statement of John F. Ray," April 23, 1864, in O. R. Series 1, vol. 32, part 1, 527; "Fort Pillow Massacre," House Report no. 65, 38th Congress, 1 session, 53; Albert Castel, "The Fort Pillow Massacre: A Fresh Examination of the Evidence,"

Civil War History 4 (March, 1958): 40–42 (quote, 42); John Cimprich, "The Fort Pillow Massacre: Assessing the Evidence," in Smith, ed. *Black Soldiers in Blue*, 154; Ward, *River Run Red*, 178–185.

10   Ward, *River Run Red*, 193–198; Report of Mack J. Leaming, January 17, 1865, in O. R. Series 1, vol. 32, part 1, 561.

11   George S. Burkhardt, *Confederate Rage, Yankee Wrath*, 5; Jason Phillips, *Diehard Rebels: the Confederate Culture of Invincibility* (Athens, GA: The University of Georgia Press, 2007), 66–67; Black soldiers taunts at rebels are from Ward, *River Run Red*, 190.

12   George Bodnia, ed., "Fort Pillow 'Massacre': Observations of a Minnesotan," *Minnesota History* (1973): 186–190; House Report no. 65, 22 (quote), 25 (quote), 27 (quote), 34 (quote) 108–109 (quote, 109), 16 (quote); Carl Adolf Lamberg to Liet. Col. T. H. Harris, April 27, 1864, in O. R. Series 1, vol. 32, part 1, 567–568; Statement of John F. Ray, April 23, 1864 in ibid., 527.

13   House Report, no. 65, 15–18, 24–25, 87.

14   House Report, no. 65, 30 (quote), 32 (quote), 18–19, 75–76; Statement of Frank Hogan, April 30, 1864, in O. R. Series 1, vol. 32, part 1, 536 (quote).

15   Statement of William J. Mays, April 18, 1864, in O. R. Series 1, vol. 33, part 1, 525; House Report 65, 45 (quote); Statement of George Huston, April 30, 1864 in O. R. Series 1, vol. 32, part 1, 536 (quote); Statement of Jerry Stewart, April 30, 1864 in O. R. Series 1, vol. 32, part 1, 538 (quote). House Report, 65, 92 (quote).

16   House Report, 65, 35–36 (quotes) 35, 42, 45, 46; Richard L. Fuchs, *An Unerring Fire: The Massacre at Fort Pillow* (Rutherford, NJ: Farleigh Dickinson University Press, 1994), 67–69; Report of Lieut. Mack J. Leaming, January 17, 1865, in O. R. Series 1, vol. 32, part 1, 562.

17   House Report 65, 82 (quote), 25–26, 20 (quote), 40–41, 107, 91–92; Statement of William J. Mays, April 18, 1864, in O. R. Series 1, vol. 32, part 1, 525.

18   House Report 63, 86–89.

19   Ward, *River Run Red*, 229–230.

20   Achilles V. Clark to "My Dearest Sisters, April 14, 1864, quoted from John Cimprich and Robert C. Mainfort, Jr., eds., "For Pillow Revisited: New Evidence About an Old Controversy," *Civil War History* 28 (1982): 299; Samuel H. Caldwell to "My Dearest Darling Wife, April 15, 1864, in ibid. 300; Report of "Vidette" in ibid, 297; House Report 65, 13.

21   Report of Lieutenant Mack J. Leaming, January 17, 1865, in O. R. Series 1, vol. 32, part 1, 562; Report of Lieuts. Francis A. Smith and William Cleary, April 18, 1864, in ibid., 565.

22   Report of Acting Master William Ferguson, April 14, 1864, in O. R. Series 1, vol. 32, part 1, 571; Report of Capt. John G. Woodruff, April 15, 1864, in ibid., 558.

23   House Report 65, 49, 83 (quote, 83).

24   Forrest to Davis, April 15, 1864, in Lynda Lasswell Crist, ed., *The Papers of Jefferson Davis* (Baton Rouge, LA: Louisiana State University Press, 1999), 10: 342–344; Forrest to Leonidas Polk, April 15, 1864, in O. R. Series 1, vol. 32, part 1, 610; James R. Chalmer to soldiers, April 20, 1864 in ibid., 622; Phillips, *Diehard Rebels*, 67.

25   John Cimprich and Robert C. Mainfort, "The Fort Pillow Massacre: A Statistical Note," *Journal of American History* 76 (December, 1989): 830–837.

3   Controversy

1   John Cimprich, "The Fort Pillow Massacre: Assessing the Evidence," John David Smith, ed., *Black Soldiers in Blue*, (Chapel Hill, NC: University of North Carolina Press, 2002), 150–152.

2   G. R. Giddings to Joshua Giddings, April 17, 1864, Joshua Giddings Papers, Ohio Historical Society, Columbus, Ohio; *Chicago Tribune*, April 16, 1864, p. 1; *New York Independent*, April 21, 1864, p. 4, May 5, 1864; Augustus L. Chetlain to Elihu B. Washburne, April 14, 1864, in *Freedom: A Documentary History of Emancipation, 1861–1867*, series 2, *The Black Military Experience*, ed. Ira Berlin (Cambridge: Cambridge University Press, 1982), 539–540; *New-York Tribune*, April 16, 1864, p. 6.

3   *Harpers*, April 30, 1864, p. 274; *Liberator* May 13, 1864, p. 2; *Indianapolis Daily Journal*, April 22, 1864, p. 2; *New York Independent*, April 21, 1864, p. 4; E. Conke to Henry Wilson, April 23, 1864, Abraham Lincoln Papers, Library of Congress; *New York Times*, April 18, 1864, p. 4; Theodore Hodgkins to Edwin S. Stanton, April 18, 1864 in *Freedom's Soldiers: The Black Military Experience in the Civil War*, Ira Berlin, Joseph P. Reidy, and Leslie S. Rowland, eds. (Cambridge: Cambridge University Press, 1998), 118–119.

4   Congressional *Globe*, 38th Congress, 1st session, 1662–1665, 1673 (quote, 1662); *New York Herald*, April 19, 1864, p. 4.

5   *The Diary of Gideon Welles*, ed. John T. Morse (Boston: Houghton Mifflin Co., 1911), 2: 23–24. The Committee on the Conduct of the War published the report on the Fort Pillow Massacre together with a report on prisoners of war on May 6, 1864. The shorter report on Fort Pillow, without testimony, appeared in many daily papers a few days before this.

6   *New York Times*, April 23, 1864, p. 4.

7   Fort Pillow Massacre, House Report No. 65, 38th Congress, 1st session, 1–7 (quoted material 2–3, 5–7).

8   Congressional *Globe*, 38th Congress, 1st session, 2108; Chicago *Tribune*, April 28, 1864, p. 1; "Address at Sanitary Fair, Baltimore, Maryland, April 18, 1864, in Roy P. Basler, ed., *The Collected Works of Abraham Lincoln* (New Brunswick, NJ: Rutgers University Press, 1953), VII, 302–303 (quote, 302).

9   William H. Seward to Lincoln, May 4, 1864, Abraham Lincoln Papers, Library of Congress; Edwin Stanton to Lincoln, May 5, 1864, ibid.

10   Welles to Lincoln, May 5, 1864, Lincoln Papers.

11   Salmon Chase to Lincoln, May 6, 1864, Lincoln Papers.

12   Montgomery Blair, to Lincoln, May 6, 1864, Lincoln Papers.

13   Edwin Bates to Lincoln, May 4, 1864, Lincoln Papers.

14   John P. Usher to Lincoln, May 6, 1864, Lincoln Papers.

15   Tap, *Over Lincoln's Shoulder*, 205; Lincoln to Stanton, May 17, 1864, *Collected Works*, VII, 345–346 (quote, 346).

16   Report of "Marion" in Mobile *Advertiser and Register*, April 17, 1864, quoted in John Cimprich and Robert C. Mainfort, eds. "Fort Pillow Revisited: New Evidence about an Old Controversy," *Civil War History* 28 (1982): 304.

17   Mason Brayman to Benjamin F. Wade, June 19, 1864, Benjamin F. Wade Papers, Library of Congress.

18   Forrest to Washburn, June 14, 1864, O. R. Series 1, volume 32, part 1, 586–587; Washburn to Forrest, June 19, 1864, in ibid., 588–589.

19   Forrest to Washburn, June 23, 1864, in ibid., 591–592, Washburn to Forrest, July 2, 1864, in ibid., 602.

20   Washburn to Stephen D. Lee, July [June] 17, 1864, in ibid., 587–588; Lee to Washburn, June 28, 1864, in ibid., 599–601.

21   House Report No. 65, 66; New York Times, April 26, 1864, p. 2; ibid., July 3, 1864, p. 7.

22   Dudley Cornish Taylor, The Sable Arm: Negro Troops in the Union Army, 1861–1865 (New York: W. W. Norton & Company, 1966), 177–178; John A. Logan, The Great Conspiracy: Its Origin and History (New York: A. R. Hart & Co., Publishers, 1886), 506; "Sergeant," 55th Massachusetts Infantry, Folly Island, South Carolina, July 26, 1864, in Edwin S. Redkey, ed., A Grand Army of Black Men: Letters from African-American Soldiers in the Union Army, 1861–1865 (New York: Cambridge University Press, 1992), 68; George W. Reed, Drummer, U.S.S. Commodore Reed, Potomac Flotilla, May [14], 1864, in Redkey, ed., Grand Army of Black Men, 273; Bruce Catton, Bruce Catton's Civil War (New York: Fairfax Press, 1984), 597; John F. Brobst to "My Dear Friend Mary, May 24, 1864, in Well Mary: Civil War Letters of a Wisconsin Volunteer, Margaret Brobst Roth, ed. (Madison, WI: University of Wisconsin Press, 1960), 56–57; Terry L. Jones, ed. The Civil War Memoirs of Captain William J. Seymour: Reminiscences of a Louisiana Tiger (Baton Rouge, LA: Louisiana State University Press, 1991), 127; The Diary of George Templeton Strong, Allan Nevins and Milton Halsey Thomas, eds., (New York: MacMillan, 1952), 3: 463–464.

23   The Diary of James T. Ayers: Civil War Recruiter, ed. John Hope Franklin (Springfield, IL: Illinois State Historical Society), 18–19.

24   "Remarks on Black Soldiers," April 30, 1864, in The Selected Papers of Thaddeus Stevens, Beverly Wilson Palmer, ed. (Pittsburgh, PA: University of Pittsburgh Press, 1997), 1: 458; J. H. B. P., [Corporal] 55th Massachusetts Infantry, Morris Island, South Carolina, May 24, 1864 in Redkey, ed., A Grand Army of Black Men, 208–210; Andrew Tate, et al. to the Union Convention of Tennessee, January 9, 1865, in Berlin, ed. Freedom's Soldiers, 144–145; Continental Monthly, August 1864, 193–195 (quotes, 193, 195).

25   Lincoln to James C. Conkling, August 26, 1863, in Basler, ed., Collected Works, 6: 407; Lincoln to Michael Hahn, March 13, 1864, in ibid., 7: 243. On the Wade-Davis Bill, see Eric Foner, Reconstruction: America's Unfinished Revolution, 1863–1877 (New York: Harper & Row, Publishers, 1988), 60–62; William C. Harris, With Charity for All: Lincoln and the Restoration of the Union (Lexington, KY: University of Kentucky Press, 1997), 186–190.

26   Frederick Douglass, The Life and Times of Frederick Douglass (New York: Citadel Press, 1983), 385–386 (quote, 386).

27   "Moses" quote from Hans L. Trefousse, Andrew Johnson: A Biography (New York: W. W. Norton & Company, 1989; Johnson quote on Douglass is from Albert Castel, The Presidency of Andrew Johnson (Lawrence, KS: The Regents Press of Kansas, 1979), 64.

28   Charles Sumner to John Bright, April 24, 1865, in *The Selected Letters of Charles Sumner*, Beverly Wilson Palmer, ed. (Boston: Northeastern University Press, 1990), 2: 297.

29   Hans L. Trefousse, *Andrew Johnson: A Biography* (New York: W. W. Norton & Company, 1989), 215–217; Thaddeus Stevens to William D. Kelley, May 30, 1865 in *Selected Papers of Thaddeus Stevens*, 2: 6; Stevens to Andrew Johnson, July 6, [186] 5, in ibid., 7; Sumner to Benjamin F. Wade, August 3, 1865, in *Selected Letters of Charles Sumner*, 2: 320–321; Letter of Hugh P. Beach, August 1, 1865 in *The Union in Crisis 1850–1877*, Robert W. Johannsen and Wendy Hamand Venet, eds. (Acton, MA: Copley Press, 2003), 304–305.

30   Foner, *Reconstruction*, 199–201; James McPherson, *Ordeal by Fire: The Civil War and Reconstruction* (New York: Alfred A. Knopf, 1982), 517–518.

31   Foner, *Reconstruction*, 271–280; McPherson, *Ordeal by Fire*, 520–523, 535–539.

32   The analysis of the popular vote in the 1868 election is from Castel, *Presidency of Andrew Johnson*, 208–209.

33   McPherson, *Ordeal By Fire*, 545–546.

34   David Donald, *Charles Sumner and The Rights of Man* (New York: Alfred A. Knopf, 1970), 516–529; McPherson, *Ordeal by Fire*, 561–572; Horace Greeley, "They Can't Buy the People," in *The Union in Crisis, 1850–1877*, 370.

35   C. Vann Woodward, *The Strange Career of Jim Crow*, second revised edition (New York: Oxford University Press, 1966), 79.

4   Historians and the Fort Pillow Massacre

1   John A. Logan, *The Great Conspiracy: Its Origins and History* (New York: A. R. Hart & Co., Publishers, 1886), 506; John G. Nicolay, *A Short Life of Abraham Lincoln* (New York: The Century Co., 1902), 351.

2   Edward A. Pollard, *The Lost Cause: A New Southern History of the War of the Confederates*, (New York: E. B. Treat & Co., Publishers, 1866), 499n.

3   Thomas Jordan and J. P. Pryor, *The Campaigns of Lieut. Gen. N. B. Forrest, and of Forrest's Cavalry* (New York: Blelock & Company, 1868), 432–448.

4   John Allen Wyeth, *Life of Nathan Bedford Forrest* (New York: Harper & Brothers, Publishers, 1899), 332–383 (quoted material 355, 353, and 378).

5   John W. Burgess, *The Civil War and the Constitution, 1859–1865* (New York: Charles Scribner's Sons, 1901), 117–118. See also William Archibald Dunning, *Reconstruction Political and Economic, 1865–1877* (New York: Harper & Brother Publishers, 1907).

6   James Ford Rhodes, *History of the United States from the Compromise of 1850 to The McKinley-Bryan Campaign of 1896* (New York: The MacMillan Company, 1920), 5: 511–513; Nathaniel Wright Stephenson, *Lincoln* (Indianapolis, IN: The Bobbs-Merrill Company Publishers, 1924), 339.

7   James G. Randall, *The Civil War and Reconstruction* (Boston: D. C. Heath & Company, 1937), 507; T. Harry Williams, "Benjamin F. Wade and the Atrocity Propaganda of the Civil War," *Ohio Archeological and Historical* Quarterly 48 (1939): 33–38; Idem., *Lincoln and the Radicals* (Madison, WI: University of Wisconsin Press, 1941), 343–346; Allan Nevins, *The War for the Union: The Organized War to Victory, 1864–1865* (New York: Charles Scribner's Sons, 1971), 25; Carl Sandburg,

Abraham Lincoln: The War Years (New York: Harcourt, Brace & Company, 1939), 3: 38.

8   Ralph Seth Henry, *"First with the Most" Forrest* (Indianapolis, IN: The Bobbs-Merrill Company, 1944), 248–268.

9   John L. Jordan, "Was There a Massacre at Fort Pillow?" *Tennessee Historical Quarterly* 6 (1947): 99–133 (quoted material, 116, 119).

10   Albert Castel. "The Fort Pillow Massacre: A Fresh Examination of the Evidence," *Civil War History* 4 (1958): 37–50 (quote, 46).

11   Shelby Foot, *The Civil War: A Narrative, Red River to Appomattox* (New York: Vintage Books, 1974), 111–112.

12   John Cimprich and Robert C. Mainfort, eds., "Fort Pillow Revisited: New Evidence about an Old Controversy," *Civil War History* 24 (1982): 293–306 (quoted material 297, 306).

13   Idem., "The Fort Pillow Massacre: A Statistical Note," *Journal of American History* 76 (1989): 830–837 (quoted material, 837).

14   Brian Steel Wills, *The Confederacy's Greatest Cavalryman: Nathan Bedford Forrest*, (Lawrence, KS: The University Press of Kansas, 1992), 169–196 (quote, 196).

15   Jack Hurst, *Nathan Bedford Forrest: A Biography* (New York: Alfred A. Knopf, 1993), 167–181.

16   Lonnie E. Maness, "The Fort Pillow Massacre: Fact or Fiction," *Tennessee Historical Quarterly* (1986): 287–315.

17   Richard L. Fuchs, *An Unerring Fire: The Massacre at Fort Pillow* (Rutherford: Farleigh Dickinson University Press, 1994), 12. Other studies that incorporate some of Fuch's assumptions on the flag of truce violations are James D. Lockett, "The Lynching Massacre of Black and White Soldiers at Fort Pillow, Tennessee, April 12, 1864," *Western Journal of Black Studies* 22 (1998): 87–91; John Gauss, *Black Flag! Black Flag!: The Battle at Fort Pillow* (Lanham, MD: University Press of America, 2003), 130–173; Andrew Ward, *River Run Red: The Fort Pillow Massacre in the American Civil War* (New York: Viking Press, 2005), 183–185.

18   John Cimprich, *Fort Pillow: A Civil War Massacre and Public Memory* (Baton Rouge, LA: Louisiana State University Press, 2005). In particular see pp. 138–139, 141–142, which deals with early efforts to establish Fort Pillow as an historic state park.

19   Ibid., 142–144 (quote, 143–144).

20   George S. Burkhardt, *Confederate Rage, Yankee Wrath: No Quarter in the Civil War* (Carbondale, IL: Southern Illinois University Press, 2007), 1.

21   Jason Phillips, *Diehard Rebels: The Confederate Culture of Invincibility* (Athens, GA: University of Georgia Press, 2007), 2, 66–67.

Conclusion

1   On the concept of "Herrenvolk Democracy," see James McPherson, *Ordeal by Fire: The Civil War and Reconstruction* (New York: Alfred A. Knopf, 1982), 32–33.

2   W. J. Cash, *The Mind of the South* (New York: Alfred A. Knopf, 1941), 131.

3   Gary W. Gallagher, *The Union War* (Cambridge, MA: Harvard University Press, 2011), 152–153.

4   Peter Irons, *A People's History of the Supreme Court* (New York: Penguin Books, 1999), 211–215, 222–232.

Documents

1   Basler, ed., *Collected Works*, 5: 356–357. Although there are two congressmen referenced in this document, their identity is not known with certainty.
2   John Cimprich and Robert C. Mainfort, Jr., "Fort Pillow Revisited: New Evidence About an Old Controversy," *Civil War History* 28 (1982): 297–299.
3   Excerpted from *The Papers of Jefferson Davis*, Lynda Lasswell Crist, ed. (Baton Rouge, LA: Louisiana State University Press, 1999): 10: 342–343.
4   James Ronald Chalmers (1831–1898) was a Brigadier General under Forrest.
5   From O. R. Series 1, vol. 32, Part 1, 528–529.
6   Revelle was mistaken about the actual participation of Forrest and Bradford in the flag of truce consultations, which were conducted by subordinates. The Confederates did not know, at the time of the truce, that Booth had been killed, and Bradford deliberately kept them in the dark on that important fact.
7   Eyewitness accounts vary on the exact time of the attack as well as the size of the rebel force. A more commonly accepted interpretation is the rebel flag of truce being presented at approximately 3:30 and the attack beginning roughly one half hour afterward.
8   A Massachusetts native who resided in Iowa, Dr. Charles Fitch was a surgeon stationed at Fort Pillow.
9   Popularly known as "Black Bob," Robert McCulloch (1820–1895) was in charge of the one of the brigades involved in the attack on Fort Pillow.
10   O. R. Series 1, Volume 32, Part 1, 534.
11   O. R. Series 1, Volume 32, Part 1, 536.
12   Captain Deloz Carson, USCHA, Company 6/D.
13   O. R. Series 1, Volume 32, Part 1, 537–538.
14   Sutlers were individuals who traveled with armies for the purpose of supplying additional items of food, drink, and other supplies.
15   O. R. Series 1, Volume 32, Part 1, 538–539.
16   One of the most plentiful rifled artillery pieces during the Civil War was the 10 pound Parrot cannon, developed by Robert P. Parrott, a onetime superintendent of the West Point Military Academy.
17   Other sources put the flag of truce a little later in the afternoon, approximately 3:30 p.m.
18   An undoubted reference to the "rebel yell," which many Confederate troops shouted prior to going into battle.
19   O. R. Series 1, Volume 32, Part 1, 571–572.
20   O. R. Series, Volume 32, Part 1, 563–565.
21   The numbers cited in this report are clearly exaggerated. Forrest reported that he had assigned 1,500 men under Brigadier General Chalmers.
22   The report's authors were confused about the chronology. According to most reports, Major Booth was killed several hours prior to the flag of truce, which Major Bradford dealt with entirely on his own.
23   Theodore Bradford was an elder brother of William F. Bradford.
24   O. R. Series 1, Volume 32, Part 1, 530–531.
25   *New York Times*, April 23, 1864, p. 4.
26   The town of Cairo, Illinois is located in southern Illinois where the Ohio River joins the Mississippi River.

27   A reference to Democratic papers sympathetic to the peace Democrat or Copperhead cause.

28   Fort Pillow Massacre, House of Representatives Report No. 65, 38th Congress, 1st session, 15.

29   Slang term for Confederate or rebel that derives from the term secession.

30   House Report No. 65, 17–18.

31   Undoubtedly a reference to the fate of Major Lionel F. Booth who was shot on the morning of April 12.

32   House Report No. 65, 18–19.

33   House Report No. 65, 25–26.

34   Term used early on in the war to described fugitive slaves who came across Union lines. At Fort Pillow, a northern man, Edward Benton, had established a plantation where a number of escaped contraband slaves labored. See Ward, *River Run Red*, 9, 42.

35   House Report No. 65, 26–27.

36   Like many witnesses, Williams' recollection of the specific timing of the battle is hazy. Since the main fight did not begin until nearly 4:00 p.m., he was most likely wounded a little later in the afternoon.

37   Probably a reference to Lieutenant John C. Ackerstrom who was identified as suffering this fate by a number of different witnesses.

38   House Report No. 65, 94–95.

39   Probably Captain Deloz Carson, Company D, 6th USCHA.

40   House Report No. 65, 13–14.

41   *New York Times*, May 8, 1864, p.3.

42   A reference to the *New York World*, a leading Democratic paper and political opponent of the Lincoln administration.

43   Charles Francis Adams was the son of President John Quincy Adams and was United States minister to England from 1861–1868.

44   William H. Seward was the former governor and Senator from New York. Lincoln's rival for the presidency in 1860, he served as Secretary of State from 1861–1869.

45   Stephen R. Mallory was Secretary of the Navy for the Confederacy and served the Davis administration for the duration of the war.

46   Benjamin F. Butler became infamous in the South when he was name commander of the Department of the Gulf after the fall of New Orleans. Widely accused of financial corruption by the residents of New Orleans, Butler was also hated because he played an early role in the training and arming of black soldiers.

47   Probably a reference to Union General John McNeil, who spent most of the Civil War in Missouri dealing with Confederate irregulars or guerrilla soldiers.

48   A native of Russia, John Basil Turchin was born Ivan Vasilovitch Turchinoff. Becoming a Brigadier General in the Union army, Turchin was hated by many southerners because of his actions at Athens, Alabama, where he let his troops sack the town as punishment for the alleged firing on his troops by southern civilians in the town.

49   James Patten Anderson was the Confederate general who was appointed to command the Confederate district of Florida in early 1864, just prior to the battle of Olustee.

50   Union General John Porter Hatch served briefly in the Department of the South as commander of the district of Florida.

51   The battle of Olustee (Florida) was the largest battle to take place in Florida during the Civil War. Union forces under Truman Seymour and Quincy Gillmore were bested by Confederate forces with heavy losses. The defeat ended an opportunity to organize a Unionist government in Florida as had been done in other Confederate states such as Louisiana, Tennessee, and Arkansas.

52   O. R. Series 1, Volume 32, Part 1, 586–587.

53   Brigadier General Abraham Buford was the commander of a division in Forrest's Cavalry.

54   Colonel Edmund Winchester Rucker was served in the 6th brigade in the division of Brigadier General James Chalmers when this letter was composed.

55   Stephen A. Hurlbut was a South Carolina native who moved to Illinois in 1845. He was a commander of the 16th corps, Army of Tennessee, and was stationed at Memphis during the writing of this letter.

56   Brigadier General Samuel D. Sturgis was commander of the Expeditionary Force, District of West Tennessee, Department of Tennessee. After a disastrous defeat at the hands of Nathan Forrest at Brice's Cross Roads, Sturgis was never given another active command during the Civil War.

57   More commonly known as the battle of Brice's Cross Roads (Mississippi), which took place on June 10, 1864 and was an overwhelming victory for Forrest's Cavalry.

58   O. R. Series 1, Volume 32, Part 1, 588–589.

59   Major General Stephen Dill Lee as the commander of the Cavalry Corps for Department of Alabama, Mississippi, and East Louisiana. At the time of this letter, he was Forrest's immediate superior.

60   Colonel William Lafayette Duckworth was a regimental commander in Forrest's Cavalry. He is credited with taking the Union garrison at Union City, Tennessee by using a threat of no quarter just prior to the battle at Fort Pillow.

61   O. R. Series 1, Volume 32, Part 1, 591–593.

62   Captain John T. Young, 24th Missouri volunteers, was taken prisoner by the Confederates at Fort Pillow. According to Young, he was later pressured to sign a statement that exonerated Forrest for his handling of the Fort Pillow battle.

63   Major General Braxton Bragg held a variety of commands for the Confederacy during the Civil war including the Army of the Mississippi and the Army of the Tennessee.

64   Colonel Fielding Hurst commanded the 6th Tennessee Cavalry.

65   S. D. Lee to C. C. Washburn, June 28, 1864, in O. R. Series 1, Volume 32, Part 1, 599–601.

66   In Washburn's reply to Lee, this particular sentence drew an angry retort:

> I will close by a reference to your statement that many of our colored soldiers "are yet wandering over the country attempting to return to their masters." If this remark is intended as a joke, it is acknowledged as a good one, but if stated as a fact, permit me to correct your misapprehensions by informing you that most of them have rejoined their respective commands, their search for their later "masters" having proved bootless; and I think I do not exaggerate in assuring you that there is not a colored soldier here who does not prefer the fate of his comrades at Fort Pillow to being returned to his "master."
>
> Washburn to Lee, July 3, 1864, in O. R. Series 1, Volume 32, part 1, 604

67   This is a reference to Captain John T. Young, 24th Missouri, who was captured at Fort Pillow.

68   O. R. Series 1, Volume 33, Part 1, 601–602.

69   The Report of the Joint Committee on the Conduct of the War on Fort Pillow.

70   General Orders No. 100 was a compilation of all the laws of warfare that would guide northern armies in their war against the Confederacy. See Burrus M. Carhan, *Acts of Justice: Lincoln's Emancipation Proclamation and the Law of War* (Lexington, KY: University of Kentucky Press, 2007), 127–130.

71   O. R. Series 1, vol. 33, Part 1, 604–605.

72   Phineas Thomas Scruggs was apparently a friend of Forrest's who the general entrusted to interview and to convince Young to sign documents favorable to Forrest. See Ward, *River Run Red*, 278.

Selected Bibliography

Adams, Virginia Matzke, ed. *On the Altar of Freedom: A Black Soldier's Civil War Letters from the Front*. Amherst, MA: University of Massachusetts Press, 1991.

Baker, Jean H. *Affairs of Party: The Political Culture of Northern Democrats in the Mid-Nineteenth Century*. Ithaca, NY: Cornell University Press, 1983.

Basler, Roy P. et al., eds. *The Collected Works of Abraham Lincoln*. 8 volumes. New Brunswick, NJ: Rutgers University Press, 1953–1955.

Berlin, Ira, Joseph P. Reidy, and Leslie S. Rowland, eds. *Freedom's Soldiers: The Black Military Experience in the Civil War*. Cambridge: Cambridge University Press, 1998.

Berwanger, Eugene. *The Frontier Against Slavery: Western Anti-Negro Prejudice and the Slavery Extension Controversy*. Urbana, IL: University of Illinois Press, 1964.

Bodnia, George, ed. "Fort Pillow 'Massacre': Observations of a Minnesotan." *Minnesota History* 6 (1973): 186–190.

Burkhardt, George S. *Confederate Rage, Yankee Wrath: No Quarter in the Civil War*. Carbondale, IL: Southern Illinois University Press, 2007.

Carnahan, Burrus M. *Act of Justice: Lincoln's Emancipation Proclamation and the Law of War*. Lexington, KY: University of Kentucky Press, 2007.

Carwardine, Richard. *Lincoln: A Life of Purpose and Power*. New York: Vintage Books, 2007.

Cash, W. J. *The Mind of the South*. New York: Alfred A. Knopf, 1941.

Castel, Albert. "The Fort Pillow Massacre: A Fresh Examination of the Evidence." *Civil War History* 4 (1958): 37–50.

——. *The Presidency of Andrew Johnson*. Lawrence, KS: The Regents Press of Kansas, 1979.

——. *Winning and Losing in the Civil War: Essays and Stories*. Columbia, SC: University of South Carolina Press, 1996.

Cimprich, John. *Fort Pillow: A Civil War Massacre and Public Memory*. Baton Rouge, LA: Louisiana State University Press, 2005.

Cimprich, John and Robert C. Mainfort, Jr. "Fort Pillow Revisited: New Evidence about an Old Controversy." *Civil War History* 28 (1982): 293–306.

——. "The Fort Pillow Massacre: A Statistical Note." *Journal of American History* 76 (1989): 830–837.

Clinton, Catherine. *Harriet Tubman: The Road To Freedom.* New York: Back Bay Books, 2004.

Cooper, William J. *"We Have The War Upon Us": The Onset of the Civil War, November 1860-April 1861.* New York: Alfred A. Knopf, 2012.

Cornish, Dudley Taylor. *The Sable Arm: Negro Troops in the Union Army.* New York: W. W. Norton & Company, 1956.

Cowden, Joanna D. *"Heaven Will Frown upon Such a Cause as This": Six Democrats Who Opposed Lincoln's War.* Lanham, MD: University Press of Maryland, 2001.

Current, Richard N., ed. *The Political Thought of Abraham Lincoln.* New York: Macmillan Publishing, 1967.

Donald, David. *Charles Sumner and The Rights of Man.* New York: Alfred A. Knopf, 1970.

——. *Lincoln.* New York: Simon & Schuster, 1995.

Douglass, Frederick. *The Life and Times of Frederick Douglass.* New York: Citadel Press, 1983.

Fitzhugh, George. *Cannibals All! or Slaves Without Masters.* C. Vann Woodward, ed. Cambridge, MA: Belknap Press, 1960.

Foner, Eric. *Free Soil, Free Labor, Free Men: The Ideology of the Republican Part Before the Civil War.* New York: Oxford University Press, 1970.

——. *The Fiery Trial: Abraham Lincoln and American Slavery.* New York: W. W. Norton & Co., 2011.

——. *Reconstruction: America's Unfinished Revolution, 1863–1877.* New York: W. W. Norton & Co., 1988.

"Fort Pillow Massacre." House Report No. 65. 38th Congress, 1st session.

Franklin, John Hope, ed. *The Diary of James T. Ayers: Civil War Recruiter.* Springfield, IL: Illinois State Historical Society.

Fuchs, Richard L. *An Unerring Fire: The Massacre at Fort Pillow.* Madison, NJ: Farleigh Dickinson University Press, 1994.

Gallagher, Gary W. *The Union War.* Cambridge, MA: Harvard University Press, 2011.

Gauss, John. *Black Flag! Black Flag!: The Battle at Fort Pillow.* Lanham, MD: University Press of America, 2003.

Gienapp, William E. *Abraham Lincoln and the Civil War: A Biography.* New York: Oxford University Press, 2002.

Glatthaar, Joseph T. *Forged in Battle: The Civil War Alliance Between Black Soldiers and White Officers.* New York: The Free Press, 1990.

Green, Michael S. *Freedom, Union, and Power: Lincoln and his Party During the Civil War.* New York: Fordham University Press, 2004.

Grimsely, Mark. *The Hard Hand of War: Union Military Policy Toward Southern Civilians, 1861–1865.* Cambridge, MA: Harvard University Press, 1995.

Guelzo, Allen C. *Lincoln and Douglas: The Debates that Defined America.* New York: Simon & Schuster, 2008.

Halpine, Charles. *The Life and Adventures, Songs, Services, and Speeches of Private Miles O'Reilly.* New York: Carlton, 1864.

Harris, William C. *With Charity for All: Lincoln and the Restoration of the Union.* Lexington, KY: University of Kentucky Press, 1997.

Henry, Ralph Seth. *"First with the Most" Forrest.* Indianapolis, IN: The Bobbs-Merrill Company, 1944.

Huch, Ronald K. "Fort Pillow Massacre: the Aftermath of Paducah." *Journal of the Illinois State Historical Society* 66 (1973): 62–70.

Irons, Peter. *A People's History of the Supreme Court.* New York: Penguin Books, 1999.

Hurst, Jack. *Nathan Bedford Forrest: A Biography.* New York: Alfred A. Knopf, 1993.

Johannsen, Robert W., ed. *The Lincoln–Douglas Debates of 1858.* New York: Oxford University Press, 1965.

——, ed. *Democracy on Trial: A Documentary History of the American Life, 1845–1877.* Second edition. Urbana, IL: University of Illinois Press, 1988.

Johannsen, Robert W. and Wendy Hamand Venet, eds. *The Union in Crisis 1850–1877.* Acton, MA: Copley Publishing, 2003.

Jones, Terry L., ed. *The Civil War Memoirs of Captain William J. Seymour: Reminiscences of a Louisiana Tiger.* Baton Rouge, LA: Louisiana State University Press, 1991.

Jordan, John L. "Was There a Massacre at Fort Pillow?" *Tennessee Historical Quarterly* 6 (1947): 99–133.

Jordan, Thomas and J. P. Pryor. *The Campaigns of Lieut. Gen. N. B. Forrest, and of Forrest's Cavalry.* New York: Blelock and Company, 1868.

Klement, Frank L. *The Copperheads of the Middle West.* Chicago, IL: University of Chicago Press, 1960.

——. "Midwestern Opposition to Lincoln's Emancipation Policy." *Journal of Negro History* 49 (1964): 169–183.

——. *Lincoln's Critics: The Copperheads of the North.* Shippensburg, PA: White Mane Books, 1999.

Litwack, Leon F. *North of Slavery: The Negro in the Free States, 1790–1860.* Chicago: University of Chicago Press, 1961.

Looby, Christophe, ed. *The Complete Civil War Journal of Thomas Wentworth Higginson.* Chicago: University of Chicago Press, 2000.

Logan, John A. *The Great Conspiracy: Its Origin and History.* New York: A. R. Hart & Co., Publishers, 1886.

Maness, Lonnie E. "The Fort Pillow Massacre: Fact or Fiction." *Tennessee Historical Quarterly* (1986): 287–315.

Marzalek, John F. *Sherman: A Soldier's Passion for Order.* New York: Free Press, 1993.

McFeely, William S. *Frederick Douglass.* New York: W. W. Norton & Company, 1991.

McPherson, James. *Ordeal by Fire: The Civil War and Reconstruction.* New York: Alfred A. Knopf, 1982.

——. *Battle Cry of Freedom: The Civil War Era.* New York: Oxford University Press, 1988.

——. *For Cause and Comrades: Why Men Fought in the Civil War.* New York: Oxford University Press, 1997.

Monroe, Dan and Bruce Tap. *Shapers of the Great Debate on the Civil War: A Biographical Dictionary*. Westport, CT: Greenwood Press, 2005.

Nevins, Allan and Milton Halsey Thomas, eds. *The Diary of George Templeton Strong*. 4 volumes. New York: Macmillan, 1952.

Palmer, Beverly Wilson, ed. *The Selected Letters of Charles Sumner*. 2 volumes. Boston: Northeastern University Press, 1990.

——. *The Selected Papers of Thaddeus Stevens*. 2 volumes. Pittsburgh, PA: University of Pittsburgh Press, 1997.

Phillips, Jason. *Diehard Rebels: The Confederate Culture of Invincibility*. Athens, GA: University of Georgia Press, 2007.

Phillips, Ulrich B. "The Central Theme of Southern History." *American Historical Review* 34 (1928): 30–43.

Quarles, Benjamin. *The Negro in the Civil War*. 1953 reprint. New York: Da Capo Press, 1989.

Redkey, Edwin S., ed. *A Grand Army of Black Men: Letters from African-American Soldiers in the Union Army, 1861–1865*. Cambridge: Cambridge University Press, 1992.

Roth, Margaret Brobst, ed. *Well Mary: Civil War Letters of a Wisconsin Volunteer*. Madison, WI: University of Wisconsin Press, 1960.

Sears, Stephen W., ed. *The Civil War Papers of George B. McClellan*. New York: Da Capo Press, 1992.

Smith, John David, ed. *Black Soldiers in Blue*. Chapel Hill, NC: University of North Carolina Press, 2002.

Tap, Bruce. *Over Lincoln's Shoulder: The Committee on the Conduct of the War*. Lawrence, KS: University Press of Kansas, 1998.

——. "'These Devils Are Not Fit to Live on God's Earth': War Crimes and the Committee on the Conduct of the War." *Civil War History* 42 (1996): 116–132.

——. "Race, Rhetoric, and Emancipation: The Election of 1862 in Illinois," *Civil War History* 39 (1993): 101–125.

Trefousse, Hans L. *Andrew Johnson: A Biography*. New York: W. W. Norton & Company, 1989.

Voegeli, V. Jacque. *Free But Not Equal: The Midwest and the Negro During the Civil War*. Chicago: University of Chicago Press, 1967.

War of Rebellion: A Compilation of the Official Records of the Union and the Confederate Armies. 70 volumes in 128. Washington, DC: 1880–1901.

Ward, Andrew. *River Run Red: The Fort Pillow Massacre in the American Civil War*. New York: Viking Press, 2005.

Weber, Jennifer L. *Copperheads: The Rise and Fall of Lincoln's Opponents*. New York: Oxford University Press, 2006.

Wiley, Bell Irvin. *The Life of Billy Yank: The Common Soldier of the Union Army*. 1952 rpt. Baton Rouge, LA: Louisiana State University Press, 1998.

Williams, T. Harry. "Benjamin F. Wade and the Atrocity Propaganda of the Civil War." *Ohio Archeological and Historical Quarterly* 48 (1939): 33–43.

——. *Lincoln and the Radicals*. Madison, WI: University of Wisconsin Press, 1941.

Williams, Walter L. "Again in Chains: The Grisly Fate of Black Prisoners." *Civil War Times Illustrated* 20 (1981): 36–43.

Woodward, C. Vann. *The Strange Career of Jim Crow*. Second revised edition. New York: Oxford University Press, 1966.

Wyeth, John Allen. *Life of Nathan Bedford Forrest*. New York: Harper & Brothers, Publishers, 1899.

Index

Note: where letters follow page numbers, "i" refers to insert and "sb" to sidebar.

1st Missouri Light Artillery 43sb
6th Tennessee Cavalry 168
7th Tennessee 48
13th Tennessee Cavalry 42–43sb, 46–51, 53, 56–61, 109, 130–131, 133, 135, 137–142, 151
20th Tennessee Cavalry 112, 127
24th Missouri 172, 183n
25th Wisconsin 82
40th Illinois 45
113th Illinois 61

abolition *see* emancipation
Ackerstrom, John 58, 139, 182n
Adams, Charles Francis 158
Addison, Sandy affidavit 132–133
Adison, Thomas 52i
African-Americans soldiers: behavior at Fort Pillow 51–58, 60–64, 66–68, 109–111, 113, 128–142, 143–157, 168–169; behavior after Fort Pillow 77–83, 159–162, 164–167, 169; Confederate policy toward 38–39, 49–50, 71, 78, 108–109, 116–117, 162; debate over recruitment as soldiers 22, 25–31, 126–127; Federal protection of 68–69, 72–75; hardships of 34–35, 36–37, 39, 98–99; and Ku Klux Klan 94–95; Lincoln fails to protect 80, 122–123; northern attitudes toward

8–10, 16–18, 27–28, 32–33, 35–36, 84–85, 91, 94, 100, 107, 123–125; recruitment 33–44, 41; relationship with Andrew Johnson 87–89; rights of 2, 9–10, 31–32, 84–87, 89–93, 97–98, 101–103; southern attitudes toward 3–6, 43–47, 52, 55, 59, 62–63, 70–71, 75–76, 113–114, 118–119, 121–122, 166–167, 183n; viewed as property 19, 21–22, 33
African-American regiments: 1st Alabama, 43sb, 144; 1st Kansas colored volunteers 30, 33, 81sb; 1st South Carolina volunteers 29, 33, 37; 2nd United States Colored Light Artillery 42–43sb, 53, 80; 6th United States Colored Heavy Artillery x, 42–43, 46, 52–56, 58, 133–134, 143–146, 148, 150, 152, 182n; 9th Louisiana volunteers x, 37; 54th Massachusetts x, 33, 36–38; 55th Massachusetts 33, 36–37, 81; Corps d'Afrique 37; Louisiana Native Guards 29, 38i
Alabama 83, 182n
Alton, IL 16
American Colonization Society 18
Anderson, Charles W. 61, 163
Anderson, James Patton 158, 182n
Andrew, John A. 33, 36
Antietam, battle of 1, 26

Arkansas x, 81sb, 122, 172n, 183n

Army of the Cumberland 44

Army of Northern Virginia 24, 79, 82

Army of the Potomac 24, 26, 80, 82, 127

Army of the Tennessee 44, 183n

Athen, AL 182n

Ayers, James T. 83

Baltimore, MD. 71

Barr, Captain 130

Bangs, Eli 58

Banks, Nathaniel 34

Bates, Edward 74

Bateau, C. R. 49

Beard, John 129

Beauregard, Pierre, G. T. 38

Bell, John 172n

Bell, Tyree 46, 48, 127

Benton, Edward 59i, 182n

Berlin, Ira 30, 35

Bingham, James 53

Bischoff, Peter 134

blacks *see* African Americans

Blair, Montgomery 73–74

Booth, Lionel F. x, 42–43, 46, 48–49,
    128, 130, 135, 138–139, 161,
    181n–182n

Boston, MA 7, 38, 69

Bourbons 97–98

Bradford, Theodore 139

Bradford, William x, 42, 46–51, 57–58, 106,
    109–110, 118, 128, 130–131, 135–136,
    139–140, 151, 161–163, 168, 181n

Brayman, Mason 76, 141

Brice's Cross Roads, battle of x, 78–79,
    122, 183n

Browning, Orville 21

Brownsville, TN 42sb, 57, 127, 140, 161,
    163, 168

Bruce, Blanche K. 90i

Buffalo, NY 67

Buford, Abraham 44, 159–160, 183n

Bureau of Colored Troops 34

Burgess, John W. 107

Burkhardt, George 39, 51, 116

Burnside, Ambrose 82

Butler, Benjamin F. ix, 23, 29–30, 34,
    158, 182n

Cailloux, Andre 38i

Caldwell, Samuel H. 60, 112

Cameron, Simon 28

Carnahan, Burrus 19, 23, 26

Carson, Deloz 133, 153, 181n–182n

Cash, W. J. 121

Castel, Albert 61, 110–111, 116–117

Catton, Bruce 87

Chalmers, James R. 8, 44, 46–48, 56, 59,
    61–63, 66, 72–74, 107, 109, 118–119,
    129, 141, 158, 163, 168, 181n, 183n

Charleston, IL 16

Charleston, SC 7, 17, 37, 47sb–48i

Chase, Salmon P. 21, 73

Chetlain, Augustus 75

Chicago *Times* 28

Chicago Tribune 67, 71

Childs, Lydia Maria 22

Cimprich, John 41, 63, 66, 76, 107,
    111–113, 115–116

City Point, VA 160

Civil Rights Act of 1866 89

Civil Rights Act of 1871 96sb

Civil Rights Act of 1875 97, 124

Civil Rights Cases 1883 xi, 97sb, 124

Clark, Achilles 112; letter 127–129

Cleary, William 49, 61, 142; report
    138–141

colonization 18

Columbia 94, 103

Columbus, KY x, 69

compromise of 1850 23

Confederacy 1, 5, 19, 21–22, 27, 30, 34,
    37, 39, 41, 43, 45, 47, 62, 64–65,
    67–68, 72–74, 80, 86, 89, 107– 108,
    116–117, 120, 122, 157, 182n–184n

Confiscation Act (First) ix, 23

Confiscation Act (Second) ix, 26–27, 41

Conkling, James 87

Connecticut 16sb, 91

contrabands ix, 29, 41, 59i, 149, 182n

Copperheads 26, 34, 64, 88, 101

Cornish, Dudley 34, 81, 111

Crittenden Compromise 12

Crittenden, John J. 12

Crittenden–Johnson Resolution ix, 20

Cummins vs. County Board of Education
    124

Davis, H. C. 170
Davis, Jefferson (Davis administration) 8–9,
    38, 62, 64, 70–72, 74, 79, 85, 90, 109,
    122–123, 129, 143, 182n
DeBow, J. B. W. 5
Delany, Martin R. 18i, 38
Democratic Party 20, 25–28, 67, 80, 85,
    90, 94, 101–104, 172n
Detroit, MI 57
Dew, Thomas R. 3
District of Columbia ix, 24, 82
Douglas, Stephen A. 13, 15
Douglass, Frederick 18, 22, 33i, 38–39,
    86–87
Dred Scott v. Sanford 14
Duckworth, W. L. x, 45, 161–163, 183n
Dunning, William 107

Edwards, Arthur 53
emancipation 1–2, 26, 85–86, 127;
    abolition by Federal government 12,
    19, 22, 67, 87, 103; abolitionist 3, 8,
    16, 18, 20–22, 29–30, 34, 37, 39, 51,
    67, 84, 87, 98–99, 121–122, 126;
    Democratic opposition 25, 27;
    Emancipation Proclamation x, 30,
    41–42, 86; gradual abolitionism 16sb,
    18; Preliminary Proclamation see
    Preliminary Emancipation
    Proclamation; Proclamation of Fremont
    ix, 20; Proclamation of Hunter ix,
    21–22, 28; and racial equality 18;
    relationship to laws of war 19;
    relationship to African-American
    recruitment 40, 45, 91; relationship to
    soldiers 35–36; resolution to border
    states 24; as war goal 8–9, 35–36
Emerson, John 14sb
election of 1860 15
election of 1868 90; Indiana 16sb, 17,
    126; Indianapolis, IN 67
Epeneter, Charles 134–135

Falls, Elias 54; statement 144–145
Fentis, Arthur 54
Ferguson, William x, 61; report 137–138
Fifteenth Amendment xi, 90–91, 123,
    125

fire-eaters 3
Fitch, Charles 59, 131
Fitzhugh, George 4, 17
Flag, Alfred 153
Foner, Eric 23
Foote, Shelby 111
Forrest, Nathan Bedford 8, 10, 43–51,
    55–56, 58–59, 61–64, 66, 70, 72–74,
    76–81, 83, 94, 96, 101, 103, 105–111,
    113–116, 118–121, 127–131, 134, 137,
    139, 141–142, 144, 146, 151, 157–160,
    162, 165–166, 168–171
Fort Donelson 24
Fort Henry 24
Fort Pickering 77, 81, 133–136
Fort Pillow: cabinet debates x, 72–75;
    casualties at 63–64, 112–113;
    Confederacy responds to 75–80, 123,
    125; Congress debates x, 68, 71;
    description of fort and location 1,
    41–44; Flag of Truce 49, 138–139;
    Forrest's attitude and tactics 45–48, 59,
    62–63, 101, 103, 105, 129–130; Forrest
    corresponds with C. C. Washburn on
    159–165, 168–169; historians attitude
    toward 11, 100–120; Joint Committee
    on the Conduct of the War
    Investigation x, 64, 68–70, 100,
    157–158; Lee and Washburn
    correspond on 165–167; Lincoln
    addresses x, 9, 65, 71, 75, 80, 94;
    northern reactions to 8, 64, 66–71;
    relationship to equal rights and race
    9–10, 84, 91, 99, 183n; slaughter of
    soldiers 53–59, 61, 122–123, 130–157;
    treatment of Confederate officers 62;
    troops stationed at x, 42
Fort Pillow Historic State Park 115–116
Fort Sumter 15, 19, 22, 172n
Fort Wagner x, 1, 37–38
Forten, James 18
Fortress Monroe 23
Fourteenth Amendment xi, 89, 97–98,
    123–125
Fox, Sgt. 150
Fredonia, NY 53
Free Labor (Free Labor ideology) 6–7,
    100, 122, 172n

Free Soil Party 7
Fremont, John C. ix, 20–21, 23
Fuchs, Richard 114–115
Fugitive Slave Act of 1793 23i
Fugitive Slave Act of 1850 2, 23i
Fulks, Nathan 56

Gallagher, Gary W. 20, 124
Garrison, William Lloyd 67
Gettysburg, battle of x, 1, 37, 120
Gibbs, Dennis 153
Giddings, Grotius 66
Giddings, Joshua 66
Gillmore, Quincy 183n
Glover, Martha 36sb
Gooch, Daniel W. x, 57, 69–70, 80, 108,
    143–146, 148, 157
Gooding, James H. 33, 36
Gordon, Stewart 52i
Grant, Ulysses 24, 75, 77sb, 79–80, 90,
    94, 96–97, 104
Greeley, Horace 26, 67, 94, 96,
    103–104

Hahn, Michael 85
Halleck, Henry W. 32
Halpine, Charles 32
Hammond, James H. 4
Harding, Duncan 54
Harrison's Landing 24–25
Hatch, John Porter 158, 183n
Hayes, Rutherford xi, 97
Henry, Ralph Seth 109, 114
Hicks, S. G. 45
Hill, Lieutenant 135
Higginson, Thomas W. 29, 37
Hodgkins, Theordore 68
Hogan, Frank 55; affidavit 133–134;
    statement 152–154
Howard, Jacob 68
Huch, Ronald 45
Hunter, Lieutenant 135–136, 150
Huntsville, AL 83
Hurlbut, Stephen x, 42, 77sb, 80, 138,
    159–160, 163, 183n
Hurst, Fielding 163, 168, 183n
Hurst, Jack 113–114
Huston, George 56

Illinois x, 13–17, 19, 21, 27, 52, 60, 67,
    69, 76–77, 83, 103, 144, 154, 181n,
    183n
Independent (New York) 67

Jackson, TN 45, 62, 161, 163, 168
Johnson, Andrew 87–89
Johnston, Joseph 24, 86
Joint Committee on the Conduct of the
    War x, 10, 64, 68, 70–71, 75–76, 80,
    106, 108–112, 127, 130, 143–145, 150,
    152, 154, 184n
Jordan, John J. 109–110, 114
Jordan, Thomas 105–106, 109
Julian, George W. 71

Kansas 13, 29
Kansas-Nebraska Act 13
Kennedy, John 53
Kirkwood, Samuel 32
Ku Klux Klan xi, 96sb, 103–105

Lane, James H. 29–30
Langston, John M. 33sb
Lecompton Constitution 14
Leaming, Mack J. 51, 57, 60
Leadbetter, Isaac 57
Lee, Robert E. 24, 26, 86, 105
Lee, Stephen D. 78–79, 86, 160, 162, 167,
    183n
Liberal Republicans 96, 104
Liberator 67
Liberty 49
Lincoln, Abraham ix–xi, 2–3, 6, 8–10, 12,
    15–16, 19–31, 36, 38–41, 45, 51,
    64–65, 68–69, 71–76, 79–80, 85, 87,
    91, 98, 104, 107, 112, 122–123, 126,
    157, 172n, 182n
Litwack, Leon 17
Logan, John A. 81, 103
Louisiana x, 7, 13–14, 29, 33–34, 37–38,
    82, 85, 88, 90, 97, 183n
Louisiana Purchase 13i

McClellan, George B. 24–26
McClure, T. W. 135
McCulloch, Robert "Black Bob" 46,
    48–49, 132–133, 141, 163, 181n

McNeil, John 158, 182n
McPherson, James 36
Maine 13i, 77, 158
Mainfort, Robert 63, 112–113, 116
Mallory, Robert 28–29
Mallory, Stephen 158, 182n
Maness, Lonnie S. 114, 116
Manassas, first battle of 20
Marmaduke, John S. 81sb
Marshall, James 46, 58–59, 106, 110, 118
Massachusetts 7, 16i, 19, 22–23, 29, 33,
    36, 67, 181n
Mays, William J. 56
Meador, James 57
Memphis Appeal 112
Memphis, TN x, 1, 41–43, 45–46, 59i,
    61, 67, 69, 77, 80–81, 133–134, 137,
    146, 150, 153, 158–160, 162–163, 165,
    168–169, 183n
Mexican War 2
Military Reconstruction Acts 89–90
Militia Act of 1862 ix, 25, 30, 36, 126
Milliken's Bend, battle of x, 1
Mississippi x, 34, 52, 81, 90, 97, 121, 146,
    150, 183n
Mississippi River 1, 37, 41–43, 48–49, 51,
    53–54, 56, 60, 105–106, 112, 119,
    181n
Missouri 2, 13i–14sb, 21, 30, 36, 59, 126,
    172n, 182n
Missouri Compromise of 1820 12, 13i, 14sb
Missouri Democrat 66
Montgomery, James 30sb
Mound City, IL x, 52i, 60, 69, 142, 144,
    154
Mudsill theory 4–6, 121
Munroe, John 132

Nast, Thomas 92, 95, 101–104
Nevins, Allan 108
New Era 43, 46, 48, 51, 54, 57–58, 60, 76,
    86, 105–106, 109–111, 118
New Jersey 16sb, 90
New Mexico Territory 3
New Orleans 7, 17, 38i; 182n
New York 7, 16sb, 18, 53, 67, 90
New York, NY 83
New York City Draft Riots 101

New York Herald 69
New York Journal of Commerce 158
New York Times 68–69, 143, 157–158
New-York Tribune 26, 67
Nicolay, John G. 103
North Carolina x, 34, 122, 172n
North Carolina Proclamation 88
Nott, Josiah 3–4

Ohio 16sb, 17, 18i, 33i, 69
Olive Branch x, 49
Olustee, battle of 122, 158, 182n–183n
Oregon 90

Paducah, KY x, 45–46, 48
Payne, John H. B. 84
Peace Democrats 26, 31, 64
Peninsula Campaign 24, 26
Pennsylvania 2, 33, 88
Penwell, John 57, 62
Petersburg, VA xi, 79–80
Phelps, John W. 29, 39
Phillips, Colonel 59i
Phillips, Jason 52, 116–117
Phillips, Ulrich B. 5
Phillips, Wendell 22
Pillow, Gideon 41
Platte Valley x, 61–62, 70, 137, 158
Plessey v. Ferguson 124
Plymouth, battle of (VA) x, 122
Poison Spring, battle of (AK) x, 81sb, 122
Pollard, Edward 105
Polk, Leonidas 62, 109
populist 98
Popular Sovereignty 13
Port Hudson, battle of (LA) x, 1, 37–38i
Preliminary Emancipation Proclamation ix,
    26–27, 30
Prosser, Gabriel 48i
Pryor, John 105–106, 109
Pulaski, TN 94, 96sb

Quincy, IL 15

Randall, James G. 108
Ray, John F. 49, 53
reconstruction xi, 9, 71, 85–91, 94–97,
    101, 105, 107, 123–124

Reed, George 82
Republican Party 3, 7–8, 12, 14–15, 18–19, 21, 23, 26, 77sb, 80, 90, 98, 101i, 121
Resolution on Fugitive Slaves 24
Revels, Hiram 90i
Revelle, Cord 140
Revelle, Hardy N. 141, 181n; statement 130–132
Rhode Island 16sb, 33
Rhodes, James Ford 110
Richmond *Enquirer* 157
Robinson, Benjamin: statement 145–146
Robinson, Charley 52
Rucker, E. W. 159, 183n

Saltville, battle of xi, 122
Sandburg, Carl 108
Saxton, Rufus 29–30
Scruggs, Pnineas T. 170, 184n
Seward, William H. 7, 19, 26, 72–73, 158, 182n
Seymour, Horatio 90
Seymour, Truman 183n
Shaw, George 53, 58; statement 148–150
Shaw, Robert Gould 38
Shiloh, battle of 120
Sherman, Thomas W. ix, 28
Sherman, William T. 35, 42, 44–45, 109
slavery ix, xi, 2–9, 12–27, 29, 31, 33, 36–39, 43, 67, 75, 77–78, 84, 87–88, 90–91, 98, 103, 121, 123, 126, 157, 161–162, 164
Smith, Francis A. 61; report with William Cleary 138–141
Smith, John David 27
Smith, Malcolm 133–134
South Carolina x, 4, 7, 21, 28–29, 37, 47sb, 48i, 52i, 82, 146, 183n
Stamps, Daniel 56–57; statement 141–142
Stanley, William 142
Stanton, Edwin M. x, 28–29, 35, 68–69, 72–73, 75, 79, 130
Stephenson, Nathaniel W. 107
Stevens, Thaddeus 29, 33, 37, 84, 88
Stewart, Jerry 56; statement 134
Stono Rebellion 48
Strong, George Templeton 83

Sturgis, Samuel 78, 81, 159–160, 165, 183n
Sumner, Charles 19, 22, 87–88, 94

Taney, Roger B. 14
Ten Percent Plan 85
Tennessee 24, 40–43, 45, 50, 55, 57, 61, 63, 76–77, 82, 84, 94, 96, 105–106, 110, 113, 115–116, 118, 121, 127, 134–135, 148, 150, 158, 160, 168–169, 172n, 183n
Thirteenth amendment xi, 84, 86
Thomas, Lorenzo 34
Thompson, Jacob 55
Thompson, John 134
Times (London) 76
Travis, Joseph 47
Tubman, Harriet 22, 30sb
Tupelo, AL 160
Turchin, John 158, 182n
Turner, Nat 3, 47–48i
Tyler, Daniel 55; statement 146–148

Ullman, Daniel 34
Union City, TN x, 42sb, 45, 183n
Usher, John P. 74
Utah Territory 3

Van Horn, Daniel 136
Vermont 16i, 29, 59
Vesey, Denmark 47–48i
"Vidette" 60
Virginia ix, xi, 3, 18, 33, 47–48i, 79, 82, 122, 172n

Wade, Benjamin F. x, 69–70, 76, 80, 88, 108, 143, 150, 152, 154
Wade-Davis bill 85
Walls, James 53
Ward, Andrew 115
Wardner, Horace 60; statement 154–157
Washburn, Cadwallader x, 77–80, 158, 165, 183n; letters 160–162, 168–169
Washburne, Elihu 67, 77sb
Washington, D. C. ix, 67, 82, 86, 89–90, 169
Washington Peace Conference 12
Watson, Thomas 98

Weaver, Henry 56; statement 135–136
Welles, Gideon 69, 72–73
Wickliffe, Charles 28
Wild, Earl 34
Wilderness, battle of 75, 79, 82
Wiley, Bell I. 35
Williams, James 81sb
Williams, Major 53, 182n; statement
    150–152
Williams, Rebecca 55, 141
Williams, T. Harry 108
Wills, Brian 113–114
Wilmot, David 2

Wilmot Proviso 2
Wilson, Captain 128
Wilson, Henry 68
Wilson, Lieutenant 130, 139
Wisconsin 91
Wisconsin state fair 6
Wisconsin territory 14sb
Woodruff, John 61
Woodward, C. Vann 98
Wyeth, John Allen 106, 109

Yates, Richard 28
Young, John T. 183n–184n; letter 169–171